A CONFUSION OF THE SPHERES

For Sissy and Uli

A Confusion of the Spheres

Kierkegaard and Wittgenstein on Philosophy and Religion

GENIA SCHÖNBAUMSFELD

OXFORD
UNIVERSITY PRESS

OXFORD

UNIVERSITY PRESS

Great Clarendon Street, Oxford OX2 6DP

Oxford University Press is a department of the University of Oxford.
It furthers the University's objective of excellence in research, scholarship,
and education by publishing worldwide in

Oxford New York

Auckland Cape Town Dar es Salaam Hong Kong Karachi
Kuala Lumpur Madrid Melbourne Mexico City Nairobi
New Delhi Shanghai Taipei Toronto

With offices in

Argentina Austria Brazil Chile Czech Republic France Greece
Guatemala Hungary Italy Japan Poland Portugal Singapore
South Korea Switzerland Thailand Turkey Ukraine Vietnam

Oxford is a registered trade mark of Oxford University Press
in the UK and in certain other countries

Published in the United States
by Oxford University Press Inc., New York

© Genia Schönbaumsfeld 2007

The moral rights of the author have been asserted
Database right Oxford University Press (maker)

First published 2007

British Library Cataloguing in Publication Data
Data available

Library of Congress Cataloging in Publication Data
Data available

Typeset by Laserwords Private Limited, Chennai, India
Printed in Great Britain
on acid-free paper by
Biddles Ltd., King's Lynn, Norfolk

ISBN 978-0-19-922982-6

1 3 5 7 9 10 8 6 4 2

Contents

An honest religious thinker is like a tightrope walker. He almost looks as though he were walking on nothing but air. His support is the slenderest imaginable. And yet it really is possible to walk on it.

Ludwig Wittgenstein, *Culture and Value*

Acknowledgements

The writing of this book was made possible by a three-year 'Hertha Firnberg' research fellowship awarded by the Austrian Science Fund. I would like to express my gratitude to this institution as well as to the Philosophy Department of the University of Vienna for providing me with an office and a congenial place in which to work during the tenure of the award. I would also like to thank Konrad Paul Liessmann for supporting my application as well as the two anonymous referees who favourably reviewed it.

This book has been greatly improved by critical comments from Brian McGuinness, Denis McManus, Stephen Mulhall, three anonymous readers for Oxford University Press, and, in particular, Aaron Ridley, whose generous provision of good advice has gone well beyond the call of duty. I also wish to thank Stephen Mulhall for supporting my application for a Visiting Fellowship at New College, Oxford, where, during the Michaelmas term of 2004, much fruitful work was conducted.

I have at one point used material previously published. Sections IV to VI of chapter 3 are based on my paper 'No New Kierkegaard', *International Philosophical Quarterly* 44/4 (2004): 519–34. My thanks to the editor for permission to draw on this material here.

Last, but not least, I would like to thank Peter Momtchiloff, Helen Gray and the staff from Oxford University Press for their help and support.

Introduction

Hegel is a Johannes *Climacus* who does not storm the heavens, like the giants, by putting mountain upon mountain, but climbs aboard them by way of his syllogisms.

Søren Kierkegaard, *Papers and Journals: A Selection*[1]

I would be afraid that you would try and give some sort of philosophical justification for Christian beliefs, as if some sort of proof was needed . . . The symbolisms of Catholicism are wonderful beyond words. But any attempt to make it into a philosophical system is offensive.

Ludwig Wittgenstein[2]

On 1 June 1310, in Paris, the French mystic Marguerite Porète was burnt at the stake for heresy. Her 'sins' consisted in affirming the primacy of faith and love over reason and propagating mystical union with God through dying to the self or 'annihilation' of the soul. In her book, *The Mirror of Simple Souls*, she had written:

> You who would read this book that I have writ
> If you will please your heed to it to lend,
> Consider well what you may say of it,
> For it is very hard to understand
> But let Humility lead you by the hand,
> She, keeper of the key to Learning's treasure-chest,
> She, the first virtue, mother to all the rest.

[1] trans. Alistair Hannay (London: Penguin, 1996), 100.
[2] Quoted by M. O'C. Drury, 'Notes on Conversations with Wittgenstein', in Rush Rhees (ed.), *Recollections of Wittgenstein* (Oxford: Oxford University Press, 1981), 102.

Men of theology and Scholars such as they
Will never understand this writing properly.
True comprehension of it only may
Those have who progress in humility;
You must let Love and Faith together be
Your guides to climb where Reason cannot come,
They who this house as mistresses do own . . .

So you too must abase your learning now,
Built only upon Reason, and your true
And perfect trust completely you must show
In the rich gifts which Love will make to you,
And Faith will cause to shine in brightest hue.
So understanding of this book they'll give
Which makes the Soul the life of Love to live.[3]

A list of fifteen 'propositions' was extracted from this book, allegedly contravening Church doctrine; and it was these that formed the basis of her condemnation.[4]

I

It is remarkable how much Porète's words—written so very long ago (in 1296 to be precise)—and the spirit that animates them chime with a number of things Kierkegaard and Wittgenstein say about religious belief. For Kierkegaard and Wittgenstein also believe that spiritual cultivation is more important for a religious understanding than intellectual adherence to a set of dogmas; they, too, believe that 'truth in the sense in which Christ is the truth is not a sum of statements, not a definition . . . , but a life'.[5] In Wittgenstein's words, 'faith is faith in what is needed by my *heart*, my *soul*, not my speculative intelligence. For it is my soul with its passions, as it were with its flesh and blood, that has to be saved, not my abstract mind. Perhaps we can say: Only *love* can believe the Resurrection. Or: it is *love* that believes the Resurrection.'[6]

---

[3] *The Mirror of Simple Souls*, translated from the French with an Introductory Interpretative Essay by Edmund Colledge, J. C. Marler and Judith Grant (Notre Dame: University of Notre Dame Press, 1999), 9.

[4] Introductory Interpretative Essay to *The Mirror of Simple Souls*, xlv–xlvi.

[5] Søren Kierkegaard, *Practice in Christianity*, ed. and trans. Howard and Edna Hong (Princeton: Princeton University Press, 1991), 205, henceforth PC.

[6] *Culture and Value*, ed. G. H. von Wright, trans. Peter Winch (Oxford: Blackwell, 1980), 33e, henceforth CV.

In the light of this, it is perhaps not entirely surprising that, her fateful end apart, parallels can be discerned between Porète's treatment at the hands of the Inquisition and the ways in which Kierkegaard's and Wittgenstein's religious thought has been regarded in much of the philosophical literature. For, just as the Inquisition seemed to find nothing wrong with the idea of distilling a body of doctrine from a work—written in the form of a dialogue between Love, Reason and the Trinity and in the language of courtly love—whose object is to show that this is precisely the wrong way in which to approach spiritual questions, so Kierkegaard and Wittgenstein have, more often than not, been treated as 'premise-authors'[7] whose intellectually disreputable claims warrant philosophical excommunication. J. L. Mackie, for example, is of this opinion. He attributes a form of 'irrationalism' to Kierkegaard which, in his words, is tantamount to playing 'a sort of intellectual Russian roulette'.[8] Alvin Plantinga shares Mackie's interpretation:

According to the most common brand of extreme fideism, however, reason and faith *conflict* or *clash* on matters of religious importance; and when they do, faith is to be preferred and reason suppressed. Thus, according to Kierkegaard, faith teaches 'the absurdity that the eternal is the historical'. He means to say, I think, that this proposition is among the deliverances of faith but absurd from the point of view of reason; and it should be accepted despite this absurdity.[9]

Nor have Wittgenstein's views on religious belief fared much better. They, too, like Kierkegaard's thought, have been condemned as 'fideistic' and as committing Wittgenstein to the thesis that religious beliefs are immune from rational criticism and support.[10] According to John

---

[7] This is Petrus Minor's (the pseudonymous author of Kierkegaard's *Book on Adler*) term for authors primarily interested in the communication of 'results'. See chapter 2 for further elaboration of this.

[8] J. L. Mackie, *The Miracle of Theism*, (Oxford: Oxford University Press, 1982), 216.

[9] 'Religious Belief as Properly Basic', in Brian Davies (ed.), *Philosophy of Religion. A Guide and Anthology* (Oxford: Oxford University Press, 2000), 91. This kind of view is, unfortunately, endemic. It cannot only be found in Kierkegaard's critics, but also in the works of sympathetic advocates who argue that faith is, literally, 'beyond' or 'against' reason. An especially prominent example of the latter is C. Steven Evans' work. See, for example, *Kierkegaard's* Fragments *and* Postscript (New York: Humanity Books (imprint of Prometheus Books), 1999) and *Faith Beyond Reason* (Michigan: William B. Eerdmans, 1998). For similar types of argument see Julia Watkin, *Historical Dictionary of Kierkegaard's Philosophy* (Maryland: The Scarecrow Press, 2001) and Patrick Gardiner, *Kierkegaard* (Oxford: Oxford University Press, 1988).

[10] See, for example, John Hyman, 'The Gospel According to Wittgenstein', in Robert Arrington and Mark Addis (eds), *Wittgenstein and Philosophy of Religion* (London: Routledge, 2001), 1–11, and Kai Nielsen's collected articles in Kai Nielsen and D. Z.

Hyman, this commitment 'has the interesting consequence that, as Wittgenstein [himself] said, "if Christianity is the truth then all the philosophy written about it is false" (*Culture and Value*, 83), but it has little else to recommend it.'[11]

It is no accident that such similar kinds of criticism should be levelled at both Kierkegaard and Wittgenstein by the philosophical Inquisition. For, as this book will show, Wittgenstein's account of religious belief is very clearly indebted to Kierkegaard's. But this is not the only parallel between them. A remarkable congruence of philosophical method also exists between both authors that makes the attempt to cash out their thought in a set of propositions as point-missing as it is to construe Porète's work as a kind of theoretical *scala paradisi*. Neither Kierkegaard nor Wittgenstein is concerned with combating a philosophical theory in order to replace it with another, but rather with undermining the philosophical misapprehensions that stand in the way of seeing that what we take to be the only available alternatives, are in fact a set of false dichotomies. That is to say, what is revolutionary in Kierkegaard's and Wittgenstein's conception is precisely to challenge the idea that as regards religious faith only two options are possible—either adherence to a set of metaphysical beliefs (with certain ways of acting following from these beliefs) or passionate commitment to a 'doctrineless' form of life; *tertium non datur* (there is no third way).

II

Part of the reason why the two philosophers who I am concerned with have been so widely misrepresented is, of course, that both pose notorious interpretative problems. The problems that they pose are, as a matter of fact, quite dissimilar: in Kierkegaard's case, the difficulties revolve around the pseudonymous and 'literary' character of many of his most important writings; while, in Wittgenstein's case, one of the most prominent issues concerns the relation between his earlier and his later work. The principal problems are different, then, but both are thorny, and whole books could be—indeed have been—written about either. The present book's purposes are different, however; and I will not be trying to

---

Phillips, *Wittgensteinian Fideism?* (London: SCM Press, 2005). The latter will be the subject of detailed discussion in chapter 4.

[11] John Hyman, op.cit., 10.

add to that literature here. Nevertheless, because there are genuine interpretative difficulties to be faced, it would probably be sensible to say a few words at the outset about the approach that I intend to take. The remarks that follow are necessarily brief and programmatic, but they should provide an indication, at least, as well as due warning perhaps, of the guiding interpretative principles that I have adopted in what follows. None of these principles, in my view, should strike anyone as very radical.

Kierkegaard's writings are all by Kierkegaard. Some of them he published under his own name; others he published under a variety of pseudonyms (sometimes presenting himself as editor); and others again, such as his journals, he didn't publish at all. But he did write all of them, and it is important to give this homely fact its proper weight if the task of interpreting him is not to lapse into one or another form of eccentricity—a genuine danger when confronted with an *oeuvre* of such diverse and unusual character. Here are four interpretative strategies that might appear to be licensed by the nature of Kierkegaard's production.

The first—let's call it the 'literal-minded reading'—is over-impressed by the fact that Kierkegaard wrote all of Kierkegaard's writings, and treats everything, whether signed or pseudonymous, published or unpublished, as a straightforward report of his views. This reading has the advantage that it takes Kierkegaard seriously, in one sense at least, as a thinker—that is, as someone who did actually have some views to report. But it doesn't take him seriously enough. In conflating the published and unpublished writings it fails to do Kierkegaard the basic courtesy, due to any writer, of distinguishing between what he thought worth reading and what he (perhaps) did not; and—still more damagingly—it fails to leave room for the possibility that there might have been some *point* to his decision to publish certain of his works pseudonymously. I will not be adopting a reading of this sort here.

The second strategy—call it the 'purely literary reading'—is the mirror image of the first, and treats all of Kierkegaard's writings as if they were some sort of high-spirited romp, pieces of the merest ventriloquism designed, as it might be, to prove that this particular author, at any rate, is well and truly dead. This reading has the advantage that it at least notices, and tries to make something of the fact, that Kierkegaard's work often has a strongly literary dimension (signalled among other things by his use of pseudonyms). But it flattens his *oeuvre* out every bit as crassly as the literal-minded reading does, while reducing him at the same time to a pointless—indeed a thoughtless—one-joke wonder. I will not be adopting this strategy either.

The third strategy, which we might term the 'killjoy reading', is alert to the literary dimension of Kierkegaard's work, but is suspicious of it, and is inclined to regard the pseudonymous writing as a kind of alarming hobby of Kierkegaard's, to be sidelined in favour of the signed works (and perhaps also of the journal entries). On this reading, Kierkegaard is to be taken seriously as a thinker—but only, or at any rate pre-eminently, when he writes in a reasonably ordinary way and does so under his own name. When he adopts an alias, he's up to something funny, and what he writes under it had better be treated with caution. A reading of this sort is certainly to be preferred to either of the other two that I have canvassed. But I will not be advancing such a reading—partly because it shares with the literal-minded reading a reluctance to entertain the possibility that what Kierkegaard is up to when he writes pseudonymously might actually be germane to his thought, and partly because, in my view at least, the pseudonymous works are often among his most interesting, and I would not wish to soft-pedal them in what follows.

Nor, finally, will I adopt a fourth strategy (mentioned here largely for the sake of completeness, and for which no label springs readily to mind), which reverses the emphasis of the killjoy reading, and gives absolute interpretative priority to the more overtly literary aspects of Kierkegaard's production, while discounting everything that he wrote under his own name (including, implicitly, his journals). It is hard to see what might be said in favour of such an approach, and no one, so far as I am aware, has ever seriously embraced it.

None of these strategies seems warranted to me, for the reasons that I have given. My own strategy—which I think might reasonably be described as 'moderate'—is different. It begins, as I have said, from the observation that Kierkegaard wrote all of Kierkegaard's writings, and from the presumption that any of them might therefore be helpful in interpreting his thought. In this much, I have some sympathy with the literal-minded approach set out above. I am, however, mindful that his writings are of different sorts; and I try to reflect that fact in the readings that I offer. So, for example, I give priority to the published works, and draw on the unpublished ones only where they corroborate or amplify something that Kierkegaard said in print. I am also convinced that there is a serious philosophical point to Kierkegaard's deployment of pseudonyms and other literary devices—I try to say what that point is in chapters 2 and 4—and so am careful not simply to conflate Kierkegaard's voice with those of his aliases. Nevertheless, and this strikes me as just as important, if hardly very surprising, certain themes, preoccupations and views are quite demonstrably shared by Kierkegaard and (at least some of) his pseudonyms; and, where this is the case, I do not hesitate to enlist Climacus, say, or Johannes *de Silentio*, as Kierkegaard's spokespersons. To refuse to do this, it seems to me, would be the merest asceticism, however apt the killjoy reading's caution may be in some respects. And by taking this approach, or so I hope to show, it is possible to give proper interpretative weight to every aspect of Kierkegaard's *oeuvre* while doing justice to, and making sense of, the fact that much of that *oeuvre* is highly 'literary' and the fact that a lot of it was published pseudonymously.

The interpretative conundrums confronting a potential exegete of Wittgenstein's work are somewhat different. The first concerns the question of how Wittgenstein's early work, the *Tractatus*—a work that notoriously declares itself to be nonsense—is to be read. This (already in itself almost insurmountable) exegetical difficulty has recently acquired a new spin given the rise to prominence of the so-called 'resolute reading' of the *Tractatus*, challenging the 'traditional' approaches taken to Wittgenstein's book that see it as promoting a self-undermining conception of attempting to say what, by the book's own lights, can only be 'shown'. The alternative vision offered by 'resolute readers' is that early Wittgenstein did not endorse—most of—what the *Tractatus* purports to be saying, but is deliberately drawing the reader into a nonsensical trap to be seen through and discarded. This reading not only has the advantage of saving Wittgenstein from refuting himself, it also confers the benefit of making the man appear less 'disjointed' in the sense that, on this reading, many of the same principles seen to be at work in Wittgenstein's *Philosophical Investigations* can already be found in the *Tractatus*. Nevertheless I will not be adopting such a reading here, for the price we have to pay for it—coming in the way of simply writing off two-thirds of what Wittgenstein actually says—strikes me as much too high.

Despite this substantial disagreement (which will be the focus of chapter 3) with 'resolute readers', however, I do share with them the sensible thought that whatever the differences between the author of the *Tractatus* and the author of the *Investigations*, 'early' and 'later' Wittgenstein are nevertheless the same person. That is to say, while I believe that many of Wittgenstein's philosophical views have clearly changed significantly in the later work—such as, for example, his thoughts on language and what lies beyond its limits—his conception of philosophy, and of the ethical dimension of the practice of philosophy, remains (or so I will argue) essentially the same.

Finally, something needs to be said about where Kierkegaard stands in relation to the development of Wittgenstein's thought. Here I intend to show that while interesting parallels can be discerned between Kierkegaard and the *Tractatus*, by far the most significant similarities between the two thinkers are to be found in Wittgenstein's later work. This explains why I have specifically devoted only one—albeit very long—chapter to a discussion of the relation between Kierkegaard and the *Tractatus* (chapter 3), while, in the other chapters, drawing mainly from Wittgenstein's post-*Tractatus* writings.

III

The aims of this book are threefold. First, to trace the extent of Kierkegaard's influence on Wittgenstein. Second, to show how remarkably like-minded the two philosophers are on such important issues as the nature of philosophy and religious belief. Third, to rectify the distortions that Kierkegaard's and Wittgenstein's views have been subjected to in the philosophical literature and to dispel the illusions that stand in the way of taking their concerted critique of the orthodox conceptions of philosophy and religion as seriously as it deserves.

The first chapter of the book will be devoted to the task of assembling biographical as well as textual evidence for the claim that Wittgenstein read and was deeply involved with Kierkegaard's work throughout his life. The second will be devoted to a discussion of the parallels to be found in Kierkegaard's and Wittgenstein's conception of philosophy. This will set the stage for a discussion, in chapters 3 and 4, of the parallels in the ways in which Kierkegaard and Wittgenstein conceive of religious belief. While it will be shown that much of the later Wittgenstein's thought on religion can be said to be directly modelled on a Kierkegaardian view, the connection between early Wittgenstein's conception and Kierkegaard's is altogether more subtle.

More specifically, it will be shown (in chapter 3) that where the parallels between the two thinkers are generally thought to be found, namely in a common doctrine of 'ineffable truth'—whether this doctrine is taken to be rejected or endorsed by both authors[12]—there aren't in

---

[12] C. Steven Evans thinks both philosophers endorse it (see Evans, *Kierkegaard's Fragments and Postscript*, 222), whereas James Conant believes Kierkegaard's and Wittgenstein's common strategy consists in the dispelling of this illusion. For an indepth discussion of the latter, see chapter 3.

fact any. This will go some way towards deflating Mackie's critique, mentioned earlier, by showing that we need not choose between a 'plain nonsense view' of religious belief—what 'resolute readers' of the *Tractatus* appear to propound—or a form of fideistic irrationalism. More will then be said about the latter type of criticism in chapter 4, where Kierkegaard's and (the later) Wittgenstein's account of religious belief will be developed and the charges of 'fideism' and 'incommensurability' examined and rejected. If this endeavour succeeds, I hope, among other things, to have pulled the rug away from under some surprisingly ingrained philosophical prejudices, and to have illuminated a potentially very rich 'third way' of approaching issues concerning religious faith. And, as the Inquisition no longer seems very active, I hope to have nothing more to fear from my efforts than scholarly censure.

1

Kierkegaard's Influence on Wittgenstein's Thought

Kierkegaard was by far the most profound thinker of the last century. Kierkegaard was a saint.

Ludwig Wittgenstein[1]

INTRODUCTION

In his biographical sketch of Wittgenstein G. H. von Wright writes, 'Wittgenstein received deeper impressions from some writers in the borderland between philosophy, religion, and poetry than from the philosophers, in the restricted sense of the word. Among the former are St. Augustine, Kierkegaard, Dostoevsky, and Tolstoy.'[2] This seems to me an accurate assessment. Indeed, it has almost become a commonplace today that Wittgenstein held Kierkegaard in incredibly high regard. Nevertheless, although many commentators take heed of this fact, few go beyond merely noting it.[3] Much, therefore, still needs to be

---

[1] Quoted by M. O'C. Drury, in Rhees, *Recollections of Wittgenstein*, 87.

[2] In Norman Malcolm, *Ludwig Wittgenstein, A Memoir* (Oxford: Oxford University Press, 2001), 19.

[3] To my knowledge only two monographs exist on this subject: Charles Creegan, *Wittgenstein and Kierkegaard — Religion, Individuality and Philosophical Method* (London: Routledge, 1989), and Mariele Nientied, *Kierkegaard und Wittgenstein — 'Hineintäuschen in das Wahre'* (Berlin: de Gruyter, 2003). In the latter book Nientied concentrates exclusively on the subject of 'indirect communication' and its inherent problems, as she believes that 'Søren Kierkegaard and Ludwig Wittgenstein neither have an academic discipline nor an era in common, and least of all a school or a domain of discourse' (Introduction, 4, translation mine). I don't see why that should matter, if it can be shown that Wittgenstein and Kierkegaard share common views on religion and the point of philosophical activity. Creegan's book, on the other hand, does not suffer from such over-hasty generalizations, but came too early to take account either of the recently

done when it comes to tracing the extent of Kierkegaard's influence on Wittgenstein and the deep-running intellectual affinities between them. The greater availability of biographical material on Wittgenstein, notably his diaries and letters, has made this task easier than it would have been only a couple of decades ago.

I believe that the main reason for the still perceptible lacuna in scholarship as regards this issue stems from the fact that what Wittgenstein cared about most—ethics, aesthetics and religion—he, in Tractarian fashion, passed over in silence, for the most part, while Kierkegaard's pseudonymous authorship is, by comparison, astonishingly prolix on these matters.[4] This fact has no doubt fuelled the common misunderstanding that Kierkegaard and Wittgenstein are engaged in radically different—even incommensurable—projects. An excellent example of this is Bertrand Russell's surprise, when he found that after the First World War Wittgenstein had, in Russell's words, 'become a complete mystic'. Russell wrote to Lady Ottoline Morrell on 20 December 1919, 'I had felt in his (Wittgenstein's) book (the *Tractatus*) a flavour of mysticism, but was astonished when I found that he has become a complete mystic. He reads people like Kierkegaard and Angelus Silesius, and he seriously contemplates becoming a monk.'[5] Even more recent critics of Wittgenstein's work, however, often either fail to see the extent to which Kierkegaard influenced Wittgenstein's views on religion or else underestimate the points of contact in their respective authorships. The following will serve as two examples.

In his perceptive account of logic and sin in the writings of Wittgenstein, Philip Shields writes:

While . . . St. Augustine, Kierkegaard, Tolstoy and William James, were clearly read by Wittgenstein and in some sense deeply admired by him, there generally appears to be little direct influence . . . No doubt there are some strands of influence in places, but, with the possible exception of Schopenhauer, Wittgenstein's views of religious matters seem to be fairly well developed long before we have clear evidence of his having read particular writers.[6]

published journals throwing new light on Wittgenstein's interest in Kierkegaard or of the current debates surrounding the interpretation of Kierkegaard's and Wittgenstein's work.

[4] The stereotyping of Kierkegaard as a 'Continental' philosopher and of Wittgenstein, despite his 'Continental' origin, as 'analytic', has no doubt also contributed to this.

[5] Quoted in *Ludwig Wittgenstein: Cambridge Letters*, ed. Brian McGuinness and G. H. von Wright (Oxford: Blackwell, 1995), 140.

[6] Philip Shields, *Logic and Sin in the Writings of Ludwig Wittgenstein* (Chicago, IL: University of Chicago Press, 1993), 7.

I am not going to take issue with this claim as regards Augustine, Tolstoy and James, but, with respect to Kierkegaard, Shields's verdict seems to me to be patently wrong. In this chapter I therefore intend to show that the evidence speaks against Shields's view.

The other common misconception—that Wittgenstein and Kierkegaard were engaged in very different enterprises—can be found, among other places, in the writings of D. Z. Phillips. Although I agree with him in rejecting James Conant's recent interpretations of the revocations to be found in Wittgenstein and Kierkegaard,[7] I think that Phillips over-emphasizes the discontinuities in Kierkegaard's and Wittgenstein's work by claiming that, in the end, the former is a purely religious author and that his writings, in this sense, are 'partisan',[8] while Wittgenstein, on the other hand, offers a 'non-partisan', 'contemplative' conception of philosophy. He says, 'I claim that a contemplative conception of philosophy is not to be found in Kierkegaard. He is a religious thinker, concerned with specific confusions concerning Christianity. Kierkegaard never doubts the categories of the aesthetic, the ethical, and the religious, whereas Wittgenstein wonders at their very possibility. An asymmetry therefore exists between their authorships.'[9] While I do not intend to demonstrate that what seems different is really the same—how ironic that would be given that Wittgenstein and Kierkegaard both chastise Hegel for doing just that[10]—I *am* going to show that the distinction Phillips draws isn't as clear-cut as he supposes.

For, firstly, Wittgenstein, too, was motivated by religious concerns. After all, he once said to Drury, 'I am not a religious man but I cannot help seeing every problem from a religious point of view.'[11] This remark rightly led Drury to wonder 'whether there are not dimensions in Wittgenstein's thought that are still largely being ignored'. 'Have I seen,' he goes on to ask himself, 'that the *Philosophical Remarks* could have

---

[7] See chapter 3.   [8] This is my term not Phillips's.

[9] D. Z. Phillips, *Philosophy's Cool Place* (New York: Cornell University Press, 1999), 14.

[10] Wittgenstein once said to Drury, 'Hegel seems to me to be always wanting to say that things which look different are really the same. Whereas my interest is in showing that things which look the same are really different. I was thinking of using as a motto for my book a quotation from *King Lear*: "I'll teach you differences."' ('Some Notes on Conversations with Wittgenstein', 157.) Wittgenstein couldn't be more in agreement with Kierkegaard on this point.

[11] For an interesting discussion of what exactly Wittgenstein could have meant by that, see Norman Malcolm, *Wittgenstein, A Religious Point of View?*, edited with a response by Peter Winch (New York: Cornell University Press, 1993).

been inscribed "to the glory of God"?[12] Or that the problems discussed in the *Philosophical Investigations* are being seen from a religious point of view?'[13] Secondly, I will be arguing that Kierkegaard was not a purely religious author in the sense that he was *only* concerned with the dispelling of the 'monstrous illusion' that Christianity exists in Christendom. Rather, I will show that Wittgenstein and Kierkegaard are united in their common aim of paving the way, in their writings, for an *authentic existence*—an existence that is free of self-deception and illusion. In both authors, I will argue, this rigorous demand is an ethical one, and, although both Wittgenstein and Kierkegaard would agree that philosophy cannot help one to become the kind of person capable of leading such a life, it can certainly clear away the conceptual confusions and obstacles that might stand in the way of leading it. Indeed, it seems to me that Wittgenstein and Kierkegaard both desire the kind of reader for whom, ideally, philosophical clarity *would* lead to *existential* clarity, that is, to a breakdown of the distinction between a 'contemplative' and a 'partisan' conception of philosophy. This, I will argue, is the ethical lynchpin uniting their work.

In other words, I intend to show that Phillips's asymmetry (just like the asymmetry between Wittgenstein's relative silence on ethico-religious matters and Kierkegaard's comparative verbosity) is only an apparent one, which ultimately reveals more, rather than less, common ground between the two thinkers. In the present chapter, though, our task will be to assemble evidence for the claim that Wittgenstein read and was deeply involved with Kierkegaard's work throughout his life. Only then will we be in a position to assess the extent to which Kierkegaard's thought left its mark on Wittgenstein's own philosophical activity.

I TESTIMONIAL EVIDENCE

There is every reason to suppose that Wittgenstein was introduced to the writings of Kierkegaard from a very early age.[14] During his

---

[12] In the introduction to the *Philosophical Remarks* Wittgenstein wrote: 'I would like to say, "This book is written to the glory of God", but nowadays this would be the trick of a cheat, i.e. it would not be correctly understood.' Quoted in Rhees, *Recollections of Wittgenstein*, 78.

[13] M. O'C. Drury, 'Some Notes on Conversations with Wittgenstein', in Rhees, op. cit., 79.

[14] This section deals primarily with evidence that Wittgenstein read Kierkegaard—testimony collated from conversations with friends, correspondence, etc.—that is not

childhood and adolescence his elder sister Margarete ('Gretl') served as his 'philosophical' mentor. In the words of Ray Monk, 'Gretl was acknowledged as the intellectual of the family, the one who kept abreast of contemporary developments in the arts and sciences, and the one most prepared to embrace new ideas and to challenge the views of her elders.'[15] Given that Kierkegaard was Gretl's favourite author[16] and was generally very much in vogue in turn-of-the-century Vienna, it would be very surprising indeed if Gretl had not drawn her younger brother's attention to Kierkegaard's works.

Be that as it may, direct evidence is certainly available that Wittgenstein was exposed to some Kierkegaard subsequently. In 1914, while spending some time in Norway, Wittgenstein first came across Ludwig von Ficker, the editor of the literary journal *Der Brenner*, which published the work of Theodor Haecker, whose German translations of Kierkegaard first introduced the Danish philosopher to an Austrian audience. Among the Kierkegaard texts that appeared in *Der Brenner* between 1913 and 1921 are the preface to *Prefaces*, the introduction to *Johannes Climacus*, the discourse 'At a Graveside' from *Three Discourses on Imagined Occasions*, the discourse 'The Thorn in the Flesh' from *Four Upbuilding Discourses*, *A Critique of the Present Age*, some journal entries from 1835 and 1836, as well as the discourse *Die Kraft Gottes in der Schwachheit des Menschen*.[17] Wittgenstein clearly read this journal and even decided, through Ficker, to donate some of his family money to Austrian artists in need. Theodor Haecker was one of the beneficiaries.[18]

Further evidence of Wittgenstein's engagement with Kierkegaard can be gleaned from his extensive correspondence during the war period. Wittgenstein's sister, Hermine, for example, writes in her letter to Ludwig from 20 November 1917:

Thank you very much for your lovely card from 13th November. You were perfectly correct in supposing that I did not receive the earlier one with your request for books, but I've just been out for them and a number of Kierkegaard volumes are already on the way. I hope they are the ones you want, because,

---

taken from Wittgenstein's own notebooks, diaries or published writings (occasional reference to some of the latter is of course unavoidable). Section II, on the other hand, deals specifically with references to Kierkegaardian themes in Wittgenstein's own writings.

[15] Ray Monk, *The Duty of Genius* (London: Vintage, 1991), 16.
[16] See Kurt Wuchterl and Adolf Hübner, *Wittgenstein* (Hamburg: Rowohlt, 1979), 30.
[17] I have so far not managed to locate an English translation of this discourse.
[18] See Monk, *Duty*, 106–9.

given that I don't know anything about him and his writings, I simply chose a few at random. The Diary of a Seducer, which I bought in a different bookshop, will follow.[19]

It is unfortunate that Hermine does not say which volumes she sent, but the fact that Wittgenstein had her send them to him at the Front speaks for itself.

Kierkegaard also comes up in the correspondence between Wittgenstein and his close wartime friend, Paul Engelmann,[20] who quotes from the *Stages on Life's Way* in one of his letters to Wittgenstein. Engelmann says, ' "If I had had faith, I would have stayed with her"[21] . . . . It seems to me that you are lacking in faith.'[22] To which Wittgenstein replies:

When you say that I do not have faith, you are quite right, except that I did not have it previously either. It is obvious that someone who wants to invent a machine to turn him into a better person, that such a one has no faith. But what should I do? One thing is clear to me: I am much too bad to ponder about myself; I will either remain a swine or I will improve and that's that! No transcendental twaddle when everything is as clear as a slap.[23]

From the notebooks and the coded diaries dating from this period it becomes clear that Wittgenstein was constantly preoccupied with spiritual matters. Although there are no direct references to Kierkegaard in these materials, it would, I think, not be an exaggeration to say that Wittgenstein was constantly suffering from a form of 'Kierkegaardian despair'. The diaries reveal that Wittgenstein was continuously tormented by his moral worthlessness and his sense of being at odds with the world. Wittgenstein believed that this kind of unhappiness—what Kierkegaard would call despair—is the sign of a bad life, the mark of someone who is incapable of doing God's will and who, as the previously cited letter suggests, lacks faith.[24]

---

[19] *Wittgenstein Familienbriefe*, ed. Brian McGuinness, Maria Ascher and Otto Pfersmann (Vienna: Hölder-Pichler-Tempsky, 1996), 48, translation mine.

[20] Wittgenstein first met Engelmann when he was at the Front in Olmütz. They became very close friends and Engelmann later collaborated with Wittgenstein on the house he built for his sister Gretl in the Kundmanngasse in Vienna. See Monk, op.cit., 150–1 and 235.

[21] This is an allusion to Kierkegaard's tortured relationship with his ex-fiancée, Regine Olsen.

[22] Letter from 8.1.1918; translation mine. In Paul Engelmann, *Ludwig Wittgenstein. Briefe und Begegnungen* (Vienna and Munich: Oldenbourg, 1970), 18.

[23] Letter from 16.1.1918. Ibid.

[24] See Ludwig Wittgenstein, *Tagebücher 1914–16*, in Werkausgabe Band 1 (Frankfurt: Suhrkamp, 1993c), 168–9. All subsequent translations mine.

In the *Notebooks* Wittgenstein equates doing God's will with coming to terms with the facts,[25] and at *Tractatus* 6.4321 he writes, 'The facts all merely belong to the task, not to the solution.'[26] On this conception of things, where life is seen as a task to be mastered (a conception that Kierkegaard shared), a lack of faith is therefore regarded as a *moral* failing.[27] This is also the reason why Wittgenstein accepted the Dostoevskyan thought that if suicide is allowed, then everything is allowed. On 10.1.1917 Wittgenstein writes, 'suicide is so to speak the elementary sin'.[28] This is so, because suicide is an evasion of the task that is life, a sign that one's life is not in harmony with the facts, or, to put it religiously, is in rebellion against the will of God. The parallels with Anti-Climacus'[29] *The Sickness Unto Death*, be they conscious or not, are striking. Anti-Climacus says, 'That is why the pagan . . . judged suicide with such singular irresponsibility, yes, praised suicide, which for spirit is the most crucial sin, escaping from existence in this way, mutinying against God . . . The point that suicide is basically a crime against God completely escapes the pagan.'[30] From what has been said so far, it seems that Wittgenstein would therefore also have agreed with the central Kierkegaardian notion that the opposite of sin is not virtue, but *faith*. Wittgenstein appears to have accepted, too, Kierkegaard's central contention that only Christianity provides a real solution to the 'problem of life',[31] as one of his coded diary entries from 1914 reveals:

Bought Nietzsche volume 8 [containing *The Antichrist*] and read around in it. Was deeply impressed by his antagonism towards Christianity. For also in his writings there is a grain of truth. To be sure, Christianity is the only *certain* way to happiness. But what if someone rejected this happiness?! Might it not be better to be ground to the dust [*zu Grunde gehen*] in the hopeless struggle against the external world? But such a life is meaningless. But why not lead a meaningless life? Is it unworthy?[32]

---

[25] See *Tagebücher*, 8.7.16, 168–9.

[26] *Werkausgabe Band 1*, 84, translation mine.

[27] For a more detailed discussion of this, see chapter 3, section VIII.

[28] *Werkausgabe Band 1*, 187.

[29] Kierkegaard's 'highest', i.e. most Christian, pseudonym.

[30] Søren Kierkegaard, *The Sickness unto Death*, ed. and trans. Howard and Edna Hong (Princeton: Princeton University Press, 1980a), 46, henceforth SUD.

[31] Of course this is also an idea to be found in Tolstoy and we know that Wittgenstein was constantly reading Tolstoy's *The Gospel in Brief* at this time. However, it is no part of my argument, here or elsewhere, to claim that Wittgenstein was only influenced by Kierkegaard in religious matters.

[32] *Geheime Tagebücher*, ed. Wilhelm Baum (Vienna: Turia and Kant, 1991), 49. Letter dated 8.12.1914, translation mine.

It seems, therefore, that at this point in his life, although he could not come to have faith himself, Wittgenstein accepted the idea that a life without faith is meaningless, that without it we are mere playthings of contingency, doomed to a life of despair and, as Kierkegaard would doubtlessly add, spiritlessness. In this revolt against contingency, we are again hard pressed not to hear echoes of Kierkegaard. In *Fear and Trembling*, for example, Kierkegaard's pseudonym, Johannes *de Silentio*, expresses the same idea as the quotation above, just more poetically: 'If a human being did not have an eternal consciousness, if underlying everything there were only a wild, fermenting power that writhing in dark passions produced everything, be it significant or insignificant, if a vast, never appeased emptiness hid beneath everything,[33] what would life be then but despair?'[34]

It seems, therefore, that Wittgenstein read much Kierkegaard both during and after the First World War (during which time he wrote the *Tractatus*). He also discussed Kierkegaard's works with his friends Paul Engelmann and Ludwig Hänsel, a fellow schoolteacher of Wittgenstein's in Trattenbach, in whose correspondence with Wittgenstein we find mention of the trouble that Hänsel had with sending Wittgenstein Kierkegaard's *Practice in Christianity*. In the notes to this volume of correspondence, the editors claim that it is certain that Wittgenstein was also reading other Kierkegaardian works at that time, for Karl Gruber, one of Wittgenstein's most talented pupils, recalls seeing books with 'weird titles' in Wittgenstein's room (and most of Kierkegaard's writings would fit that description). One of them contained the word 'anxiety' and it is sensible to assume that this was Kierkegaard's *The Concept of Anxiety*.[35]

More frequent direct references to the Danish thinker, however, only start to abound in Wittgenstein's later remarks to friends. Especially rich sources of these are the recorded conversations that Wittgenstein had with Maurice Drury,[36] Norman Malcolm[37] and O. K. Bouwsma.[38] I will attempt to present a synoptic view of the most important themes

---

[33] This is also reminiscent of Pascal's oft-quoted aphorism: 'Le silence éternel de ces espaces infinis m'effraie.'

[34] *Fear and Trembling*, ed. and trans. Howard and Edna Hong (Princeton: Princeton University Press, 1983), 15, henceforth FT.

[35] See *Ludwig Hänsel—Ludwig Wittgenstein. Eine Freundschaft*, ed. Ilse Somavilla, Anton Unterkircher and Christian Paul Berger (Innsbruck: Haymon, 1994), 56 and 278. See also Wuchterl and Hübner, *Wittgenstein*, 96.

[36] See Rhees, *Recollections*.   [37] See Malcolm, *Memoir*.

[38] See O. K. Bouwsma, *Wittgenstein. Conversations 1949–51*, ed. J. L. Craft and Ronald E. Hustwit, (Indianapolis, IN: Hackett, 1986).

that emerge from these remarks, starting with Drury's account, followed by Malcolm's and Bouwsma's.

In 'Some Notes on Conversations with Wittgenstein' Drury mentions the first time that Wittgenstein spoke to him about Kierkegaard. Wittgenstein says, 'Kierkegaard was by far the most profound thinker of the last century. Kierkegaard was a saint.'[39] This statement is remarkable in two ways. First, Wittgenstein was not prone to use superlatives, especially not of other philosophers. Second, the juxtaposition of 'profound thinker' and 'saint' is interesting, as it reveals how closely entwined the philosophical and the ethical dimensions of someone's character are for Wittgenstein. A 'profound thinker' is not simply a person who has 'profound' thoughts, but someone whose life expresses—or is emblematic of—these thoughts. Kierkegaard would have wholeheartedly agreed. Wittgenstein and Kierkegaard concur, in other words, that there is no profundity without authenticity and that it is therefore imperative for the philosopher to strive for both. It seems to me that much of Wittgenstein's great admiration for Kierkegaard derives from his thinking that Kierkegaard, more than perhaps any other philosopher, managed to make both his life and his work into an 'existence-communication'.

Drury then relates how Wittgenstein went on to speak of the three existence-spheres that dominate Kierkegaard's writing: 'the aesthetic, where the objective is to get the maximum enjoyment out of this life; the ethical, where the concept of duty demands renunciation; and the religious, where this very renunciation itself becomes a source of joy'. About the latter Wittgenstein says—and here again the 'personal' and the 'philosophical' aspects of a problem appear to merge—'Concerning this last category I don't pretend to understand how it is possible. I have never been able to deny myself anything, not even a cup of coffee if I wanted it. Mind you I don't believe what Kierkegaard believed, but of this I am certain, that we are not here in order to have a good time.'[40] The latter remark again reveals what has already been noted with respect to the 'earlier' Wittgenstein, that although he did not (quite) come to have faith himself, he did regard his life and work from a 'religious point of view', that is, as Anti-Climacus would say, as a task to be mastered 'before God' (SUD 79–82) and therefore in the most ethically rigorous way possible.[41]

---

[39] See note 1.   [40] Rhees, *Recollections*, 87–8.

[41] Wittgenstein (especially the 'early' one) often did not make a distinction at all between what he called the 'ethical' (or 'Ethics' with a capital 'E') and the religious. See,

Drury's records, however, not only show that Wittgenstein agreed with Kierkegaard about the ethical dimension of philosophy, but that he also shared many of Kierkegaard's views on the nature of religious belief. Here is an especially good example. On one occasion Drury discussed with Wittgenstein his intention to become a priest to which Wittgenstein reacted sceptically. He said, 'I would be afraid that you would try and give some sort of philosophical justification for Christian beliefs, as if some sort of proof was needed . . . The symbolisms of Catholicism are wonderful beyond words. But any attempt to make it into a philosophical system is offensive.'[42] Here one would be forgiven for thinking that it is Johannes Climacus, the author of *Concluding Unscientific Postscript*,[43] who is doing the talking.

This impression is reinforced by the following two remarks which again reveal that Wittgenstein shared with Kierkegaard a disdain for giving religion a 'rational' foundation and making it 'more probable': 'But the New Testament doesn't have to be proved to be true by historians either. It would make no difference if there had never been a historical person as Jesus is portrayed in the Gospels; though I don't think any competent authority doubts that there really was such a person.'[44] And in a similar vein: 'If you can accept the miracle that God became man, then all these difficulties are as nothing. For then it is impossible for me to say what form the record of such an event should take.'[45] The views Wittgenstein expresses here are identical to those propounded by Climacus in CUP, where an entire chapter is devoted to 'The Historical Point of View', in order to show that history is irrelevant to faith. Climacus says:

Thus everything is assumed to be in order with regard to the Holy Scriptures—what then? Has the person who did not believe come a single step closer to faith? No, not a single step. Faith does not result from straightforward

---

for example, *Tagebücher*, 11.6.1916, 167 (translation mine): 'What do I know about God and the purpose of life? I know that this world is . . . That something is problematical about it which we call its meaning. That this does not lie within the world, but outside it . . . That life is the world. That my will penetrates the world. That my will is good or evil. That Good or Evil are therefore somehow connected with the meaning of the world. The meaning of life, i.e. the meaning of the world, we can call God.' See also *A Lecture on Ethics*, in Ludwig Wittgenstein, *Philosophical Occasions*, ed. James Klagge and Alfred Nordmann (Indianapolis, IN: Hackett, 1993a), 36–44.

[42] Rhees, *Recollections*, 102.

[43] Søren Kierkegaard, *Concluding Unscientific Postscript to* Philosophical Fragments, ed. and trans. Howard and Edna Hong (Princeton: Princeton University Press, 1992a); henceforth CUP.

[44] *Recollections*, 101.   [45] Ibid., 164.

scholarly deliberation, nor does it come directly; on the contrary, in this objectivity one loses that infinite, personal, impassioned interestedness, which is the condition of faith . . . if passion is taken away, faith no longer exists, and certainty and passion do not hitch up as a team. (CUP 29)

That the *Postscript* was often on Wittgenstein's mind is also borne out by Drury's recalling how Wittgenstein once quoted to him the following remark of Lessing's:

If God held closed in his right hand all truth, and in his left the single and untiring striving after truth, adding even that I always and forever make mistakes, and said to me: Choose! I should fall humbly before his left hand and say: Father grant me! the pure truth is for you alone.[46]

It is curious that Drury, who knew the work of Kierkegaard well, does not go on to mention that this quote by Lessing occupies a central place in CUP, which is where Wittgenstein might have originally got it from. This episode also shows that Wittgenstein, who, according to Drury, 'quoted with great emphasis Lessing's remark', seems to be in agreement with its spirit: a rejection of philosophical *hubris* and system-mongering. Kierkegaard naturally quotes it as a gibe against his favourite adversary, Hegel:

When Lessing said these words, the system was presumably not finished; alas, and now he is dead! If he were living now, now when the system has been completed for the most part or is at least in the works and will be finished by next Sunday, believe me, Lessing would have clutched it with both hands. (CUP 106)

That Wittgenstein knew the *Postcript* well and greatly esteemed it is also corroborated by Norman Malcolm who says the following about Wittgenstein's conception of religion:

I believe that Wittgenstein was prepared by his own character and experience to comprehend the idea of a judging and redeeming God. But any cosmological conception of a Deity, derived from the notions of cause or infinity, would be repugnant to him. He was impatient with 'proofs' of the existence of God, and with attempts to give religion a *rational* foundation. When I once quoted to him a remark of Kierkegaard's to this effect: 'How can it be that Christ does not exist, since I know that He has saved me?', Wittgenstein exclaimed: 'You see! It isn't a question of *proving* anything!'

Malcolm continues, 'Kierkegaard he [Wittgenstein] also esteemed. He referred to him, with something of awe in his expression, as a "really religious" man. He had read the *Concluding Unscientific Postscript*—but found it "too deep" for him.[47] By the latter Wittgenstein meant, I think, that this work exhibits a level of religiousness which he felt to be beyond him. As Malcolm says:

I suspect that he regarded religious belief as based on qualities of character and will that he himself did not possess. Of Smythies and Anscombe, both of whom had become Roman Catholics, he once said to me: 'I could not possibly bring myself to believe all the things that they believe.' I think that in this remark he was not disparaging their belief. It was rather an observation about his own capacity.[48]

These remarks again suggest a strong affinity between Wittgenstein and Kierkegaard: both believe that coming to be religious cannot be the result of a philosophical argument and is not tantamount to accepting a metaphysical theory. Rather, it is a matter of becoming a certain sort of person—one conscious of his sins and prepared to accept the help of a redeemer. On this view, therefore, only the *ethical* can lead one to religion,[49] not metaphysical speculation.

In this respect it is interesting to note that in 1983, in the 'Notes' to the second edition of his *Memoir*, Malcolm (as a result of finding that religious remarks permeate *Culture and Value* and that religious thoughts and feelings dominate Drury's 'Conversations with Wittgenstein') modifies his earlier claim, made in 1958, that Wittgenstein was not a religious man.[50] Malcolm says, 'Thus, if it is right to say that Wittgenstein was not a religious person, there must be weighed against this the fact that his reflections about himself and mankind, and even about the aims of his intensive philosophical work, were penetrated by thoughts and feelings of a religious character.'[51] And it should have become apparent by now that Wittgenstein's religious thoughts are clearly inspired by, and therefore cannot be seen in isolation from, his admiration for Kierkegaard.

Naturally, Wittgenstein also said some 'critical' things about Kierkegaard. Here is an example from a letter to Malcolm from 1948. Wittgenstein says, 'I've never read the *Works of Love*. Kierkegaard is far

---

[47] *Memoir*, 59–60.   [48] Ibid., 60.

[49] In this respect Kierkegaard's and Wittgenstein's conception also has strong affinities with Kant's.

[50] With the publication of *Denkbewegungen* (Wittgenstein's diaries 1930–2 and 1936–7) this assessment is thrown even more into question.

[51] *Memoir*, 83.

too deep for me, anyhow. He bewilders me without working the good effects which he would in *deeper* souls.'[52] This remark again reveals that Wittgenstein regarded Kierkegaard as being on a higher spiritual and religious level than himself, a fact that Wittgenstein sometimes seemed to feel ambivalent about. This is, for instance, brought out in the following comment made to Bouwsma, although the latter is not entirely confident about its correctness: 'Kierkegaard is very serious. But he [Wittgenstein] could not read him much. He got hints. He did not want another man's thought all chewed. A word or two was sometimes enough. But Kierkegaard struck him almost as like a snob, too high, for him, not touching the details of common life.'[53] It is interesting to compare this remark, made in 1949, with the following diary entry from 1937: 'Nothing is as difficult for me as modesty. I am noticing this again now that I am reading Kierkegaard. Nothing is as difficult for me as feeling inferior; although it is only a matter of seeing things in their true light.'[54] Although I don't want to put too much weight on this remark, I do think that it perhaps helps to explain Wittgenstein's relative reticence as regards acknowledging his intellectual debt to Kierkegaard. If Wittgenstein did indeed feel 'inferior' to Kierkegaard, he may have wanted to downplay the influence that the latter had on him. This view is also given some plausibility by H. D. P. Lee's report that '(Wittgenstein) told me that he learned Danish in order to be able to read Kierkegaard in the original,[55] and clearly had a great admiration for him, though I never remember him speaking about him in detail.'[56]

II REFERENCES TO KIERKEGAARD
IN WITTGENSTEIN'S WRITINGS[57]

Apart from the *Tractatus* Wittgenstein published nothing—with the exception of a book review and 'Some Remarks on Logical Form'—during

---

[52] *Memoir*, 106.   [53] O. K. Bouwsma, op.cit., 46.

[54] Ludwig Wittgenstein, *Denkbewegungen*, ed. Ilse Somavilla (Frankfurt: Fischer, 1999), 81, translation mine (ibid. all the others taken from this work).

[55] This is also corroborated by Maurice Drury who says, 'When some years later Kierkegaard was translated into English, largely by Walter Lowrie, Wittgenstein was displeased with the poor style of this translator. He completely failed to reproduce the elegance of the original Danish' (in Rhees, *Recollections*, 88).

[56] H. D. P. Lee, 'Wittgenstein 1929–31', *Philosophy* 54 (1979): 218.

[57] This includes discussion of obviously Kierkegaardian themes, even where Kierkegaard is not mentioned directly by name.

his lifetime. His second major work, the *Philosophical Investigations*,[58] was published posthumously in 1953 and throughout his lifetime Wittgenstein remained dissatisfied with the book he kept attempting to write and which, apart from the first part, remained fragmentary. He once said to Drury, 'It is impossible for me to say in my book one word about all that music has meant in my life. How then can I hope to be understood?'[59] This remark might equally well be applied to religion. While the concluding, 'mystical' remarks in the *Tractatus* are notorious, in the *Investigations* there is only a single allusion to theology—§373: 'Grammar tells what kind of object anything is. (Theology as grammar.)'—and yet it is clear from everything that has been said so far that religion and religious thoughts occupied a central place in Wittgenstein's life. The fact that Wittgenstein remained silent about these matters in his most influential work should therefore not be seen, as it often has been, as an indication that these things did not greatly concern him. In fact, *Culture and Value*, as well as the recently published diaries from the thirties (some of whose entries overlap with remarks in CV), testify to Wittgenstein's lifelong involvement with religious issues. We can therefore only speculate as to what the reasons might have been for Wittgenstein's reticence.[60] Perhaps he did not find a natural way of incorporating the remarks he made, for example, in CV into the PI; perhaps his intense desire to do these problems justice demanded such exacting standards that Wittgenstein, with characteristic modesty, felt that he could not possibly meet them (after all, he was extremely critical of his own work in general). In this respect, Wittgenstein may have wanted, in Tractarian fashion, to confine himself to silence, rather than to 'dirty a flower with muddy hands'.[61]

Although we have found in the previous section that there are many points of contact between Kierkegaard and the early Wittgenstein, Kierkegaard's influence on Wittgenstein's later views on religion appears to have been much more profound. Given that the *Tractatus* and the *Tractatus*-inspired *Lecture on Ethics* will be the subject of detailed

[58] Ed. G. E. M. Anscombe, Rush Rhees and G. H. von Wright (Oxford: Blackwell, 1958), trans. G. E. M. Anscombe; henceforth PI.

[59] Rhees, op.cit., 79.

[60] None of this implies, of course, that Wittgenstein's philosophy in general doesn't have important implications for the philosophy of religion.

[61] This is what Wittgenstein, while his student in Cambridge, once said to Russell, when the latter chastised him for not stating any arguments for his point of view. To which Russell replied 'that he had better acquire a slave to state the arguments'. See Monk, op.cit., 54.

discussion later on and there aren't any direct references to Kierkegaard in these works,[62] I will move straight on to a discussion of the diaries from the thirties, which contain a plethora of remarks that very clearly allude to the Dane. Indeed, most of the entries revolving around spiritual matters (and these make up more than half of the text) deal overtly with Kierkegaardian issues. I will give a few examples and will then move on to a discussion of CV, the *Lectures and Conversations on Religious Belief* and Wittgenstein's *Remarks on Frazer's* Golden Bough.

The following entry, for instance, immediately calls to mind Anti-Climacus' *Practice in Christianity*:

To know oneself is awful, because one knows at the same time the living requirement and that one falls short of it. But there are no better means for coming to know oneself than by seeing the paragon [*den Vollkommenen*]. This is why the paragon must cause a storm of outrage in human beings, if they don't want utterly to humble themselves. I think the words 'Blessed is he who is not offended at me' [Mat 11:6] mean: blessed is he who can endure the sight of the paragon. For you would have to sink down into the dust before him, and you don't like doing that.[63]

The theme of 'offence' dominates the whole of *Practice in Christianity* and an entire chapter of this work is devoted to Matthew 11:6 'Blessed is he who is not offended at me.' We already know that Wittgenstein was reading this book in 1921 and there seems to be no doubt that he went back to it in 1937.

In the diaries there is also textual evidence to support the claim that Wittgenstein read *The Concept of Anxiety, Philosophical Fragments* and *The Sickness Unto Death*:

God as a historical event in the world is as paradoxical, exactly as paradoxical, as that a certain action in my life has been at such and such a point sinful. This means that a moment [*ein Augenblick*] of *my* history's having eternal validity is not more or less paradoxical than that a moment or a certain period of time in world history should have eternal validity.[64]

---

[62] An exception is the following remark from the *Lecture on Ethics*: 'And I will make my point still more acute by saying "It is the paradox that an experience, a fact, should seem to have supernatural value"' (in *Philosophical Occasions*, 43). 'It is the paradox' is a very Kierkegaardian turn of phrase, a connection Wittgenstein himself noticed (see the end of section II above). It also calls to mind Lessing's remark that 'contingent historical truths can never become a demonstration of eternal truths of reason', which is the subject of discussion on 93–106 of CUP.

[63] *Denkbewegungen*, 95.   [64] Ibid., 63.

This is a succinct reformulation of two of the central ideas—the paradoxical nature of Christ and the paradoxical nature of sin—pervading all the aforementioned writings. Indeed, Wittgenstein is even employing Kierkegaard's own concepts: 'paradox', 'sin', 'the moment', 'eternal validity' and even Hegel's term—'world history'. Wittgenstein's reaction to these ideas is also thoroughly Kierkegaardian: 'If I now think about my sins and that I have performed these actions is only a hypothesis, why do I repent of them as if no doubt about them were possible? That I now remember them is my evidence and the basis for my repentance and the reproach that I am too cowardly to confess them.'[65] That the consciousness of sin can't be approached hypothetically, as if a subject for scientific enquiry, is the main contention of Vigilius Haufniensis, the pseudonymous author of Kierkegaard's *The Concept of Anxiety*.

The editor of the diaries, Ilse Somavilla, suggests that Wittgenstein also seems to have read Constantin Constantius' (a further Kierkegaardian pseudonym) *Repetition*,[66] as she believes that this is what Wittgenstein is referring to when he says in the following entry from 1931: 'What show I, so to speak, put on in the theatre (Kierkegaard) in my soul doesn't make its condition any more beautiful but rather more reprehensible. And still I go on believing that its condition can be ameliorated by a beautiful scene in the theatre.'[67] Somavilla thinks that this is an allusion to Constantius' rumination about the theatre audience at the Königstädter Theatre in Berlin, in Part One of *Repetition*, but it is far from clear that Wittgenstein had this in mind. In fact, it is much more plausible to assume that Wittgenstein's comment is directed at the following passage in CUP:

A king sometimes has a royal theatre solely for himself, but this difference, which excludes ordinary citizens, is accidental. Not so when we speak of God and the royal theatre he has for himself. Accordingly, the individual's ethical development is the little private theatre where God certainly is the spectator, but where on occasion the individual also is himself a spectator, although essentially he is supposed to be an actor, not, however, one who deceives but one who discloses, just as all ethical development consists in becoming disclosed before God. (CUP 157–8)

But even if it can't be settled once and for all which Kierkegaardian work Wittgenstein was, in the end, really referring to, the entry itself

---

[65] Ibid. I have reproduced the awkward grammar of the original German sentence.
[66] Ibid., 132.   [67] Ibid., 54.

at least clearly shows that Wittgenstein generally regarded Kierkegaard's writings as a kind of ethical admonishment—one that he often found disturbing: 'My conscience is tormenting me and is preventing me from working. I have been reading in Kierkegaard's writings and this has made me even more anxious than I was already.'[68] This again illustrates how deep and how personal Wittgenstein's engagement with Kierkegaard was. He clearly did not regard him as simply a philosopher, but as a kind of moral and religious 'paradigm' against which he had to measure himself, often, according to Wittgenstein himself, to his own detriment, for, after all, as Wittgenstein said to Drury, Kierkegaard was 'a saint'.

This comes out even more strongly in an earlier journal entry from 1922 which has recently been found between scraps of paper in the Brenner Archives in Innsbruck. In it Wittgenstein recounts the following experience:

I suddenly felt my complete nothingness and saw that God could demand of me what He wills on the condition that my life would immediately become meaningless if I didn't obey. . . I felt totally annihilated and in the hands of God who could at every moment do with me as He wills. I felt that God could at any time force me immediately to confess my crimes [*Gemeinheiten*]. That he could at any moment force me to take the worst upon myself and that I am not prepared to take the worst upon myself. That I am not now prepared to renounce friendship and all earthly happiness. . . As I said, tonight I saw my complete nothingness. God has deigned to show it to me. During the whole time I kept thinking about Kierkegaard and that my condition is 'fear and trembling'.[69]

This is rather striking—not only does the entry contain an obvious reference to the Danish philosopher, but it is almost as if Kierkegaard himself had written it. Wittgenstein here identifies doing God's will with what Johannes *de Silentio*, in FT, calls the 'last stage before faith': 'infinite resignation'—renouncing all finite (relative) ends. But although Wittgenstein believes that disobedience will make his life meaningless, he cannot force himself to comply with God's commands. In spite of this, however, Climacus would probably say that Wittgenstein is nevertheless poised on the brink of faith, for the feeling of complete self-annihilation before God that Wittgenstein mentions is, according to Climacus, one of the most decisive features of religiousness: 'Religiously,

---

68 *Denkbewegungen*, 77.
69 13.1.1922. In *Licht und Schatten*, ed. Ilse Somavilla (Innsbruck: Haymon, 2004), translation mine. I am grateful to Allan Janik for drawing my attention to this passage.

the task is to comprehend that a person is nothing at all before God or to be nothing at all and thereby to be before God, and he continually insists upon having his incapability before him, and its disappearance is the disappearance of religiousness' (CUP 461).

Although the diaries give the impression that Wittgenstein was generally in agreement with Kierkegaard's conception of things, there are two passages—one from 1931, the other from 1937—where Wittgenstein doesn't seem entirely to share Kierkegaard's vision. Here is the first:

Kierkegaard's writings are teasing and this is of course their intention, although I am not sure whether the exact effect they produce in me is intentional. Undoubtedly, the person who is teasing me is forcing me to take notice of his cause and if this cause is important, then this is a good thing. Nevertheless, there is something in me that rejects this teasing... The idea that someone uses a trick in order to make me do something is unpleasant. I am sure that this (using the trick) requires great courage and that I wouldn't in the least have such courage, but it is questionable whether, if I had this courage, I would have the right to employ it. I *believe* that what would also be required, apart from the courage, is a lack of love for one's neighbour. One could say: What you call loving your neighbour is selfishness. Well, then I know no love without selfishness, for I cannot meddle with the eternal blessedness [*Seligkeit*] of someone else. I can only say: I will love him in such a way as I—who am concerned about my soul—would wish that he would love me.[70]

Here we have a disagreement about philosophical method, which is important, as it provides evidence against James Conant's[71] view that the *Tractatus*, like Kierkegaard's *Postscript*, is an exercise in 'deceiving the reader into the truth'. Such an endeavour, as this remark suggests, would, I believe, be alien to Wittgenstein,[72] for he seems to regard it as in some sense 'unethical'.

The second passage runs as follows:

I think that the word 'belief' has caused much mischief in religion. All these intractable thoughts about 'paradox', the *eternal* meaningfulness of a *historical* state of affairs etc. However, if instead of saying 'belief in Christ' you say 'love of Christ', then the paradox vanishes, the vexation of the understanding ceases... Not that one could now say: Yes, now everything

---

[70] Ibid., 62.

[71] See James Conant, 'Kierkegaard, Wittgenstein and Nonsense', in Ted Cohen, Paul Guyer and Hilary Putnam (eds), *Pursuits of Reason* (Lubbock, TX: Texas Technical University Press, 1993), 195–224.

[72] For a detailed discussion of this point, see chapter 3.

is simple or comprehensible. Nothing is comprehensible, but it is no longer incomprehensible either.[73]

Although Wittgenstein doesn't mention Kierkegaard by name in this remark, he clearly has him and his frequent use of his central category, 'paradox', in mind. Wittgenstein seems rightly worried here that this concept can give rise to all sorts of misunderstandings. He may also be rejecting the implications of his own earlier endorsement of the idea that Kierkegaard's concept of paradox is analogous to what he, Wittgenstein, called the ineffable in the *Tractatus* and to what he meant by 'running up against the limits of language' in the *Lecture on Ethics*. It may therefore indicate that he is rejecting what he once said to Waismann—'Man has the urge to thrust against the limits of language . . . Kierkegaard, too, recognized this thrust and even described it in much the same way (as a thrust against paradox).'[74]—for, after all, as Wittgenstein came to realize, 'language is not a cage'.[75] The criticism implicit in Wittgenstein's aforementioned remark from the diaries may therefore be directed as much at himself and at his perhaps earlier reading of Kierkegaard as at the latter himself.

Much of what Wittgenstein says in the diaries also accords well with the remarks he makes about Kierkegaard in CV. In a passage from 1937, for example, Wittgenstein says:

Kierkegaard writes: If Christianity were so easy and cosy, why should God in his Scriptures have set Heaven and Earth in motion and threatened with *eternal* punishments?—Question: But in that case why is this Scripture so unclear? If we want to warn someone of a terrible danger, do we go about it by telling him a riddle whose solution will be the warning?—But who is to say that the Scripture really is unclear? Isn't it possible that it was essential in this case to 'tell a riddle'? And that, on the other hand, giving a more direct warning would necessarily have had the *wrong* effect? God has *four* people recount the life of his incarnate Son, in each case differently and with inconsistencies—but might we not say: It is important that this narrative should not be more than quite averagely historically plausible *just so that* this should not be taken as the essential, decisive thing? So that the *letter* should not be believed more strongly than is proper and the *spirit* may receive its due . . . The Spirit puts what is essential, essential for your life, into these words. The point is precisely

[73] *Denkbewegungen*, 103–4.

[74] *Ludwig Wittgenstein und der Wiener Kreis*, conversations recorded by Friedrich Waismann, ed. Brian McGuinness (Frankfurt: Suhrkamp, 1984), 68, translation mine.

[75] Ibid., 117. This remark occurs almost exactly a year after the previous one: the first is from 30 December 1929; the second from 17 December 1930.

that you are only SUPPOSED to see clearly what appears clearly even in *this* representation. (I am not sure how far all this is exactly in the spirit of Kierkegaard.) (CV 31e–32e)

Wittgenstein's point of departure in this remark seems to be a phrase from Kierkegaard's *Attack Upon 'Christendom'*, which Wittgenstein must have read:

if what we mean by being a Christian really is being a Christian—what then is God? He is the most comical being that ever lived, His word the most comical book that ever has come to light: to set heaven and earth in motion . . . , so threaten with hell, with eternal punishment . . . in order to attain what we understand by being Christians [i.e. to bring about what we already are anyway].[76]

Wittgenstein's reflections on this issue strike me as being very much in the spirit of Kierkegaard, although they call to mind Anti-Climacus' diatribes in *Practice in Christianity* against the 'direct recognizability' of Jesus Christ and his insistence on the 'incognito' of the Son of God, rather than anything Kierkegaard says in the *Attack*. Here is Anti-Climacus on a closely related theme:

They [the pastors] say that Christ himself has directly said that he was God, the only begotten Son of the Father. They reject with horror any concealment as unworthy of Christ, as vanity and conceit in connection with so earnest a matter, the most earnest of all matters, the salvation of mankind. They maintain that Christ has given us a direct answer to a direct question. (PC 135)

But:

it is easily seen that direct communication is an impossibility when one is so kind as to take the communicator into account . . . In relation to unrecognizability or for someone in unrecognizability, direct communication is an impossibility, because the direct communication does indeed directly state what one essentially is—but unrecognizability means not to be in the character of what one essentially is. Thus there is a contradiction that nevertheless makes direct communication indirect, that is, makes direct communication impossible. (PC 133)

What Anti-Climacus is saying here is that because there is an 'infinite qualitative distinction' between being God and being an individual human being, Christ, who claims to be both, is a 'sign of contradiction'. Given that there is nothing in itself remarkable about Christ, he is also,

---

[76] Kierkegaard's *The Attack Upon Christendom*, translated, with an introduction, by Walter Lowrie (Princeton: Princeton University Press, 1968), 110.

in this much, 'incognito' (that is, it is not 'directly perceivable' that he is also God). Therefore, whatever such a person says will *eo ipso* be indirect communication and to that extent ambiguous (that is, it can either be taken as coming from God or from a mere human being and there are no objective criteria enabling one to adjudicate between the two options). Even the miracles that Christ is supposed to have performed are not a species of 'direct communication', as 'the miracle can demonstrate nothing, for if you do not believe him [Christ] to be who he says he is, then you deny the miracle. The miracle can make aware—now you are in the tension, and it depends upon what you choose, offence or faith; it is your heart that must be disclosed' (PC 97).

In other words, Anti-Climacus agrees with Wittgenstein that the 'riddle' is the essential thing. Given that no outward signs whatever can determine once and for all who Christ was, it simply does not matter, on this conception, whether there are inconsistencies in the Gospels or not. For even the most consistent and most historically accurate account could not 'prove' more, in this respect, than the more deficient ones. It is exactly as Wittgenstein said to Drury, 'If you can accept the miracle that God became man, then all these difficulties are as nothing. For then it is impossible for me to say what form the record of such an event should take.'[77]

Similar themes are to be found throughout CV. I will give two more examples. Here is another remark from 1937, which, like the previous one quoted from the diaries of the same year, seeks to understand what Climacus/Kierkegaard is saying, without employing the concept of paradox:

Christianity is not based on a historical truth; rather, it offers us a (historical) narrative and says: now believe! But not, believe this narrative with the belief appropriate to a historical narrative, rather: believe through thick and thin, which you can only do as a result of a life. *Here you have a narrative, don't take the same attitude to it as you take to other historical narratives.* Make a *quite different* place in your life for it.—There is nothing *paradoxical* about that! (CV 32e)

In 1946 we again find Wittgenstein agreeing with Kierkegaard that Christianity is not a theory and that faith is consequently not a matter of assenting to a sum of tenets. He says:

I believe that one of the things Christianity says is that sound doctrines are all useless. That you have to change your *life*. (Or the *direction* of your life.) . . . The point is that a sound doctrine need not *take hold* of you; you can follow it as you would a doctor's prescription.—But here you need something to move you and turn you in a new direction...Once you have been turned round, you must *stay* turned round. Wisdom is passionless. But faith by contrast is what Kierkegaard calls a *passion*. (CV 53e)

This remark clearly echoes the following passage from Climacus' earlier book, *Philosophical Fragments*[78]—'Inasmuch as he was untruth, he was continually in the process of departing from the truth; as a result of receiving the condition in the moment, his course took the opposite direction, or he was turned around. Let us call this change *conversion*' (PF 18)—but also seems to be influenced by what Climacus says about 'subjective appropriation' and the 'existential' dimension of faith in the *Postscript*:

The way of objective reflection turns the subjective individual into something accidental and thereby turns existence into an indifferent, vanishing something. The way to objective truth goes away from the subject, and while the subject and subjectivity become indifferent, the truth becomes indifferent, and that is precisely its objective validity, because the interest, just like the decision is subjectivity. (CUP 193)

In other words, Wittgenstein and Kierkegaard agree that 'objective' or speculative thought ('wisdom') is incapable of solving 'the problem of life', because what is needed here is something that 'takes hold of you', something that engages you ethically as an individual. The teachings of Christ are supposed radically to change the way you live, not your theoretical commitments. For, as Wittgenstein says in another remark, 'it is my soul with its passions, as it were with its flesh and blood, that has to be saved, not my abstract mind' (CV 33e).

Some of the themes only touched upon in CV are developed further in the *Lectures and Conversations on Religious Belief*[79] and here, too, the parallels with Kierkegaard are extremely striking.[80] Compare, for

---

[78] *Philosophical Fragments*, ed. and trans. Howard and Edna Hong (Princeton: Princeton University Press, 1985); henceforth PF.

[79] In *Lectures and Conversations on Aesthetics, Psychology and Religious Belief*, ed. Cyril Barrett, compiled from notes taken by Yorick Smythies, Rush Rhees, and James Taylor (Oxford: Blackwell, 1966); henceforth LC.

[80] Although Wittgenstein does not refer to Kierkegaard by name at any point in the LC, Kierkegaard does get an oblique reference towards the end of the lectures: 'A great writer said that, when he was a boy, his father set him a task, and he suddenly felt that nothing, not even death, could take away the responsibility [in doing this task]; this was his duty to do, and that even death couldn't stop it being his duty. He said that

example what Wittgenstein says about Father O'Hara, who is 'one of those people who make it [religious belief] a question of science' (LC 57), with what Climacus says about 'objective Christianity' in CUP. Here is Wittgenstein:

I would definitely call O'Hara unreasonable. I would say, if this is religious belief, then it's all superstition. But I would ridicule it, not by saying it is based on insufficient evidence. I would say: here is a man who is cheating himself. You can say: this man is ridiculous because he believes, and bases it on weak reasons. (LC 59)

Climacus, characteristically, is rather more long-winded, but is essentially saying the same thing:

When an individual infinitely, impassionedly interested in his own eternal happiness [*Salighed*] is placed in relation to the Church theory in such a way that he intends to base his eternal happiness on it, he becomes comic. He becomes comic not because he is infinitely, impassionedly interested . . . but he becomes comic because the objectivity is incongruous with his interest. If the historical aspect of the Creed (that it is from the apostles etc.) is to be decisive, then every iota must be infinitely insisted upon, and since this can be attained only *approximando*, the individual finds himself in the contradiction of tying, that is, wanting to tie his eternal happiness to it and not being able to do so because the approximation is never finished . . . The individual is tragic because of his passion and comic because of staking it on an approximation. (CUP 43)

Interestingly, in connection with these questions, Wittgenstein even employs another very central Kierkegaardian term, the 'absurd'. He says, 'Where what is said sounds a bit absurd I would say: "Yes, in this case insufficient evidence." If altogether absurd,[81] then I wouldn't' (LC 60). On the face of it, this seems an incredible claim to make. But if it is juxtaposed with what Wittgenstein says about bent-rule following, both

---

this was, in a way, a proof for the immortality of the soul—because if this lives on [the responsibility won't die]. The idea is given by what we call the proof. Well, if this is the idea, [all right]' (LC 70). This story is, of course, Kierkegaard's own. In the passage about evidence Wittgenstein also uses the example of Napoleon, which is the example Climacus/Kierkegaard uses to make the selfsame point in *Philosophical Fragments*: 'It has been said a thousand times by intelligent people that indubitability is not enough in this case. Even if there is as much evidence as for Napoleon. Because the indubitability wouldn't be enough to make me change my whole life' (LC 57). By 'intelligent people' Wittgenstein presumably primarily means Kierkegaard.

[81] I don't mean to imply that Wittgenstein is using the term in anything like as complex a way as Kierkegaard does, but I do think it testifies to a similar underlying thought.

in the LC and in the PI, it will start to make some sense. Further down in the LC Wittgenstein says:

> If you compare it with anything in Science which we call evidence, you can't credit that anyone could soberly argue: 'Well, I had this dream . . . therefore . . . Last Judgement'.[82] You might say: 'For a blunder, that's too big.' If you suddenly wrote numbers down on the blackboard, and then said: 'Now, I'm going to add,' and then said: '2 and 21 is 13' etc. I'd say: 'This is no blunder.' (LC 61–2)

In other words, what Wittgenstein is saying is that if you believe that religious beliefs are based on 'evidence' in the way that scientific beliefs can be said to be based on evidence, then you are either cheating yourself or you are mad. For, if you *really* believed that one *could* soberly argue 'dream—therefore Last Judgement' or 'miracles—therefore Son of God', then this is no ordinary mistake—no simple blunder, but rather an intellectual aberration. But given that we don't (necessarily) want to come to the conclusion that all religious people are mad, an alternative explanation must be found: 'There are cases where I'd say he's mad, or he's making fun. Then there might be cases where I look for an entirely different interpretation altogether' (LC 62). The 'entirely different interpretation' might comprise, for example, a refusal to interpret religious beliefs as being in any way *analogous* to scientific beliefs. In other words, the person concerned isn't (necessarily) mad, but is rather engaged in a different kind of activity: 'Whether a thing is a blunder or not—it is a blunder in a particular system . . . You could also say that where we are reasonable, they are not reasonable—meaning they don't use *reason* here' (LC 59). Again, the parallels with Climacus' views are striking:

> Suppose that Christianity does not at all want to be understood; suppose that, in order to express this and to prevent anyone, misguided, from taking the road of objectivity, it has proclaimed itself to be the paradox. Suppose that it wants to be only for existing persons and essentially for persons existing in inwardness, in the inwardness of faith, which cannot be expressed more definitely than this: it is the absurd,[83] adhered to firmly with the passion of the infinite. (CUP 214)

In other words, the term 'absurd' plays a similar role in Wittgenstein's and Kierkegaard's thought about religious belief. In both authors the

---

82 Wittgenstein is surely exaggerating here. It is very unlikely that any religious person would argue in this way. Despite the exaggeration, though, I think it is possible to see what Wittgenstein is driving at.

83 By 'absurd' Climacus means something resistant to 'objectification' (and consequently Hegelian 'mediation'). See chapter 3.

term is supposed to alert us to the fact that something *different*—not something irrational—is going on in the case of religion which makes it impossible simply to assimilate it to ordinary (empirical or scientific) endeavours. As Wittgenstein says, 'Why shouldn't one form of life culminate in an utterance of belief in a Last Judgement? But I couldn't either say "Yes" or "No" to the statement that there will be such a thing. Nor "Perhaps", nor "I'm not sure". It is a statement which may not allow of any such answer' (LC 58).[84] This is so, Kierkegaard would doubtless add, because given that Christianity is not a philosophical theory, the issue of the Last Judgement, for example, can only arise for someone who actually wants to be a Christian; that is, it has to arise subjectively, for from the objective (speculative) point of view, it couldn't, on this conception, even be asked. Therefore, according to the view that Wittgenstein and Kierkegaard share, saying either 'yes' or 'no' to it would be equally misguided.

That religious beliefs and practices can't simply be reduced to a form of false (or bizarre) science, is also the predominant theme of Wittgenstein's *Remarks on Frazer's* Golden Bough:[85]

Frazer's account of the magical and religious views of mankind is unsatisfactory: it makes these views look like *errors*. Was Augustine in error, then, when he called upon God on every page of the *Confessions*? But—one might say—if he was not in error, surely the Buddhist holy man was—or anyone else—whose religion gives expression to completely different views. But *none* of them was in error, except when he set forth a theory. (PO 119)

Wittgenstein's invective against scientism is very reminiscent of Kierkegaard's recurring critique of the 'speculative point of view'. Both the 'scientistic' and the 'speculative' approach to religion, by making it out to be some kind of theory, distort religious beliefs and practices to such an extent that they either, in Hegel's case, in the end, abolish Christianity, or else make it impossible to see these practices as anything but sheer 'stupidity' (Frazer). Wittgenstein complains: 'Frazer is much more savage than most of his savages, for they are not as far removed from the understanding of a spiritual matter as a twentieth-century Englishman. *His* explanations of primitive practices are much cruder than the meaning of these practices themselves' (PO 131). Kierkegaard, naturally, is just as acerbic. This is Climacus' voice:

---

[84] See chapter 4 for a more detailed discussion of these points.
[85] In *Philosophical Occasions*, 118–55; henceforth PO.

Speculative thought has understood everything, everything, everything! The ecclesiastical speaker still exercises some restraint; he admits that he has not yet understood everything; he admits that he is striving (poor fellow, that is a confusion of categories!). 'If there is anyone who has understood everything,' he says, 'then I admit . . . that I have not understood it and cannot demonstrate everything, and we lesser ones . . . must be content with faith.' (Poor, misunderstood, supreme passion: faith—that you have to be content with such a defender; poor preacher-fellow, that you do not know what the question is! Poor intellectual pauper . . . who cannot quite make it in scholarship and science but who has faith, because that he has, the faith that turned fishermen into apostles, the faith that can move mountains—if one has it!) (CUP 31)

Here Climacus is criticizing the type of person who believes that faith is inferior to speculative philosophy and who consequently assumes that faith and speculative philosophy are continuous with each other in the sense that they both, presumably, aim at 'objective knowledge' (the God's eye view of the world), the one (speculative philosophy) just a trifle more successfully than the other (faith). This, just as, in Wittgenstein's words, 'making it a question of science', Climacus calls a confusion of categories. The latter is another key Kierkegaardian term which is also strikingly reminiscent of the later Wittgenstein's 'grammatical distinctions'. Wittgenstein probably noticed this similarity himself, for, towards the end of his life, he once said to Drury:

You are quite right [in saying that Kierkegaard seems always to be making one aware of new categories], that is exactly what Kierkegaard does, he introduces new categories. I couldn't read him again now. He is too long-winded; he keeps on saying the same thing over and over again. When I read him I always wanted to say, 'Oh all right, I agree, I agree, but please get on with it.'[86]

With this avowal of agreement and mild exasperation, I propose to end my survey of Wittgenstein's engagement with Kierkegaard. Naturally, there is much more to be said about each of the cited works, but—lest I incur the same judgement as Kierkegaard—this will have to wait for subsequent chapters.

CONCLUSION

The over-arching aim of this chapter has been to undermine Philip Shields's contention that Kierkegaard had little direct influence on

---

[86] Rhees, op.cit., 88.

Wittgenstein. A survey of all the available evidence shows not only that Wittgenstein was an avid and admiring reader of Kierkegaard, but also that Kierkegaard keeps coming up time and again in almost all of Wittgenstein's reflections about religious belief. Furthermore, these reflections themselves show such remarkable affinities with those of Kierkegaard that it is nigh on impossible not to speak of a direct influence—especially now that we know exactly how much Kierkegaard Wittgenstein actually read. In the words of Ronald Hustwit, Wittgenstein owes a debt to Kierkegaard 'to the extent that any original thinker could owe anything to anyone'.[87] In the light of all this, Shields's thesis is simply untenable.

I also hope to have gone some way towards showing how difficult it is to separate Wittgenstein's 'personal' reflections (about philosophy and religion) from his 'philosophical' ones (on the same topics). Any account, therefore, that drives a firm wedge between the two, as does that of Phillips, for instance, must remain dangerously one-sided. In the next chapter I will be looking at Wittgenstein's and Kierkegaard's views on the point of their own philosophical activity, in order to get a clearer idea of how an ethical conception of the latter informs the works of both thinkers. More will then be said about Phillips's view.

[87] Ronald Hustwit, 'Wittgenstein's Interest in Kierkegaard', in *Wittgenstein Studies* 2 (1997): 10 (text file).

2

The Point of Kierkegaard's and Wittgenstein's Philosophical Authorship

Such works are mirrors: when an ape looks in, no apostle can look out.

Georg Christoph Lichtenberg. Quoted as a motto in Kierkegaard's *Stages on Life's Way*[1]

INTRODUCTION

In the previous chapter I said that Wittgenstein and Kierkegaard agree that a 'profound thinker' is not simply someone who has 'profound' thoughts, but a person whose life expresses—or is emblematic of—these thoughts. For both philosophers profundity and authenticity are internally connected and nowhere more so than in philosophical authorship. This is what distinguishes their work from what Kierkegaard calls 'premise-authors'—authors who are primarily interested in communicating results without paying attention to the method they employ and without understanding themselves in their work. Petrus Minor, the pseudonymous author of the posthumously published *Book on Adler* puts it like this:

And what is profundity really? It is the deep existential carrying out of an idea that through the relationship of conscience is related to God. Nowadays people think that it is very glorious if someone is so fortunate as to be struck by a profound *thought*, to make a profound remark, now and then *horis successivis* to compile something profound that in every other hour one *existentially* denies.

---

[1] Quoted as a motto to 'In Vino Veritas' by William Afham, one of the pseudonymous authors of Kierkegaard's *Stages on Life's Way*, ed. and trans. Howard and Edna Hong (Princeton: Princeton University Press, 1988b), 8; henceforth SLW. Wittgenstein was also a great admirer of Lichtenberg and quotes him, for example, in CV 65e.

No, just as perseverance . . . is the true virtue, so also profundity is not an utterance, a statement, but an existing. The profound mind is not an aesthetic qualification with regard to genius but is essentially an ethical qualification.[2]

This remark encapsulates in a nutshell the main strands of what is peculiar to both Wittgenstein's and Kierkegaard's conception of philosophical authorship and also provides the key to understanding what Wittgenstein meant when he said that the *Philosophical Remarks* could have been inscribed to the 'glory of God'. I will therefore begin this chapter, using the aforementioned quotation as a point of departure, by tracing the most important parallels in Wittgenstein's and Kierkegaard's conception of philosophy.[3] I will then go on to assess D. Z. Phillips's objections to the kind of 'symmetrical'[4] reading of Kierkegaard's and Wittgenstein's philosophical authorship that I shall be proposing—a subject already briefly touched upon in the first chapter—and attempt to show that they either misfire or are perfectly innocuous.

I PARALLELS IN KIERKEGAARD'S AND WITTGENSTEIN'S CONCEPTION OF PHILOSOPHY

Profundity, Petrus Minor says, is an ethical qualification. There are many ramifications to this remark (ones which I hope will become clear in the course of this chapter), but we can get an initial purchase on its meaning by juxtaposing it with something that Wittgenstein says in *Culture and Value*:

You must say something new and yet it must all be old. In fact you must confine yourself to saying old things—and *all the same* it must be something new! . . . A poet too has constantly to ask himself: 'but is what I am writing really true?'—and this does not necessarily mean: 'is this how it happens in

---

[2] *The Book on Adler*, ed. and trans. Howard and Edna Hong (Princeton: Princeton University Press, 1998a), 164; henceforth BA. Adolph Adler was a Danish theologian, pastor and writer who claimed to have had a revelation from Christ and was dismissed from office on the grounds that he was not of sound mind.

[3] In this chapter I will be dealing almost exclusively with the affinities between Kierkegaard and the 'later' Wittgenstein; points of contact between Kierkegaard and the *Tractatus*, as well as the question of how these relate to Wittgenstein's later work, will be discussed in the next one.

[4] 'Symmetry' does not imply 'identity'. It is no part of my concern, here or elsewhere, to argue that there is a 'perfect fit' between Kierkegaard's and Wittgenstein's philosophical endeavours.

reality?' Yes, you have got to assemble bits of old material. But into a *building*. (CV 40e)

What Wittgenstein means by this, I believe, is that for an author to be profound he or she need not necessarily string together astonishingly new ideas, but rather offer the reader a new perspective on the same old facts; to provide a *Weltanschauung* that, as it were, casts novel light on ancient darkness. In other words, the newness or originality of the building does not consist of the materials used, but lies in *how* the building is actually constructed. That is to say, Kierkegaard and Wittgenstein seem to agree that the main thing in philosophical authorship isn't primarily the content—the 'what'—but rather the *method* or the 'how': profundity is not a function of the novelty of the philosophical claims advanced, but is rather a result of the way in which existing problems are addressed. This distinguishes their conception from that of Petrus Minor's 'premise-author' who is content with the 'what' alone—as long as new theses are propounded, everything is all right. Or to continue with the earlier analogy: as long as ever new materials are used, the premise-author doesn't care whether the building in the end collapses. Petrus Minor puts it rather more acerbically:

One takes an author like that, on whose head, just as on matches, a phosphorescent substance has been placed: a proposal for a project, a suggestion; one takes him by the legs and strikes him on a newspaper, and then there are three or four columns. And premises without conclusions actually have a striking resemblance to phosphorescence—both go off in a puff. (BA 10)

The premise-author, to use a Wittgensteinian phrase, doesn't himself know his way about, and the multiplying of premises (claims, theses) is supposed to hide this fact. This predicament, Petrus Minor believes, stems from the premise-author's lack of a world-view and the absence of the author's understanding himself in this world-view. That is to say, the premise-author gives pride of place to an accumulation of knowledge (without really knowing to what end he accumulates it), instead of arranging what we have always known in such a way that the problems lose their sting. The 'essential author', on the other hand (Petrus Minor's counterpart to the premise-author), recognizes a philosophical disease for what it is and instead of satisfying the 'demand of the times' (such as, say, the demand for 'progress') by indulging in more thesis-spinning—'stok(ing) the fire under the boiler with the flammability of the premises' (BA 11)—attempts to extinguish the flames by taking the matches away from the reader. In this respect,

Petrus' view of philosophical authorship harmonizes perfectly with that of another Kierkegaardian pseudonym, Johannes Climacus, which is perhaps not very surprising, given that Kierkegaard once intended the Climber as the pseudonymous author of the *Book on Adler*.[5] In CUP Climacus says of his book that it is written for 'people in the know, whose trouble is that they know too much.' He claims:

When this is the case, the art of being able to *communicate* eventually becomes the art of being able to *take away* or to trick something away from someone . . . When a man has filled his mouth so full of food that for this reason he cannot eat and it must end with his dying of hunger, does giving food to him consist in stuffing his mouth even more or, instead, in taking a little away so that he can eat? (CUP 274)

Kierkegaard and Wittgenstein agree, in other words, that the ethical task of philosophy is not to give the reader what she *wants*, but rather what she *needs*. Even employing the same metaphor as Climacus, Wittgenstein says, 'A present-day teacher of philosophy doesn't select food for his pupil with the aim of flattering his taste, but with the aim of changing it' (CV 17e). That is to say, the 'essential' (genuine or authentic) author recognizes what his audience's confusion consists in and attempts to offer a remedy by undermining, or 'tricking away', the philosophical preconceptions that gave rise to it. Such a task, however, cannot be accomplished 'directly'—by, for example, writing a conventional philosophical treatise—for as Kierkegaard says in *The Point of View*, 'there is nothing that requires as gentle a treatment as the removal of an illusion'.[6] Given that Kierkegaard and Wittgenstein both believe that the problem is not an absence of knowledge, but rather the lack of a clear view of it, what has to be overcome is a 'difficulty having to do with the will, rather than with the intellect' (CV 17e). In other words, for both authors, the problem is not primarily intellectual, but *ethical*—a resistance of the will needs to be surmounted. For, as Kierkegaard says in PV, there is a great difference between these two situations:

one who is ignorant and must be given some knowledge . . . and one who is under a delusion that must first be taken away . . . direct communication presupposes that the recipient's ability to receive is entirely in order, but here

---

    [5] See the 'Historical Introduction' to the *Book on Adler*, xii.
    [6] *The Point of View*, ed. and trans. Howard and Edna Hong (Princeton: Princeton University Press, 1998b), 43; henceforth PV.

this is simply not the case—indeed, here a delusion is an obstacle. That means a corrosive must first be used, but this corrosive is the negative, but the negative in connection with communicating is precisely to deceive. (PV 53–4)

Although Wittgenstein would probably not want to call this indirect method a 'deception', he would not, I think, object to Kierkegaard's notion that a 'corrosive' must first be applied. Indeed, he seems to have just that in mind when he says at PI §118:

Where does our investigation get its importance from, since it seems only to destroy everything interesting, that is, all that is great and important? (As it were all the buildings, leaving behind only bits of stone and rubble.) What we are destroying is nothing but houses of cards and we are clearing up the ground of language on which they stand.

Wittgenstein and Kierkegaard share the view, in other words, that if one of philosophy's main tasks is the removal of illusions, then the writing of philosophy can no longer be straightforwardly didactic. For it would be self-defeating to set out the reader's delusions in propositional form and to combat them using standard philosophical arguments, as the reader must, first of all, be prised away from the attachment she feels towards her philosophical captivity. She must, that is, be brought to see that what she is attached to is merely a house of cards—a will o'the wisp—not a substantial philosophical thesis standing in need of refutation. Kierkegaard's and Wittgenstein's philosophical method is designed to match this conception. Neither author seeks to substitute one philosophical preconception for another—one thesis for another—but to hold up a mirror to the reader that will show her that however beautiful her reflection might be, it is a false image not worthy of her attachment. Such an attempt is simultaneously philosophical and ethical, both on the part of the reader as well as on the author's, for the latter must strive, as Wittgenstein says, 'to be *no more* than a mirror' (CV 18e, emphasis added), while the former must renounce some of her most ingrained ways of thinking, in order to 'put it right' (ibid.) Both enterprises therefore involve forms of self-denial and self-overcoming.

That is to say, just as a looking-glass has no 'point of view' and 'adds' nothing to the way things are, so Wittgenstein's and Kierkegaard's writing 'simply puts everything before us, and neither explains nor deduces anything' (PI §126). Given that, on Kierkegaard's and Wittgenstein's conception, there are no longer any results—in the sense of 'new' information—directly to communicate, there is also nothing to 'explain' (in the sense of constructing a theoretical system). This is the significance of Wittgenstein's notorious remark that 'if one tried to advance *theses* in philosophy, it would never be possible to debate them, because everyone would agree to them' (PI §128). And this doesn't mean that we are left with nothing—as one might fear—but rather with a change in perspective that will no longer make us succumb to certain kinds of temptation. The result of philosophy, if Kierkegaard and Wittgenstein are correct, is therefore not philosophical propositions, but, as the *Tractatus* famously put it, 'seeing the world aright' (TLP 6.54).

In this respect, Wittgenstein's and Kierkegaard's conception of philosophy is radically anti-metaphysical and anti-foundationalist. Neither philosopher believes that metaphysics can deliver on its promises and supply a presuppositionless vantage-point from which we can view the world. Indeed, Wittgenstein regards the very idea of such a vantage-point as fundamentally incoherent; and while Kierkegaard does not go as far as exposing the nonsensicality of such a 'view from nowhere' in his authorship, his conception, for all practical purposes, comes down to the same: to view the world *sub specie aeternitatis* is impossible for an existing individual and every attempt to do so becomes, in the end, comical:

It is from this side [from the side of existence] that an objection must first be made to modern speculative thought, that it has not a false presupposition but a comic presupposition, occasioned by its having forgotten in a kind of world-historical absentmindedness what it means to be a human being, not what it means to be a human being in general, for even speculators might be swayed to consider that sort of thing, but what it means that we, you and I and he, are human beings, each one on his own. (CUP 120)[7]

Philosophical problems, Wittgenstein and Kierkegaard believe, cannot be divorced from the specific context of human life in which they occur. Let us be human, Johannes Climacus urges, not fantastical beings who confuse themselves with speculative thought and world-history. Wittgenstein makes a similar request when he says that:

When philosophers use a word—'knowledge', 'being', 'object', 'I', 'proposition', 'name'—and try to grasp the *essence* of the thing, one must always ask oneself: is the word ever actually used in this way in the language-game which is its original home?—What *we* do is to bring words back from their metaphysical to their everyday use. (PI §116)

---

[7] Compare this with what Wittgenstein says at PI §111: 'Let us ask ourselves: why do we feel a grammatical joke to be *deep*? (And that is what the depth of philosophy is.)'

Hence, both philosophers are interested in what is *actually* going on, rather than in what the metaphysician hopes to see. Given that neither of them believes that a neutral standpoint is available from which we can watch the passing show, the philosopher must get into the thick of things and leave the rarefied spheres of metaphysical contemplation in favour of the 'rough ground' (PI §107).

'To imagine a language,' says Wittgenstein, 'means to imagine a form of life' (PI §19). Kierkegaard's pseudonyms have something similar in mind when they talk of the different 'existence-spheres' or 'stages of life'. In the 'Letter to the reader' from *Stages on Life's Way* Frater Taciturnus says:

There are three existence-spheres: the aesthetic, the ethical, the religious. The metaphysical is abstraction, and there is no human being who exists metaphysically. The metaphysical, the ontological, is, but it does not exist, for when it exists it does so in the aesthetic, in the ethical, in the religious, and when it is, it is the abstraction from or a *prius* to the aesthetic, the ethical, the religious' (SLW 476)

Following Stanley Cavell,[8] who was probably one of the first to note this parallel, I propose to identify Kierkegaard's existence-spheres with Wittgenstein's concept of a 'form of life'. Kierkegaard's 'subjective thinker', Johannes Climacus' way of characterizing the 'essential author', depicts existence-possibilities and attempts to show, in what he calls 'qualitative dialectic', how the same concept can take on different meanings depending on the 'existential' context in which it is employed. Cavell brings this out very well when he says:

For example, an examination of the concept of *silence* will show that the word means different things—that silence is different things—depending on whether the context is the silence of nature, the silence of shyness, the silence of the liar or hypocrite, the short silence of the man who cannot hold his tongue, the long silence of the hero or the apostle, or the eternal silence of the Knight of Faith. And the specific meaning of the word in each of those contexts is determined by tracing its specific contrasts with the others—the way its use in one context 'negates' its use in another, so to speak.[9]

In *Fear and Trembling*, for instance, half of the book is devoted to contrasting 'aesthetic' silence with 'religious' silence. And this is not

---

[8] See Stanley Cavell, 'Kierkegaard's *On Authority and Revelation*', in *Søren Kierkegaard —Critical Assessments of Leading Philosophers*, vol. 1, ed. Daniel Conway with K. E. Gover (London: Routledge, 2002), 37–50. Reprint of an essay from 1969.

[9] Ibid., 42.

just an idiosyncratic interest on Kierkegaard's part, but is an extremely important enterprise, as he believes, like Wittgenstein, that philosophical problems arise primarily from a confusion of categories: from thinking that a word always means the same and plays an identical role regardless of a substantive change in context. This is how Kierkegaard describes his philosophical procedure in a draft for BA:

It [*The Book on Adler*] contains developments of concepts and in my opinion very essential developments of concepts. I could very well have presented these in contrast to the confusion of concepts in our age without including Mag. Adler. But I consider it extremely fortunate to have someone who quite accurately manifests the confusion of the whole age, so one can make the development of a concept into a clinical demonstration. (BA 321)

It is striking how similar this is to Wittgenstein's conception of philosophy as conceptual clarification. In the *Investigations* Wittgenstein also uses a particular person's picture of concept-formation, Augustine's for example (PI §1), as a 'clinical demonstration' of a widespread philosophical confusion. Hence, although Kierkegaard in BA is concerned with the elucidation of the concept of what it means to have a revelation, that is, he is elucidating a religious concept, whereas most of the concepts that Wittgenstein talks about in PI come from a secular context, the method the two philosophers employ is clearly the same. They are both trying to teach the reader differences and this is done not by constructing a theory, but by paying attention to the existence-sphere or form of life in which the relevant concepts live. In this respect, Kierkegaard would happily endorse Wittgenstein's remark that 'we remain unconscious of the prodigious diversity of all the everyday language-games because the clothing of our language makes everything alike' (PI 224).

That is to say, Kierkegaard would also agree with Wittgenstein that often, in the words of Cavell, 'a question which appears to need settling by empirical means or through presenting a formal argument is really a conceptual question, a question of grammar. (This is one way of putting the whole effort of the book on Adler.)'[10] Thus, Petrus Minor, in the latter work, is not concerned with establishing whether, empirically or metaphysically, a revelation is possible, but what it would actually *mean* to call something a revelation today. This is an exercise, as Cavell says following Kant, in the 'a priori possibility of applying the concepts in general'.[11] The procedure that Petrus Minor employs

---

[10] 'Kierkegaard's *On Authority and Revelation*', 42   [11] Ibid., 41.

therefore accords well with Wittgenstein's claim that 'one might also give the name "philosophy" to what is possible *before* all new discoveries and inventions' (PI §126).

The questions that most of Kierkegaard's pseudonyms are addressing are therefore simultaneously philosophical and religious: it is impossible to get a clear view of what the religious questions really come down to when philosophical confusions about them stand in the way. Believing that a revelation can be proven by evidence, for example, would be one such confusion. What Kierkegaard calls 'the monstrous illusion' in PV—the belief that Christendom and Christianity are co-extensive—is another. The whole of the *Postscript*, on the other hand, is devoted to a discussion of 'where the misunderstanding between speculative thought and Christianity lies' (CUP 241). And the latter is an especially interesting problem, not only because Climacus believes that Hegelianism has made a philosophical travesty of faith,[12] but also because he takes this to be symptomatic of a much deeper *malaise*. He says:

I need not report my many mistakes, but it finally became clear to me that the deviation of speculative thought and, based thereupon, its presumed right to reduce faith to a factor might not be something accidental, might be located far deeper in the orientation of the whole age—most likely in this, that because of much knowledge people have entirely forgotten what it means to *exist* and what *inwardness* is. (CUP 241–2)

The parallels with Wittgenstein couldn't be stronger. Compare what he says, for example, in the sketch for a foreword to *Philosophical Remarks*:

This book is written for those who are in sympathy with the spirit in which it is written. This is not, I believe, the spirit of the main current of European and American civilization. The spirit of this civilization makes itself manifest in the industry, architecture and music of our time, in its fascism and socialism, and it is alien and uncongenial to the author. (CV 6e)

In other words, Kierkegaard and Wittgenstein both believe that there is an intimate connection between 'the orientation of a whole age' and its

---

[12] Whether Kierkegaard's pseudonyms are entirely fair to Hegel is a question I shall not be addressing. In many ways, the word 'Hegel' can be regarded as a philosophical place-holder that goes proxy for someone exhibiting the kinds of philosophical tendencies that Kierkegaard's pseudonyms are criticizing. And to these criticisms it is, in the end, irrelevant whether the 'real Hegel' actually exhibited them or not. For an interesting study of Kierkegaard's relation to Hegel, see Mark C. Taylor, *Journeys to Selfhood. Hegel and Kierkegaard* (New York: Fordham University Press, 2000).

philosophical problems. For philosophical confusions don't come out of nowhere, but are spawned by a certain way of looking at things. This is why Kierkegaard and Wittgenstein think that one's *Weltanschauung* is so important. Both philosophers believe that their respective ages—and it is remarkable that, although Kierkegaard and Wittgenstein are roughly half a century apart, their criticisms of a progress-worshipping, technological culture are next to identical—suffer from an intellectual disease that continuously gives birth to ever more endemic viruses in the guise of scientism and system-building. Weaning the reader from these philosophical confusions by offering them a 'perspicuous representation' of the 'qualitative distinctions' that their way of thinking obscures, is therefore an important task, not only because clarity is an end in itself, but also because these confusions can have very real and very serious consequences for the person in thrall to them. For example, as Climacus says, 'To be an idealist in imagination is not at all difficult, but to have to *exist* as an idealist is an extremely rigorous life-task, because existing is precisely the objection to it' (CUP 353). Compare Wittgenstein's remark at *Zettel* §414:

But the idealist will teach his children the word 'chair' after all, for of course he wants to teach them to do this and that, e.g. to fetch a chair. Then where will be the difference between what the idealist-educated children say and the realist ones? Won't the difference only be one of battle cry?

In other words, Kierkegaard and Wittgenstein are at one in their aim of trying to expose the *fraudulence* of metaphysics. Both want to show that it constructs edifices in which no one can dwell using only the *appearance* of building blocks. But it is not that metaphysical speculation doesn't agree with common sense and this is why we have to reject it—that is, Kierkegaard and Wittgenstein are not advocating a form of pragmatism, as some commentators have supposed. Rather, what they try to show is that metaphysics' pretensions are fantastical and confused by exposing (among other things) the speculative philosopher's tendency to disregard practice and context, confuse conceptual with factual questions and cleave to the false ideal of the 'God's eye' view of the world.

Kierkegaard and Wittgenstein not only agree, however, that in metaphysical system-building 'language has gone on holiday' (PI §38), they also think that metaphysical speculation is inimical to a consideration of the really important questions such as the 'problems of life'—that is, how to live and how to act. The reason for this is, as Climacus says, that although a system of logic can be given, attempting to give a system of existence à la Hegel[13] is an absurdity (CUP 118). But too intimate an association with world-history can allow us to lose sight of this fact:

Modern speculative thought has mustered everything to enable the individual to transcend himself objectively, but this just cannot be done. Existence exercises its constraint, and if philosophers nowadays had not become pencil-pushers serving the trifling busyness of fantastical thinking, it would have discerned that suicide is the only somewhat practical interpretation of its attempt. (CUP 197)

That is to say, and as Climacus repeatedly points out in CUP, anything is possible in 'pure thought', even, allegedly, cancelling the principle of contradiction. Existence, however, is not so accommodating; there is nothing in between to be and not to be. The ongoing process of existing—what Kierkegaard's pseudonyms call the process of 'becoming'—cannot therefore be fitted into timeless metaphysical categories except by dint of denying the existence of our selves altogether. But such a form of self-forgetfulness is not only philosophically fraudulent, according to Climacus, it is also ethically suspect. I think that Wittgenstein meant something similar when he said to Russell, 'How can I be a logician before I am a human being?'[14] In fact, Wittgenstein here seems to be endorsing the typically Climacian dictum: 'first, then, the ethical, to become subjective, then the world-historical' (CUP 159). In other words, neither author believes that there is anything wrong with the disinterested 'world-historical' vantage-point per se; it is only when constant preoccupation with it makes one fancy that one is no longer a human being but 'three-eighths of a paragraph' (CUP 145) in the world-historical 'system' that this impulse becomes pernicious. For, as Climacus says:

the observer sees world history in purely metaphysical categories, and he sees it speculatively as the immanence of cause and effect, ground and consequent. Whether he is able to discern a *telos* for the whole human race, I do not decide, but that *telos* is not the ethical *telos*, which is for individuals, but is a metaphysical *telos*. Insofar as the individuals participate in the history of the human race by their deeds, the observer does not see these deeds as traced back to the individuals and to the ethical but sees them as traced away from the individuals and to the totality. (CUP 155)

Hence, if we take up the world-historical vantage-point, the ethical will become indifferent, for what we see from this perspective is a mere

---

[13] Hegel attempted this by introducing movement into logic.
[14] Quoted in Rush Rhees, *Ludwig Wittgenstein. Personal Recollections* (Oxford: Oxford University Press, 1984), 211.

contingent unfolding of events according to the laws of cause and effect. But to abstract from subjectivity in this way is effectively to negate our humanity: it is 'objectively' to reduce us to little more than physical automata reacting to external stimuli. The ultimate consequence of such a view is nihilism,[15] for, on such a conception, the ethically central notions of agency and responsibility can no longer get a foothold.[16] Climacus is therefore warning us against the reductionism implicit in taking this standpoint for a paradigm with universal validity and many of Wittgenstein's criticisms of Frazer, in his *Remarks on Frazer's* Golden Bough, come from exactly the same direction.

For both authors, then, every philosophical misconception also has an ethical dimension. This is the significance of Wittgenstein's remark that a philosophical mistake is like a character failing. Hypocrisy and confusion in thought are connected to hypocrisy and confusion in life. James Conant brings this out very well when he says:

One can, if one will, take the words 'perspicuity' and 'clarity' to stand for things Wittgenstein struggles to attain in philosophy. And one can, with equal justification, take the words 'honesty' and '*Anständigkeit*' [decency] to stand for things Wittgenstein thinks everyone should struggle to attain in life. If you do not think of yourself as ever practising philosophy, then you may take yourself only to have reason to think of yourself as caught up in the second of these two kinds of struggle. If you evidently do practise philosophy, but most decidedly not in the spirit of Wittgenstein, then these two struggles may strike you as utterly independent of one another . . . But if you wish to think of yourself as practising philosophy in anything like the spirit of Wittgenstein, then these two aspects must become for you—as they did for Wittgenstein—twin aspects of a single struggle, each partially constitutive of the other.[17]

Philosophical problems, on Kierkegaard's and Wittgenstein's conception, cannot, therefore, be completely insulated from 'personal problems', as Phillips, for example, maintains, since, although a philosophical problem is not a 'personal' problem in the sense that love-sickness, for instance, is a personal problem, a philosophical problem is nonetheless 'personal' in the sense that the *struggle* with it is personal and revelatory

---

[15] This is also Wittgenstein's view in the *Tractatus* which makes him locate value 'outside the world'. See the next chapter.

[16] See, for example, P. F. Strawson's 'Freedom and Resentment' in A. P. Martinich and David Sosa (eds), *Analytic Philosophy. An Anthology* (Oxford: Blackwell, 2001), 287–300.

[17] 'On Going the Bloody *Hard* Way in Philosophy', in John Whittaker (ed.), *The Possibilities of Sense* (Basingstoke: Palgrave, 2002b), 90.

of the kind of person and philosopher one is. And this is one of the main reasons why Petrus Minor says that profundity is not an aesthetic qualification but an ethical one and Wittgenstein says that 'working in philosophy—like work in architecture in many respects—is really more a working on oneself. On one's own interpretation. On one's way of seeing things. (And what one expects of them.)' (CV 16e).

This connection between purity of heart and purity of thought, so to speak, comes out even more strongly in the Preface to *Philosophical Remarks*:

I would like to say, 'this book is written to the glory of God', but nowadays this would be the trick of a cheat, i.e. it would not be correctly understood. It means the book was written in good will, and so far as it was not but was written from vanity etc., the author would wish to see it condemned. He can not make it more free of these impurities than he is himself.[18] [19]

Peter Winch sums up the implications of this passage very nicely when he says:

The last sentence: 'He can not make it more free of these impurities than he is himself', seems to me especially important in its implication that the 'purity' of the writer and the character of the writing are connected—and not just in a

---

[18] In his book, *Logic and Sin in the Writings of Ludwig Wittgenstein*, Philip Shields gives a different gloss to this remark. He does not read it, like I do, as primarily an ethical remark concerning authenticity in philosophical writing, but as a straightforwardly 'religious' statement. He says, 'Our language is there, thrust upon us, and it is an occasion for both deep respect and dread, even worship and loathing, as though it were both created as a gift from God and infected subsequently with original sin. One must engage it and even embrace it, but with a will that is transformed and resistant to certain prevalent temptations. This, I would suggest, is the key to the striking and enigmatic remark Wittgenstein makes in the foreword to the *Philosophical Remarks*' (93). This strikes me as highly problematical, for there is nothing in the PI themselves to suggest that Wittgenstein thought that language is to be viewed as a 'gift from God'. In fact, the line 'It means the book is written in good will, and in so far as it is not so written, but out of vanity, etc., the author would wish to see it condemned' makes it quite clear that the point of the whole remark is to contrast 'writing to the glory of God' with 'writing to one's own glory'. That is to say, Wittgenstein is making an ethical, not a religious point, otherwise he needn't have qualified the sentence 'This book is written to the glory of God' with 'but nowadays this would be the trick of a cheat'. For only for someone like Bach, who could, given his theistic commitments, construe it as a straightforwardly religious remark, would it not be 'the trick of a cheat'. Naturally, this does not preclude the thought that there is something religious or quasi-religious in Wittgenstein's conception of ethics, but this is an altogether different matter (see the next chapter). For a related discussion, see Peter Winch's response to Norman Malcolm (whose claims about the 'religious dimension' in Wittgenstein's work are strikingly similar to those of Shields), in *A Religious Point of View?*, 108–32.

[19] Rhees, *Recollections of Wittgenstein*, 78.

contingent way, but internally. It would not be easy to make such a claim with many, perhaps most, types of writing; but whether or not the point does have a more general application, I believe that for Wittgenstein philosophical writing was a special case.[20]

In other words, it is not merely the 'external' fact that philosophical confusions can have bad consequences for a person's life (or for other domains of discourse) that makes Kierkegaard's and Wittgenstein's conception of philosophy into an ethical one that connects philosophy and life (or work and author); rather, and much more importantly, it is philosophical clarity *itself* that has, in the eyes of both thinkers, an ethical dimension or that functions as an imperative simultaneously philosophical and ethical. And, if this is so, we can see why Wittgenstein and Kierkegaard agree that a 'profound thinker' is not someone who thinks 'profound' thoughts, but rather someone whose life expresses or is emblematic of these thoughts. For, on such a conception, in the end, it is (conceptually) impossible *not* to go the 'bloody hard way'[21] in both philosophy and in the attitude one takes towards one's life in general. That is to say, it is impossible, according to Wittgenstein and Kierkegaard, to be a superficial person, but not to be, at the same time, a shallow thinker. Consider, for example, the following passage:

But what does it mean to have *actually* reflected oneself out of the immediate without having become a master in the comic? Well, it means that one is lying. What does it mean to give assurances that one has reflected oneself out and to communicate this in direct form as information—what does it mean? Well, it means that one is lying. (CUP 281)

Climacus could hardly put it more bluntly that he not only believes that thinking one can *reflect* oneself out of an *existence-sphere* is a philosophical mistake, but rather that it is a moral failing too: it is a *lie*, no less. This suggests that it is not so much that the Hegelian philosopher lacks the philosophical acumen to discern what is mistaken about his view, but rather that he in some sense wants to conceal (from himself and others) what on another level he knows perfectly well.[22] For the

---

[20] See Peter Winch's response to Norman Malcolm, in *A Religious Point of View?*, 131.

[21] 'Rush Rhees tells us: "Wittgenstein used to say to me, 'Go the bloody *hard* way'."' Quoted in Conant, 'On Going the Bloody *Hard* Way', 85.

[22] This is the familiar problem of having a certain 'awareness' of the fact that one is deceiving oneself, a problem which ceases to be paradoxical if we distinguish between different levels of self-knowledge. See Conant, op.cit., 93–5. Of course, being *incapable* of seeing something (rather than just deceiving oneself about it) can also be a mark of superficiality.

sake of the success of the system, as it were, he *wants* his view to be true and is therefore being dishonest both with himself and with his readers. Similarly, when Climacus criticizes the *hubris* or the absentmindedness of the Hegelian philosopher, these are *both* philosophical as well as ethical criticisms.[23] Compare Wittgenstein's criticism of Schopenhauer: 'Schopenhauer is quite a *crude* mind, one might say. I.e. though he has refinement, this suddenly becomes exhausted at a certain level and then he is as crude as the crudest. Where real depth starts, his comes to an end. One could say of Schopenhauer: he never searches his conscience' (CV 36e).

Naturally, this internal relation between the 'purity' of the writer and the character of the writing has important implications for the style in which a philosophical work is written. It is, for example, one of the main reasons for Kierkegaard's choosing to write under pseudonyms. In 'A First and Last Explanation' that Kierkegaard appended to CUP (as, at the time, he intended the *Postscript* to be his last work), he says:

My pseudonymity or polyonymity has not had an *accidental* basis in my *person* but an *essential* basis in the *production* itself . . . What has been written, then, is mine, but only insofar as I, by means of audible lines, have placed the life-view of the creat*ing*, poetically actual individuality in his mouth, for my relation is even more remote than that of a poet, who *poetizes* characters and yet in the preface is *himself* the *author*. That is, I am impersonally or personally in the third person a *souffleur* who has poetically produced the *authors*, whose *prefaces* in turn are their productions, as their *names* are also. (CUP 625–6)

Clues as to what Kierkegaard means when he speaks of his pseudonymity having an essential basis in the production itself are scattered throughout CUP and are to be found primarily in the sections where Climacus speaks of the 'subjective thinker's' form of communication. Especially promising is the following passage:

The subjective *thinker's form*, the form of his communication, is his *style*. His form must be just as manifold as are the opposites that he holds together. The systematic *eins, zwei, drei* is an abstract form that also must inevitably run into trouble whenever it is to be applied to the concrete . . . But just as he [the subjective thinker] himself is not a poet, not an ethicist, not a dialectician, so also his form is none of theirs directly. His form must first and last be related to

---

[23] And this of course also means that the two are not *identical*, otherwise we would have no more than an uninformative tautology.

existence, and in this regard he must have at his disposal the poetic, the ethical, the dialectical, the religious. (CUP 357)

We have already encountered some of the reasons why Kierkegaard and Wittgenstein think that philosophy can't be didactic. We have seen that both authors eschew metaphysical system-building and that philosophical authorship is consequently not a matter of communicating results, but that the point of the activity is ethical: what both thinkers ultimately want to achieve is a self-transformation of the reader. It is therefore important that the style employed in philosophical composition so conceived reflects these aims. Kierkegaard's way of doing this is through the creation of poetical personae (pseudonyms) who quite literally *exist* in the life-view they are trying to depict. Thus, in the first volume of *Either/Or*, for example, the reader is confronted by the aesthete A, the master doubter, who questions the sense of everything. Precisely because A takes his philosophical doubts seriously—contrary to the fraudulent Hegelians who believe they have conquered an imaginary doubt in an imaginary system—he lives as a sophisticated hedonist, which, he believes, is all one can do in the face of the 'disenchantment of the world'.[24]

According to Judge William, the advocate of ethical self-choice and the author of the letters to the aesthete in the second part of *Either/Or*, A's viewpoint has serious shortcomings. William's main objection is that the aesthete lacks a proper self, as he relates to life only as a sum of possibilities, which, if they are actualized at all, are done so purely according to whim. Consequently, the aesthete is the 'poet of chance', but in virtue of this very fact his life lacks an 'eternal' dimension: it possesses no unifying principle which could give it meaning over and above being a simple succession of moments. The aesthete does not relate to anything outside himself (to other persons or to an ideal) and his self therefore fragments into a mere set of moods. Therefore, strictly speaking, the aesthete doesn't really *exist*.

Either/Or does not present the reader with a verdict on the matter of whose viewpoint, the aesthete's or the Judge's, is superior. In this respect there is no didacticizing: both parties have their say; that is all. In the 'Glance at Danish Literature' in CUP, where, funnily enough, a pseudonym comments on other pseudonyms, Climacus offers us an interpretation of the significance of this:

---

[24] Interestingly, Kierkegaard's aesthete bears a certain resemblance to Richard Rorty's ironist. See Rorty, *Contingency, Irony and Solidarity* (Cambridge: Cambridge University Press, 1989).

Either/Or, the title of which is in itself indicative,[25] has the existence-relation between the aesthetic and the ethical materialize into existence in the existing individuality. This to me is the book's indirect polemic against speculative thought, which is indifferent to existence. That there is no conclusion and no final decision is an indirect expression for truth as inwardness and in this way perhaps a polemic against truth as knowledge . . . The absence of an author [of the whole work] is a means of distancing. (CUP 252)

The last sentence of the latter passage is significant, for what it reveals is that one of the main motivations for the pseudonymous strategy as a whole is to create, so to speak, the *absence* of an author. Given that Kierkegaard, like Wittgenstein, aims at the self-transformation of the reader who must herself be brought to recognize the deformities of her own thinking, the pseudonymous strategy is designed so as to grant maximal ethical and intellectual independence to the reader. Kierkegaard is therefore like a sophisticated stage director who orchestrates the play between the different pseudonymous characters without, however, identifying with any one of them. In this respect, pseudonymity creates authorial distance and at the same time allows the pseudonymous character to come as close as possible to the reader. And in order to achieve this, the subjective thinker, as Climacus says, must have at his disposal the poetic, the ethical, the dialectical, the religious, but without he himself being any one of these. This is the reason why Kierkegaard's works are so multifaceted and resist easy classification: depending on what kind of person the relevant pseudonymous author is, they contain, *inter alia*, fictional prose, poetry, literary essays, philosophy and dialectics as well as theology. In this way, Kierkegaard can also deflect possible charges of hypocrisy: given that none of the pseudonyms are identical to Kierkegaard himself, no one can legitimately claim that Kierkegaard's personal existence is at odds with that portrayed by an individual pseudonym.[26] Thus, Kierkegaard's strategy ensures that there is a perfect coincidence between the 'purity' of the (pseudonymous) writer and the 'purity' of the production.[27]

[25] The title, *Either/Or*, is a dig at Hegel's claim to have annulled the principle of contradiction.

[26] Something that would be an odd reproach to make anyway, in light of the fact that the three existence-spheres depicted in the authorship are mutually exclusive.

[27] The intimate connection between Kierkegaard's strategy and its ethical point also ought to be sufficient to counter charges of 'aestheticism'—that Kierkegaard is 'unserious' because he identifies with none of the options he depicts.

There is a connection between this strategy and Wittgenstein's (otherwise) rather puzzling remark from *Culture and Value*:

I think I summed up my attitude to philosophy when I said: philosophy ought really to be written only as a *poetic composition*. It must, as it seems to me, be possible to gather from this how far my thinking belongs to the present, future or past. For I was thereby revealing myself as someone who cannot quite do what he would like to do. (CV 24e)

What Wittgenstein has in mind here is, I think, similar to Climacus' claim that 'wherever the subjective is of importance in knowledge and *appropriation* is therefore the main point, communication is a *work of art*' (CUP 79, italics added). As we have already seen, Kierkegaard and Wittgenstein want to transform our whole way of looking at things instead of getting the reader to assent to a sum of novel propositions. The important thing, as Climacus says, is the appropriation of a new perspective, not an accumulation of more systematic knowledge. When this is the case, both authors seem to be urging, the writing of philosophy must become more like the creation of a work of art than the construction of a theoretical edifice. For simply stating 'directly', as it were, what one's intentions are and what one wants the reader to do, won't do the trick:

When I had comprehended this, it also became clear to me that if I wanted to communicate anything about this, the main point must be that my presentation would be made in an *indirect* form. That is, if inwardness is truth, results are nothing but junk with which we should not bother one another, and wanting to communicate results is an unnatural association of one person with another, inasmuch as every human being is spirit and truth is the *self-activity of appropriation*, which a result hinders. (CUP 242, italics added)

In other words, Kierkegaard and Wittgenstein both want the reader to *do* something, but it is part of the ethical nature of this task that it can't be captured in an instruction manual. As Wittgenstein says, 'I don't try to make you *believe* something you don't believe, but to make you *do* something you won't do.'[28] For both philosophers want to foster, not rote-reciters, but readers who think for themselves. Consequently, Kierkegaard's and Wittgenstein's intentions must manifest themselves 'indirectly' in the *form* of their respective works. In this sense,

---

[28] Quoted by Rush Rhees in *Discussions of Wittgenstein* (Bristol: Thoemmes Press, 1996), 43.

Kierkegaard's and Wittgenstein's writing has an important *maieutic* dimension (rather than being straightforwardly didactic): it is supposed to bring out, by way of Socratic 'midwifery', what the reader has always known, but has somehow lost sight of by becoming entangled in a misleading picture. As Wittgenstein says, 'The work of the philosopher consists in assembling reminders for a particular purpose' (PI §127). It is for these reasons that both authors believe that their philosophical authorship is more akin to an *artistic* rather than a scientific endeavour, for, contrary to science, where results can be given without attention to the way in which one gives them, in Kierkegaard's and Wittgenstein's work there is an *internal* relation between form and content—it is impossible to have one without the other.[29] And this does not imply that their writing therefore has no 'cognitive' content, but merely that the *point* of their productions can't be cashed out in propositions.[30] This is, I think, what Wittgenstein means when he says that 'people nowadays think that scientists exist to instruct them, poets, musicians, etc. to give them pleasure. The idea *that these have something to teach them*—that does not occur to them' (CV 36e).

Consequently, we need not endorse the either/or that Louis Mackey, for instance, seems to confront us with: either poetry or propositions.[31] I think that Kierkegaard and Wittgenstein primarily see their philosophical activity as conceptual elucidation ('qualitative dialectic') that may at times, depending on the problems being addressed, call for 'poetic' treatment and the use of literary devices (in this respect some of Kierkegaard's writings—*Philosophical Fragments* and *Concluding Unscientific Postscript to* Philosophical Fragments, as their titles already ironically indicate—are more obviously 'philosophical' than others). For example, when Wittgenstein is tracing alternatives to our use of concepts, in order to contrast this with how these concepts are *actually* employed, he is engaging in a 'poetic composition' of sorts (see, for instance, PI §283, §284, §297). And Kierkegaard does a very similar thing, when he imagines the different ways the same story might have gone—when he is, as he calls it, involved in 'imaginary construction' or 'psychological experimentation'. A good example of this is the biblical

---

[29] Of course if one thinks that philosophy is more like science in that its aim—as the traditional conception would have it—is to present the reader with a *body of knowledge*, then much of this, as well as the ethical point of the activity, will be lost on one.

[30] See also chapter 4, section III, the passages on 'internal' and 'external' understanding.

[31] See *Kierkegaard: A Kind of Poet* (Philadelphia: University of Pennsylvania Press, 1972), especially chapter 6.

account of the trial of Abraham, with its many variations, that Johannes *de Silentio* introduces in FT in order to throw light on the concept of faith.

Naturally, despite these similarities, Kierkegaard's and Wittgenstein's style of writing is also importantly different. For one, Wittgenstein writes in numbered aphorisms while Kierkegaard writes (largely) in continuous prose[32] and, as already mentioned, employs a plethora of different philosophical and literary styles. What is more, Wittgenstein's style is marked by an absence of the Dane's incisive deployment of humour and irony. Nevertheless, there is great similarity between the two when it comes to the use of epigrammatic expressions, dialogue,[33] metaphor and striking analogy. I will give just a couple of examples of this. Here is one of my favourite Kierkegaardian aphorisms, which could also have come from the pen of Wittgenstein: 'What philosophers say about actuality is often just as disappointing as it is when one reads on a sign in a secondhand shop: Pressing Done Here. If a person were to bring his clothes to be pressed, he would be duped, for the sign is merely for sale' (*Either/Or* I, 32). Compare what Wittgenstein says at CV 17e:

Philosophers often behave like little children who scribble some marks on a piece of paper at random and then ask the grown-up 'What's that?'—It happened like this: the grown-up had drawn pictures for the child several times and said: 'this is a man', 'this is a house', etc. And then the child makes some marks too and asks: what's *this* then?

Wittgenstein once said, 'What I invent are new similes'[34] (CV 19e), and this would also be an apt characterization of one of the main features of Kierkegaard's style. Indeed, there are so many examples of this in each author's work that it is hard to know which ones to choose. Here are

---

[32] The 'Diapsalmata' in the first vol. of *Either/Or* are an exception.

[33] In *Philosophical Fragments*, for example, there is an interlocutor who constantly objects to what Climacus is saying and even accuses him of plagiarism. This is very reminiscent of the role that Wittgenstein's alter ego plays in PI.

[34] One of the most striking features of the PI is indeed the abundance of novel and unusual comparisons. Thus, in the opening sections of that work alone, language is compared with the playing of games (PI §31–3), the different functions of items in a toolbox (PI §11), an ancient city (PI §18), the various levers in a locomotive (PI §12), etc. Many of the other similes have become famous catchphrases. For example, 'The confusions which occupy us arise when language is like an engine idling, not when it is doing work'(PI §132); 'What is your aim in philosophy?—To show the fly the way out of the fly-bottle'(PI §309); 'A whole cloud of philosophy condensed into a drop of grammar' (PI p. 222), etc.

two, both of which are concerned with showing the emptiness of certain philosophical endeavours. Wittgenstein says at PI §414—referring to the attempt of fixing the meaning of a word by introspection—'You think that after all you must be weaving a piece of cloth: because you are sitting at a loom—even if it is empty—and going through the motions of weaving.' Compare this with Climacus' criticism of attempting proofs of the immortality of the soul: 'The astounding labour of the system in demonstrating immortality is wasted effort and a contradiction . . . It is like wanting to paint Mars in the armour that makes him invisible' (CUP 174).

This concern with (and often great similarity of) style is connected, as we have already seen, to both authors' conception of philosophy and their consequent emphasis on the 'how' rather than the 'what' of their work (see the beginning of this section). The most explicit formulation of this is given by Wittgenstein in the preface to the *Tractatus*:

This book will perhaps only be understood by those who have themselves already thought the thoughts which are expressed in it—or similar thoughts. It is therefore not a text-book. Its object would be attained if it afforded pleasure to one who read it with understanding . . . If this work has a value it consists in two things. First that in it thoughts are expressed, and this value will be the greater the better the thoughts are expressed. The more the nail has been hit on the head.—Here I am conscious that I have fallen far short of the possible.[35]

Frege, one of the earliest readers of the *Tractatus*, found this exceedingly puzzling. In a letter to Wittgenstein from 1919 he writes: 'The pleasure of reading your book can therefore no longer be aroused by the content which is already known, but only by the peculiar form given to it by the author. The book thereby becomes an artistic rather than a scientific achievement; what is said in it takes second place to the way in which it is said.'[36]

Frege is right that the book is (primarily) an artistic rather than a scientific achievement, but wrong to think that its content is specifiable *independently* of the form given to it by the author. Consequently, it is not that the content is irrelevant, because it is already known, but rather that it is (conceptually) impossible to have *this* content without *that* style. Hence, hitting the nail on the head, as it were, isn't merely an artistic achievement, as Frege seems to think, but just as much an ethical one, because *authentic* writing, on Kierkegaard's and Wittgenstein's

---

[35] Translation by C. K. Ogden.   [36] Quoted in Monk, *Duty*, 174.

conception, must simultaneously fulfil the *maieutic* purpose of enabling the reader to recognize herself in it as well as do justice to the *facts*. For without these there would be nothing to recognize and no nail to hit.[37] This is why Wittgenstein says, 'The choice of our words is so important, because the point is to hit upon the physiognomy of the thing exactly, because only the exactly aimed thought can lead to the correct track' (PO 165). That is to say, style is of paramount importance, when the point of philosophical activity is 'to find the liberating word [*das erlösende Wort*], that is, the word that finally permits us to grasp what up until now has intangibly weighed down our consciousness' (PO 165).

In a sense, Kierkegaard and Wittgenstein both see themselves as physicians of the soul who attempt to cure the ailments (confusions) of the understanding by presenting a new perspective that will dissolve the philosophical problems: 'There is not *a* philosophical method, though there are indeed methods, like different therapies' (PI §133). Compare what Petrus Minor says in BA:

A physician at a sickbed is one thing, and a sick person, one who has leaped out of bed and by becoming an author, immediately describing his symptoms, obviously confuses being sick with being a physician, is something else. Perhaps he can give utterance to his condition in the illness and in glowing colours present himself in a way altogether different from the way the physician does in his description, since to know no solution and deliverance provides a distinctive passionate elasticity in comparison with the composed language of the person who knows the solution. But nevertheless there is a decisive qualitative difference between being sick and being a physician, and this difference is exactly the same as the decisive qualitative difference between being a *premise-author* and an *essential author*. (BA 17–18)

In other words, what Petrus Minor appears to be saying here is that in authentic writing the artistic will be tempered by the rigour of the ethical, for only when this is the case is it possible to depict, in Wittgenstein's words, 'the physiognomy of the thing exactly'. Both philosophers, it seems to me, would agree, therefore, that there is no truth without *truthfulness*, and that it is in the *style* (or spirit) of the production that truthfulness manifests itself. As Wittgenstein says:

no one *can* speak the truth; if he has still not mastered himself. He *cannot* speak it;—but not because he is not clever enough yet. The truth can be spoken only by someone who is already *at home* in it; not by someone who still lives in

---

[37] In other words, Kierkegaard and Wittgenstein are *not*, contrary to what is often assumed, propagating a form of relativism or anti-realism.

falsehood and reaches out from falsehood towards truth on just one occasion. (CV 35e)

This means that the essential author, if he is to merit this designation, must himself *exist* in the truth that he intends to communicate and this may require (much) self-restraint. To refrain, for example, from artistic flourishes or from didacticizing (direct communication) is a form of ethical self-denial, for, as Wittgenstein says, it can be as difficult not to use an expression as it is to hold back tears (PO 161)—hence the intimate connection, manifest in the style of the work, between the purity of the writer and the purity of the production. Ultimately, it is (primarily) for this reason that Petrus Minor says that the profound mind is not an aesthetic qualification with regard to genius but is essentially an ethical qualification. And this dovetails nicely with another remark of Wittgenstein's: 'The measure of genius is character,—even though character on its own does not amount to genius. Genius is not "talent *plus* character", but character manifesting itself in the form of a special talent' (ibid.).

It is for these reasons also that Kierkegaard and Wittgenstein take their works to be addressed as much to themselves as to their readership: 'The genuine subjective existing thinker is always just as negative as he is positive... He is, therefore, never a teacher, but a learner... he is continually striving' (CUP 85). As we have already seen, Kierkegaard even goes so far as to claim that he is not the author of the pseudonymous works, but a fellow reader and therefore occupies no privileged position as to the interpretation of his writings. In this respect, Kierkegaard writes 'without authority'—a motto that Wittgenstein, too, would surely want to endorse. Consequently, the indirect form of communication that Kierkegaard and Wittgenstein employ respects the ethical integrity of the reader by giving the 'self-activity of appropriation' pride of place. For it is this which will in the end decide whether what we see in the looking-glass is the image of an ape, or the image of an apostle. The mirror itself is silent on this point.

II OBJECTIONS TO A 'SYMMETRICAL READING'

In the previous section I tried to show that there are deep-running affinities between Wittgenstein's and Kierkegaard's conceptions of philosophical authorship. I will now address the objections to such a 'symmetrical reading' that have been expressed by D. Z. Phillips in his book, *Philosophy's Cool Place*. In this work, Phillips directs these objections primarily against James Conant and what the latter says in his article 'Putting Two and Two Together',[38] but they apply equally to anyone who believes that the similarities between Wittgenstein's and Kierkegaard's conception of philosophy are more important than the differences. In the following chapter I will be voicing my own disagreements with Conant's interpretation, which, however, have nothing to do with a 'symmetrical reading' as such, but are concerned with Conant's specific reading of the revocations to be found in the *Tractatus* and in CUP.

As we have already seen in the previous chapter, Phillips believes that there is an important asymmetry between Kierkegaard's and Wittgenstein's conception of philosophy: Wittgenstein's, according to Phillips, is 'contemplative' while Kierkegaard's isn't. In the first chapter of his book Phillips describes a 'contemplative conception' as one which rejects the traditional pursuit of philosophy of finding a single account of reality, but without falling into a form of relativism as a result. In this much, a contemplative conception seeks an answer to the question: 'How can philosophy give an account of reality which shows that it is necessary to go beyond simply noting differences between various modes of discourse, without invoking a common measure of "the real" or assuming that all modes of discourse have a common subject, namely, Reality?'[39] In other words, Phillips is concerned with the question of how philosophy can still be a *serious* activity once the traditional conception that philosophy can provide us with knowledge of the most basic features of the world or of Reality has been abandoned. Phillips argues that Wittgenstein's 'contemplative conception of philosophy' provides such an answer while Kierkegaard's doesn't, for the following three reasons.

First, Phillips believes that Kierkegaard was primarily a religious thinker concerned with specific confusions about Christianity. In exploring them, Phillips argues, Kierkegaard 'brings many conceptual distinctions to our attention. We can call them philosophical distinctions if we want to, but Kierkegaard's interest in making them is not primarily philosophical. He is, above all, a religious thinker,

---

[38] James Conant, 'Putting Two and Two Together: Kierkegaard, Wittgenstein and the Point of View for Their Work as Authors', in Timothy Tessin and Mario von der Ruhr (eds), *Philosophy and the Grammar of Religious Belief* (London: Macmillan, 1995).

[39] *Philosophy's Cool Place*, 11.

which is why, I argue, we do not find a contemplative conception of philosophy in his work.'[40] Second, according to Phillips, 'if we accept that Kierkegaard's conceptual clarifications were occasioned by his concern about the 'monstrous illusion', his conception of philosophy in such clarifications is obvious: it is an underlabourer conception of philosophy'.[41] In Wittgenstein, on the other hand, Phillips claims, 'philosophy is not *for* anything, in that sense; its concerns are distinctively its own'.[42] Third, Phillips argues that 'Kierkegaard did not want the sense of Christianity confused with the sense of other things, but he did not question the sense that he saw in Christianity and those other things. Wittgenstein, on the other hand, wonders at the possibility of there being sense in things at all.'[43] In other words, for Phillips, Kierkegaard's conception is non-contemplative, because Kierkegaard isn't puzzled 'about how discourse is at all possible—the puzzle that is the hallmark of a contemplative conception of philosophy'.[44] In what follows I will comment on each of these three theses in turn and attempt to show—as promised in the introduction to this chapter—that they are either implausible or perfectly harmless.

II.1 Kierkegaard—First and Foremost a Religious Thinker?

The question of how to read Kierkegaard's work is notorious, and it is compounded by the fact that the 'directions' on how to read it that Kierkegaard supplies in the course of his authorship are in conflict with one another. Let us recall, for example, what Kierkegaard said in 'A First and Last Explanation' that he appended to the *Postscript*:

Thus in the pseudonymous books there is not a single word by me. I have no opinion about them except as a third party, no knowledge of their meaning except as a reader,[45] not the remotest private relation to them, since it is impossible to have that to a doubly reflected communication. A single word by me personally would be an arrogating self-forgetfulness that, regarded dialectically, would be guilty of having essentially annihilated the pseudonymous authors by this one word. (CUP 625–6)

---

[40] Ibid., 25.   [41] Ibid.   [42] Ibid., 63.   [43] Ibid., 39.
[44] Ibid., 24.
[45] Kierkegaard's saying that he has no knowledge of his own works except as a reader is of course to be taken with a pinch of salt. Nevertheless Kierkegaard's attempt to dissociate himself from the pseudonymous works strikes me as perfectly sincere. So from the fact that he is exaggerating, it does not follow that he does not mean that we should not conflate him with his pseudonymous author.

Compare this with the (sole) evidence that Phillips cites for his view that Kierkegaard is primarily a religious thinker:

Supposing that a reader understands perfectly and appraises critically the individual aesthetic productions, he will nevertheless totally misunderstand me, inasmuch as he does not understand the religious totality in my whole work as an author. Suppose, then, another understands my works in the totality of their religious reference, but does not understand a single one of the aesthetic productions contained in them—I would say that the lack of understanding is not an essential lack.[46]

There is an obvious tension between this remark from PV and the one from CUP. In the latter Kierkegaard is telling us that he is to be regarded as merely a *reader* of his (pseudonymous) works, in the former he is, *qua author*, giving us instructions on how to read his whole production. This discrepancy is exacerbated by what Climacus says in the body of CUP:

I am pleased that the pseudonymous authors, presumably aware of the relation of indirect communication to truth as inwardness, have themselves not said anything or misused a preface to take an official position on the production, as if in a purely legal sense an author were the best interpreter of his own words, as if it could help a reader that an author 'intended this and that' when it was not carried out; or as if it were certain that it had been carried out, since the author says so in the preface. (CUP 252)

PV, in other words, where Kierkegaard claims that his authorship was religious from first to last, blithely contradicts everything that Climacus says here. In it (PV) Kierkegaard is very much taking an 'official position on the production' and he insists, as well, that the overall religious intentions—'the religious totality in my whole work as an author'—have been carried out simply because 'the author says so in the preface', as it were.

Furthermore, Kierkegaard's account of his strategy in PV also flies in the face of what Climacus says about indirect communication in CUP. As we have already seen in the previous section, Climacus rejects metaphysical system-building and the communicating of results in favour of the *appropriation* of a new perspective. That is to say, for Climacus, the point of philosophical authorship is ethical: he aims at a self-transformation of the reader. It is to this end that he

---

[46] *Cool Place*, 25–6. Phillips quotes Walter Lowrie's translation of *The Point of View for My Work as an Author* (Oxford: Oxford University Press, 1939), 6.

employs the indirect method, *not* in order to conceal secret religious intentions, as Kierkegaard claims in PV. In 'A Glance at Danish Literature', for example, where the latest pseudonym, Climacus, is commenting on all the earlier ones, we find nothing about the elaborate deception that Kierkegaard, *qua* author of all the pseudonymous works, supposedly employs in order to dispel the 'monstrous illusion', but rather a reiteration of Climacus' dictum of the relation between indirect communication and truth as inwardness.

In the light of all this, whom are we supposed to believe: the author of CUP and the 'First and Last Explanation' or the author of PV (Phillips seems to be unaware that there even is a conflict[47])? In order to answer this question I propose to enlist the help of Joakim Garff[48] who has made a very convincing study of the inconsistencies to be found in PV.

PV, as it now appears in the Hong edition, actually consists of two autobiographical pieces: the barely twenty-page long *On my Work as an Author*, composed, as Garff says, in 1849 but not published until the summer of 1851, and the much more substantial *The Point of View for my Work as an Author*, composed in the course of 1848 to await posthumous publication.[49] In the former work Kierkegaard says the following about how his total production should be read:

The movement the authorship describes is: *from* 'the poet', from the aesthetic—*from* 'the philosopher', from the speculative—*to* the indication of the most inward qualification of the essentially Christian; **from** the pseudonymous *Either/Or*, **through** *Concluding Postscript*, with *my name as editor*, **to** *Discourses at the Communion on Fridays* . . . This movement was traversed or delineated *uno tenore*, in one breath, if I dare say so—thus the authorship, regarded as a *totality*, is religious from first to last, something anyone can see, if he wants to see, must also see. (PV 5–6)

And in the *Point of View* Kierkegaard classifies his 'total production' in the following way:

First division (aesthetic writing): *Either/Or, Fear and Trembling, The Concept of Anxiety, Prefaces, Philosophical Fragments, Stages on Life's Way*—together with eighteen upbuilding discourses, which came out successively. Second

---

47 Phillips cites the quotation from CUP 625–6 in his 'Authorship and Authenticity' (in *Wittgenstein and Religion* (London: Macmillan, 1993), 205), but at the same time has no qualms about simply reading the quotation from PV 'straight'.
48 'The Eyes of Argus—The point of view and points of view with respect to Kierkegaard's "Activity as an Author"', in *Søren Kierkegaard—Critical Assessments of Leading Philosophers*, 71–96.
49 Ibid., 74–5.

division: *Concluding Unscientific Postscript*. Third division (only religious writing): *Upbuilding Discourses in Various Spirits, Works of Love, Christian Discourses*—together with a little aesthetic article: *The Crisis and a Crisis in the Life of an Actress*. (PV 29)

This classification is striking in a number of ways.

First of all, as Garff points out, the 'totality' that Kierkegaard lists here is not identical to his 'total production'. Garff says:

For example, the youthfully libellous book on Hans Christian Andersen, *From the Papers of One Still Living*, and the ironic dissertation *On the Concept of Irony* have been passed over in silence, just as one seeks in vain to find the journal articles which Kierkegaard acknowledged in a 'First and Last Explanation'. The most striking thing, however, is that the overview omits mention of *A Literary Review*. . . The fact that 'the totality of the authorship' and 'the total production' are not identical is thus due to the overview's concern for equilibrium and evenhandedness: the '*Third group* (only religious productions)' is already burdened with one aesthetic work and must thus not be burdened any further—and certainly not by anything so cumbersome as flagrantly aesthetic juvenilia.[50]

It seems, therefore, that Kierkegaard is simply rewriting history, as it were, by careful editing out of works that don't fit his plan. Second, the eighteen upbuilding discourses which Kierkegaard classifies as aesthetic in the *Point of View* are classified as *religious* in *On my Work as an Author*. As Garff says, 'It thus seems paradoxical that the establishment of this *aesthetic* symmetry requires that a work, which is classified as *aesthetic* at one point, must be classified as *religious* at another, and it is no less paradoxical that this symmetry is established precisely in order to defend against an *aesthetic* impression.'[51] This shows, I think, that the designations 'aesthetic' and 'religious' are, in the end, fairly arbitrary, for the eighteen upbuilding discourses strike one as by far more 'obviously religious' than some of the works that Kierkegaard labels thus (and yet Kierkegaard is prepared to call them 'aesthetic' when the need arises).[52] Third, in *On my Activity as an Author*, Kierkegaard says that the aesthetic writing was pseudonymous in order to conceal its religious aims, while the directly religious writing carried his name (PV 7), but, in spite of this,

---

[50] 'The Eyes of Argus—The point of view and points of view with respect to Kierkegaard's "Activity as an Author" ', 76.

[51] Ibid., 77.

[52] It is also mystifying why *Eighteen Upbuilding Discourses* are classified as 'aesthetic' whereas *Upbuilding Discourses in Various Spirits* aren't, unless, again, this is done purely for aesthetic reasons.

he assigns the more or less concurrently written, and obviously religious, *The Sickness Unto Death* (published in 1849) and *Practice in Christianity* (published in 1850), to a pseudonym, namely to Anti-Climacus. Aware of this inconsistency, Kierkegaard has the following to say about it (in a footnote):

> Later, however, there appeared a new pseudonym: Anti-Climacus. But the very fact that it is a pseudonym signifies that he is, inversely, coming to a halt, as the name (*Anti*-Climacus) indeed suggests. All the previous pseudonymity is lower than 'the upbuilding author'; the new pseudonym is a higher pseudonymity. But indeed 'a halt is made' in this way: something higher is shown, which simply forces me back within my boundary, judging me, that my life does not meet so high a requirement and that consequently the communication is something poetical. (PV 6)

Be that as it may, Kierkegaard is clearly moving the goalposts here, for in the main text of *On my Work* he is claiming that pseudonymity is supposed to hide (indirectly present) religious intentions, whereas in the footnote he is saying that pseudonymity is supposed to indicate that his own life does not match up to that of the pseudonym. So this is not so much an *explanation* of the deviation, but rather an *accentuation* of it.[53]

What, then, are we to make of all these dizzying, mutually exclusive, claims? The first moral to draw here is that PV, due to its many inconsistencies—if not to say dishonesties—simply cannot be read as if it were the definitive interpretation of Kierkegaard's *oeuvre*. We mustn't, therefore, fall into the trap of taking what Kierkegaard says in PV completely at face value. The question is: why does Kierkegaard mislead us? A possible explanation is that given that Kierkegaard repeatedly thought of ending his authorship (initially with CUP) in order to become a rural pastor, he wanted to ensure, as it were, that he had the relevant credentials. To this end he had to pretend that the so-called 'aesthetic works' were only a deception or a necessary 'emptying out' (PV 77)—that, in other words, his authorship was 'religious from first to last' (PV 6) as would befit a future man of God. Perhaps Kierkegaard also wanted, for whatever reason, to impose retrospective unity on his whole production, to make it into a coherent whole with a conscious design. In this respect he may have fallen prey to a self-generated intentional fallacy. That this might be what's going on is something that Kierkegaard himself (almost) acknowledges: 'To that

---

[53] In the light of this, it does not much matter that the decision to assign pseudonyms to SUD and PC was a last-minute decision.

extent, then, what was developed earlier, that all the aesthetic writing is a deception, proves to be in one sense not entirely true, since this expression conceded a little too much along the line of consciousness' (PV 77). In fact, Kierkegaard was quite aware that PV is in many respects a distortion, for he says in a journal entry ' "The Point of View for My Work as an Author" must not be published, no, no!. . . The fact that I cannot give the full truth in portraying myself signifies that essentially I am a poet[54]—and here I shall remain' (PV 175).

Paradoxically, in order to 'solve' the problem of the untruthfulness of PV, Kierkegaard even flirts, for a while, with the idea of assigning it to a pseudonym. In a journal entry Kierkegaard says:

Moreover, what I have written can very well be used—if I do indeed continue to be an author—but then I must assign it to a poet, a pseudonym. For example—

by
the poet Johannes de Silentio
edited
by
S. Kierkegaard

But this is the best evidence that 'The Point of View for My Work as an Author' cannot be published. It must be made into something by a third party: A Possible Explanation of Magister Kierkegaard's Authorship, that is, so it is no longer the same book at all. For the point of it was my personal story. (PV 177)

Here Kierkegaard is in effect spilling the beans about the real character of *The Point of View*: far from being *the* point of view on how Kierkegaard's authorship is to be taken, it is merely a *possible* (albeit a bit inaccurate!) explanation of Magister Kierkegaard's Authorship. In other words, PV is only one point of view among the many others that Kierkegaard offers throughout the course of his production and consequently occupies no privileged vantage-point. And in the light of its many inconsistencies, PV seems a much less reliable guide to what Kierkegaard has really been up to than the 'points of view' offered in CUP and in 'A First and Last Explanation'.[55] For we must not forget that these are, in the end, also

---

[54] Kierkegaard calls himself a poet rather than a philosopher, in order to distinguish himself from the systematicians such as Hegel and the German Idealists. This does not imply that Kierkegaard is a poet in the ordinary sense of that term.

[55] This does not imply, however, that PV can just be ignored. Despite being in many ways a distortion, PV does provide interesting insights into Kierkegaard's conception of himself and his authorship at a certain point in time and also gives us, as we saw

Kierkegaard's viewpoints, even if they come, in the case of CUP, in the guise of Johannes Climacus.[56] If we have to choose, therefore, between the 'point of view' offered in 'A First and Last Explanation' and *The Point of View*, I suggest we choose the former, for here, at least, we are spared the fallacious claim that it is certain that the book's intentions have been carried out, 'since the author says so in the preface' (CUP 252) and, one might add, since he tinkers with the evidence. For CUP, contrary to PV, does do, as it were, exactly what it says on the tin.

So, PV not only contradicts most of CUP, but is also at odds with the more or less concurrently written 'Ethical-Religious Essays' which make up parts of the posthumously published *Book on Adler*.[57] In one of these, 'The Difference between a Genius and an Apostle', Kierkegaard—as in the aforementioned journal entry—identifies himself with the poet or genius and says:

The lyrical author cares only about the production, enjoys the joy of the production, perhaps often through pain and effort, but he has nothing to do with others. He does not write *in order to*, in order to enlighten people, in order to help them onto the right road, in order to accomplish something—in short, he does not write: *in order to*. And so it is with every genius. No genius has an 'in order to'; the apostle *absolutely paradoxically* has an 'in order to'. (BA 188)

In other words, what Kierkegaard is saying here is that the writing of the 'genius' has no end outside itself. That is to say, although, as I have argued in the previous section, it does have an *ethical* end—namely, the self-transformation of the reader—this end is not *extrinsic* to the production itself in the sense that an apostle's 'leading people to Christianity' by being a 'witness to the truth' would be (see the following section). Hence, the apostle has, so to speak, 'divine authority', but the genius doesn't.

It seems, then, that in PV, by referring to himself as a 'spy in a higher service' (PV 87), that is, God's, Kierkegaard *almost* confuses himself

in the second section of this chapter, valuable insight into Kierkegaard's conception of philosophical authorship. So, although PV cannot straightforwardly be accepted as the definitive guide to Kierkegaard's entire production, this is not, as it were, to 'write it off altogether.

[56] In other words, the mere fact that PV is a 'signed' work whereas CUP isn't, is not reason enough, especially in the light of PV's inconsistencies, to prefer its account to the one offered in CUP.

[57] As should have emerged from the previous section, BA is a much more reliable guide to Kierkegaard's conception of philosophical authorship than PV.

with—or would like his readers to confuse him with—an apostle.[58] But neither Kierkegaard nor the reader is served by the attempt to squeeze Kierkegaard's multifaceted work into a single mould.[59] The fact that Kierkegaard tries this himself in PV is no good reason for following suit.

Consequently, given that the sole evidence that Phillips cites for his view that Kierkegaard is first and foremost a religious author and that his conceptual clarifications 'have their place in an authorship that is primarily religious rather than philosophical'[60] is the *one* quotation from PV, and given that there are good reasons to think that the latter work is not to be trusted, it follows that, by itself, this is not sufficient to prove Phillips's thesis. What is more, the most recently quoted remark from BA also casts serious doubt on Phillips's second claim that what serves to distinguish Wittgenstein from Kierkegaard is that in the former's case 'philosophy is not *for* anything . . . ; its concerns are distinctively its own'. For what Kierkegaard (in the guise of Petrus Minor) is saying at the end of BA seems to be very close to Wittgenstein's claim that 'the philosopher is not a citizen of any community of ideas; that's what makes him a philosopher' (*Zettel* §455)—a remark that Phillips quotes as corroboration of his view[61] that Wittgenstein, contrary to Kierkegaard, does not have an 'underlabourer conception of philosophy'. It is to this claim that I'll now turn.

II.2 An 'Underlabourer' Conception of Philosophy?

Phillips thinks that in Kierkegaard philosophy is subservient to religion whereas in Wittgenstein philosophy is an end in itself; it is not a *preliminary* to anything (such as the Christian life). In order to substantiate this claim Phillips says that:

In this respect, it is interesting to note that Kierkegaard's main interest was in the confusions of those who thought they were Christians when they were

---

[58] See, in this respect, especially chapter III of PV, the megalomaniacal 'Governance and My Authorship'. Although here, too, Kierkegaard claims to be 'without authority', I think that it would not be an exaggeration to say that he is, nevertheless, flirting with the 'extraordinary'.

[59] If one wanted to impose an overall thematic unity on Kierkegaard's works, it would be far more perspicacious to argue that what Kierkegaard provides in the course of his authorship is a number of possible existential responses to the problem of *scepticism*. For an interesting development of this interpretative strategy, see Kristin Kaufmann, *Vom Zweifel zur Verzweiflung. Grundbegriffe der Existenzphilosophie Søren Kierkegaards* (Würzburg: Königshausen and Neumann, 2002).

[60] *Philosophy's Cool Place*, 24.   [61] Ibid., 59.

not. He does not discuss those who are philosophically confused about their faith while they are believers. . . These neglected cases show the important *independent* source of philosophical confusion. The contemplative character of Wittgenstein's inquiries cannot be appreciated if this independence is not recognized.[62]

This is simply false. Kierkegaard *does* discuss those 'who are philosophically confused about their faith while they are believers'. They are the orthodox, who believe that they possess a 'higher understanding' of Christianity or else take it literally (see, for example, CUP 562–3 and 594–5). Naturally, as it then turns out, it is next to impossible to distinguish 'the confusions of those who thought they were Christians when they were not' from 'those who are philosophically confused about their faith while they are believers', for the second group ends up collapsing into the first one: neither is Christian in Kierkegaard's sense at all, as each turns out to be confused about what Christianity is. The orthodox confuse Christianity with paganism—with what Climacus terms 'direct recognizability'—and are therefore just as little Christians in Kierkegaard's sense as the ordinary Danes who pay lip service to religion by going to church once a week, but otherwise have their life in completely different categories. At the end of the *Postscript* Climacus says:

Direct recognizability is paganism; all solemn assurances that this is indeed Christ and that he is the true God are futile as soon as it ends with direct recognizability. A mythological figure is directly distinguishable. If one charges an orthodox with this, he becomes furious and flares up: Yes, but Christ is indeed the true God. . . one can see that in his gentle countenance. But if one can see it in him, then he is *eo ipso* a mythological figure. (CUP 600)

Phillips's distinction, therefore, between 'those who thought they were Christians when they were not' and 'those who are philosophically confused about their faith while they are believers' doesn't make much sense, given that the upshot of Climacus' argument in CUP is that (most probably) *all* Christians in Christendom are 'philosophically confused about their faith' and that consequently the number of (real) believers in Christendom may be *nil*. This is why Climacus says in the Conclusion to CUP: 'The present work has made it difficult to become a Christian, so difficult that the number of Christians

---

[62] Ibid., 44.

among the cultured[63] in Christendom will perhaps not even be very great—perhaps, because I cannot know something like that' (CUP 587). Naturally, this is an extraordinarily radical claim, but whether Climacus is right or not isn't what's currently at issue. At any rate, Phillips's distinction cannot, if we take Climacus seriously, be maintained and neither can his concomitant claim that Kierkegaard doesn't recognize the important source of independent philosophical confusion because he doesn't address 'those who are philosophically confused about their faith while they are believers'. For, in the end, being 'philosophically confused about one's faith' and 'being a believer' in the strict sense are, for Kierkegaard, mutually exclusive. And this, it seems to me, is quite a substantial philosophical claim that significantly undermines Phillips's contention that philosophy plays a subsidiary role in Kierkegaard's work.

Of course, as Phillips (and indeed Kierkegaard) keeps emphasizing, philosophical clarity about Christianity does not, of itself, turn one into a Christian. But this has no bearing on the converse claim which is at least as important to Kierkegaard, namely, that philosophical confusion about Christianity blocks the way to becoming one. That is to say, philosophical clarity is not (by itself) sufficient for a life-change, but philosophical confusion alone can obstruct it. Consequently, it seems to me, Phillips is wrong to attribute *complete* independence to philosophical problems (be they Wittgenstein's or Kierkegaard's).

What appears to be driving Phillips's insistence on the complete independence of philosophical problems is the thought that if this is not guaranteed, then we are, in effect, assigning to philosophy an instrumental role and must consequently inevitably settle, like Locke, for an 'underlabourer conception' of philosophy. This, too, is surely false. To show that philosophical distinctions have important implications for other domains of discourse (such as, for example, for religion) is surely not, per se, to *instrumentalize* philosophy. Neither is it to say that philosophy is therefore a 'preliminary to clear-sighted living', a view that Phillips (unfairly) attributes to Conant.[64] Something can both be an end in itself *and* have positive side-effects, as it were. For instance, an artist completely devoted to his art will dedicate his life to it both because he cannot do otherwise and because it may make him happy. But this does

---

[63] I don't think Climacus' claim is restricted to the 'cultured' or 'learned', for the so-called 'simple people' are surely just as prone (or perhaps even more prone) to confusing Christianity with paganism.

[64] *Philosophy's Cool Place*, 59.

not imply that art therefore is the *preliminary* to a happy life. Similarly, to say that 'philosophy is important because of the insights it gives you' is *not* thereby to say that consequently philosophy is merely a *means* to attaining such insight—a claim that rightly worries Phillips.[65]

Furthermore, and much more importantly, it is itself a philosophical *confusion* to think that one can, in the end, neatly separate these two—'philosophical' and 'personal'—aspects of a philosophical problem. For example, when I said in the previous section that philosophical clarity functions simultaneously as a philosophical and an ethical injunction in Kierkegaard's and Wittgenstein's work, I did *not* thereby mean to suggest that the ethical point of their philosophical activity is somehow *extrinsic* to philosophy (and specifiable independently of it)—as if you could bring about the same end without the philosophy by, say, inventing a machine, as Wittgenstein writes in one of his letters to Engelmann,[66] that turns you, at the same time, into a better person as well as a better philosopher! Nothing I have said therefore implies the absurd view that 'philosophical confusion' is to be equated with 'confused living'.[67] Phillips only seems to think it does, because he believes that the ethical self-transformation Kierkegaard and Wittgenstein aim at must be regarded as external to the pursuit of philosophy itself. It is, however, just *this* dichotomy (between an 'external' and—so to speak—an 'internal' conception, or between a 'partisan' and a 'contemplative' conception) that Kierkegaard and Wittgenstein seek to undermine. For to think that these two aspects can, in the end, be completely divorced from each other is like Frege believing that the content of the *Tractatus* is specifiable (completely) independently of the form given to it by the author.

Consequently, Phillips is right when he says that 'in saying "You cannot write anything about yourself that is more truthful than you yourself are", "Nothing is so difficult as not deceiving oneself" . . . and "Working in philosophy is really more like working on oneself", Wittgenstein is referring to difficulties in *doing philosophy*, difficulties in giving the problems the kind of attention philosophy asks of us.'[68] He is wrong, however, when he takes this to imply that 'the hold these "ways of thinking" have is not personal, nor is the source of their temptation. They are ways of thinking to which *anyone* can be susceptible, because their power is in the language that we speak.'[69]

[65] Ibid., 47.   [66] See chapter 1, note 23.
[67] *Philosophy's Cool Place*, 45.   [68] Ibid., 46.   [69] Ibid.

Although it is true of course that these are ways of thinking to which anyone can be susceptible, as I already said in the previous section, this does not mean that therefore the struggle with these ways of thinking is not personal. In fact, were it *not* (in some obvious sense) personal, then the kinds of criticism Wittgenstein and Kierkegaard make of other philosophers (such as, for example, of Schopenhauer and Hegel; see section II), as well as of themselves, would simply strike us—as Conant correctly points out in a brief response to Phillips[70]—as non sequiturs. I therefore agree with Conant that:

> erecting an opposition here between mutually exclusive categories of 'the personal' and 'the philosophical' will block the way to understanding why Wittgenstein thinks that work in philosophy (properly conducted) is a kind of working on oneself, and why he thinks that one cannot be any more honest in one's philosophical thinking than one can be with oneself, and why he thinks that the greatness of a philosophical work is expressive of the greatness of the particular human being that is its author.[71]

And the same, I have tried to show in section II, is true of Kierkegaard.

That Phillips seems to be blind to this stems from his preconceived idea that Kierkegaard is only interested in philosophical problems so far as they have religious consequences. But this view is simply not borne out by the evidence, for much of Climacus' (philosophical) criticism of Hegelianism, for example, has nothing at all directly to do with the dispelling of the 'monstrous illusion', but rather serves as a philosophical/ethical critique of 'the present age' in the manner of Wittgenstein. Consider, for example:

> Every age has its own: the immorality of our age is perhaps not lust and pleasure and sensuality, but rather a pantheistic, debauched contempt for individual human beings . . . This may account for the many attempts to hold fast to Hegel even by people who have seen the dubiousness of his philosophy. People fear that by becoming an individual existing human being one will vanish without a trace so that not even the daily newspapers, still less the critical journals and even less the world-historical speculative thinkers, will be able to catch sight of one. (CUP 355)

In other words, Climacus would *completely* agree with what Phillips says of Wittgenstein's conception:

> Wittgenstein also recognized that the age in which he philosophized was uncongenial to a contemplative conception of philosophy. When he says that it

---

[70] 'On Going the Bloody *Hard* Way', 87.   [71] Ibid., 88.

is 'possible for the sickness of philosophical problems to get cured only through a changed mode of thought and life', he is not saying . . . that a shoddiness in how we speak is, at the same time, a shoddiness in how we live. Rather, he is saying that an age's conception of what an intellectual problem is can be shoddy and that shoddiness consists precisely in the inability to see a problem in terms other than seeking answers to it, seeking solutions, getting things done. This is a sickness in the very conception of what a philosophical problem is.[72]

Indeed, this just is what Climacus has in mind when he criticizes Hegelianism for its failure to view the pursuit of philosophy in *ethical* terms and to be concerned only with 'objectivity' and 'paragraph-pomposity' (CUP 281)—something that, Climacus thinks, manifests itself especially in Hegelianism's deep-seated contempt for humour:[73]

It is another matter with the abstract thinker inasmuch as, without having understood himself and the relation of abstract thinking to existence, he either follows the inclination of a talent or is trained to be something of the sort. I know very well that people usually admire the artist-life of a person who follows his talent without accounting to himself for what it means to be human, so that the admirer forgets him in admiration over his work of art. But I also know that the tragedy of an existing person of that sort is that he is a variant and the differential is not personally reflected in the ethical. I also know that in Greece a thinker was not a stunted existing person who produced works of art, but he himself was an existing work of art. Surely, to be a thinker should least of all mean to be a variant from being a human being. If it is taken for granted that an abstract thinker lacks a sense of the comic, this is *eo ipso* proof that all his thinking is the feat of a perhaps outstanding talent but not of a human being who in an eminent sense has existed as a human being. (CUP 303)

And this just could not be closer to what Wittgenstein had in mind when he said that 'the measure of genius is character,—even though character on its own does not amount to genius. Genius is not "talent *plus* character", but character manifesting itself in the form of a special talent' (CV 35e).

---

[72] *Philosophy's Cool Place*, 46.

[73] 'That subjectivity, inwardness, is truth, is my thesis; that the pseudonymous authors relate themselves to it is easy enough to see, if in no other way, then in their eye for the comic . . . When an age is as thoroughly reflective as ours and as ours is said to be, then if this is true the comic must have been discovered by everyone . . . But assistant professors are so devoid of comic power that it is shocking; even Hegel, according to the assurance of a zealous Hegelian, is utterly devoid of a sense for the comic. A ludicrous sullenness and paragraph-pomposity that give an assistant professor a remarkable likeness to a Holberg bookkeeper are called earnestness by assistant professors. Anyone who does not have this appalling ceremoniousness is light-minded. Perhaps.' (CUP 281)

Consequently, just as on Kierkegaard's and Wittgenstein's conception it is impossible to drive a firm wedge between the character of the thinker and his thought, so it is also impossible to drive a firm wedge between 'an age's conception of what an intellectual problem is' and the way in which this age *lives*. Phillips's dichotomy therefore turns out, in the end, to be a false one, and far from showing that there is an asymmetry between Wittgenstein's and Kierkegaard's conception of philosophy, their concerted rejection of it shows us precisely how like-minded they actually are. Hence, Phillips has provided us with no good reasons for adopting the either/or—either a 'contemplative' or an 'underlabourer' conception of philosophy—that he presents us with, nor for casting doubt on a 'symmetrical reading' of Wittgenstein's and Kierkegaard's philosophical method. Indeed, what I said at the end of the introduction to the first chapter still holds true, namely, that Kierkegaard and Wittgenstein both desire the kind of reader for whom, *pace* Phillips, philosophical clarity and 'existential' (ethical) clarity become one. The kind of reader, in other words, for whom Phillips's dichotomy ceases to be a dichotomy.

So far, then, Phillips has not been successful in showing that there is an important asymmetry between Kierkegaard's and Wittgenstein's conception of philosophy. Let us therefore now examine Phillips's final and most important claim that what serves to distinguish Wittgenstein's from Kierkegaard's conception of philosophy is that Wittgenstein's revolves around 'wondering at the possibility of discourse' while Kierkegaard's doesn't.

II.3 'Wondering at the Possibility of Discourse'

Although Phillips agrees that Wittgenstein and Kierkegaard are both concerned with marking off different modes of discourse, he believes that Wittgenstein goes further than his Danish counterpart by wondering at how discourse is at all possible. What does this mean? Phillips explains:

difficulties about language itself are not the same as difficulties that involve confusions *between* different uses of language. For example, in dealing with the latter, you take for granted that the person you are teaching differences to can already speak. But in being puzzled about language, what is being taken for granted? Scepticism, at its deepest, as Plato knew, is scepticism about the possibility of discourse. These matters are easily confused, because part of the reason for confusion about the possibility of discourse may well reside in the kind of attention or lack of attention given to specific modes of discourse.

Absorbed as he is in clarifying categories for religious purposes, these wider issues are of little interest to Kierkegaard.[74]

What Phillips is saying here seems to be this: Kierkegaard isn't interested in general philosophical questions, such as, for example, what it means to say something, because his philosophical interests are animated exclusively by his religious concerns and therefore never extend beyond them. Given that the main thrust of this argument depends for much of its force on theses one and two, above, which have already been shown to be problematical, we need only focus here on whether it is true to say that we find no 'scepticism about the possibility of discourse' in Kierkegaard. And in order to get a firmer grip on what, according to Phillips, this comes down to, let us recall the following remark:

Kierkegaard did not want the sense of Christianity confused with the sense of other things, but he did not question the sense that he saw in Christianity and those other things. Wittgenstein, on the other hand, wonders at the possibility of there being sense in things at all.[75]

There are two ways of reading this passage, and between them they present Phillips with a dilemma. If we take literally the assertion that Kierkegaard 'did not question the sense that he saw in Christianity and those other things', then this claim is simply false. If, on the other hand, we take Phillips to mean that Kierkegaard isn't concerned with questions in philosophical logic—and he often writes as if this is what he means[76]—as Wittgenstein was, then this claim is obviously true, but trivial.[77] For it boils down to little more than asserting that Kierkegaard isn't Wittgenstein. And there would, of course, be little point in comparing the two philosophers, if they really were identical. Indeed, it is the very fact that Kierkegaard's and Wittgenstein's subject matter is often so very different that makes the similarities between them all the more striking. We can therefore, it seems to me, safely dismiss this horn of the dilemma and turn to the first one.

Short of repeating his familiar point that Kierkegaard is first and foremost a religious author,[78] Phillips presents no evidence at all for his

---

[74] Ibid., 37–8.   [75] Ibid., 39.   [76] See, for example, op.cit., 49.

[77] Although Kierkegaard does discuss and criticize Hegel's conception of logic in both PF and CUP.

[78] In what follows I will not be arguing against the view that Kierkegaard was a religious thinker. Of course he was. What I am taking issue with is Phillips's idea that someone cannot be both a religious thinker and a serious philosopher, as well as with his

view that Kierkegaard never questions the sense he sees in Christianity and other things. This is rather baffling, as Kierkegaard's existential dialectic as a whole seems to me to be directed precisely at the question of how it is possible to find sense in things. In fact, most Kierkegaardian pseudonyms are preoccupied, in one way or another, with doubt, and attempt to find some sort of 'existential'—that is to say, *liveable*—solution to it. The aesthete, for example, in virtue of his wholesale scepticism about finding sense in *anything*, opts for a sophisticated hedonism. His counterpart, the Kantian-inspired ethicist, takes this to be a pseudo-solution and proposes, instead, ethical self-choice. Anti-Climacus, on the other hand, believes that the only 'radical cure' for despair—the 'existential' equivalent of scepticism—is the Christian faith, while Climacus, his *alter ego*, precisely because he has made faith so difficult, is unable to see how it can be acquired. All of these—by no means exhaustive—views present distinct 'existential answers' to the sceptical predicament.

One of Kierkegaard's best philosophical insights—one, incidentally, that he again shares with Wittgenstein—is that sceptical doubt cannot be halted by *reflection*, but only by existential resolution, that is, by what Kierkegaard called a 'leap'. Compare this with Wittgenstein's remark at CV 31e: 'Language—I want to say—is a refinement, "in the beginning was the deed" '. Consequently, while Kierkegaard has respect for the Greek sceptic's aspiration to *ataraxia*, he has little or none for the Hegelian system that, to his mind, attempts to overcome philosophical doubt *in thought* and thereby only shows that the philosopher engaged in such an enterprise has never seriously doubted at all. An unfinished early work, *Johannes Climacus or De Omnibus Dubitandum Est*, was intended by Kierkegaard to reveal the fraudulence and intellectual dishonesty involved in the Hegelian system's claim to have started with and conquered doubt, and interestingly, this (fragmentary) work contains no discernible religious aims at all. It is directed exclusively at a perennial philosophical problem. (Many of the issues only skirted in *De Omnibus* are later taken up again by the 'grown-up' Climacus in PF and CUP.)

In the light of this, it would seem that the main difference between Kierkegaard and Wittgenstein, according to Phillips, really comes down

---

claim that Kierkegaard's production attempts to push the reader towards Christianity. The first contention, as we shall see, presupposes an essentialism about philosophical authorship; the second undermines the ethical point of Kierkegaard's work.

to this: 'Wittgenstein's conception of philosophy is contemplative in that its aim is to bring us to an understanding of what it is to have a world picture. . . But Wittgenstein is not *establishing* a world picture, least of all trying to tell us which is the *right* world picture.'[79] Naturally, the implication of this remark is that although Phillips thinks that Kierkegaard's qualitative dialectic doesn't, of itself, 'push people toward Christianity',[80] Kierkegaard *is*, in the end, trying to tell us which is the *right* world picture: 'As we have seen, for Kierkegaard, as a religious thinker, marking off a category from its neighbours has the purpose of clarifying the nature of a path that leads to a city whose builder and maker is God, whether the path is taken or rejected.'[81] This must, therefore, in the end, imply—Phillips's disclaimer notwithstanding—that Kierkegaard's work is a Christian apologetics of sorts. But such an interpretation falls foul of two objections. First, Kierkegaard was highly critical of any attempt to 'defend' Christianity. Second, such an account flies in the face of the aspirations Kierkegaard had for his pseudonymous strategy as a whole and is consequently at odds with the conception of philosophical authorship that I have taken both Kierkegaard and Wittgenstein to promote. I will take these points in turn.

That Kierkegaard was contemptuous of any traditional attempt to 'defend' Christianity, is, I take it, fairly uncontentious. But in case we should need any proof of this, here is just one (especially vitriolic) example coming from the mouth of Anti-Climacus:

Now we see how extraordinarily stupid . . . it is to defend Christianity, how little knowledge of human nature it manifests, how it connives even if unconsciously, with offence by making Christianity out to be some poor, miserable thing that in the end has to be rescued by a champion. Therefore, it is certain and true that the first one to come up with the idea of defending Christianity in Christendom is *de facto* a Judas No. 2: he, too, betrays with a kiss, except that his treason is the treason of stupidity. To defend something is always to disparage it . . . he who defends [Christianity] has never believed it. If he believes, then the enthusiasm of faith is not a defence. (SUD 87)

We have already seen that Kierkegaard and Wittgenstein both think that Christianity is not a metaphysical theory to be argued for and believed, but an existence-communication to be appropriated and put into practice.[82] What this means is that, if the two authors are right, then

---

[79] *Cool Place*, 54.   [80] Ibid., 28.   [81] Ibid., 59.
[82] This conception will be discussed at length in chapters 3 and 4. For the sake of the current argument, I am presupposing that these claims have been substantiated.

the Christian faith cannot be reduced to a set of theses that can become the subject matter of academic discussion and hence there is also no such thing as offering a philosophical defence of it. For a believer, according to Kierkegaard's pseudonyms, is a 'happy lover', not an apologist.

So far Phillips would presumably agree, since I take it that he wouldn't want to argue that what Kierkegaard is offering us is an apologetics in this traditional sense.[83] When Phillips therefore claims that 'Kierkegaard's hope was that when aesthetic and ethical perspectives are seen for what they are, those who confused them with Christianity would realize the error of their ways and turn to Christianity',[84] he must have something different in mind. Perhaps there is a weaker sense of 'defence' to appeal to. We might, for example, say that to 'defend' Christianity can also mean, as Kierkegaard himself says in PV, the attempt 'to deceive the reader into the religious'. This could be construed as, so to speak, an 'indirect'—or 'existential'—'defence' of the Christian religion. But this move fares no better than the first one, for if this is again taken to imply that the point of Kierkegaard's whole authorship is to show us the superiority of the Christian form of life, then, as already suggested, this undermines the rationale of the pseudonymous strategy.

In the previous sections I have already discussed the connection between Climacus' conception of truth as inwardness and the necessity of using a method of indirect communication in some detail, so I will

---

[83] C. Stephen Evans, on the other hand, comes close to attempting something like this. In his essay, 'Apologetic Arguments in *Philosophical Fragments*' (in *International Kierkegaard Commentary*, vol. 7, ed. Robert Perkins (Macon, GA: Mercer University Press, 1994), for example, he claims that Climacus (in PF) is not rejecting apologetic arguments outright, but only the 'classical' ones that presuppose foundationalism and that make faith and offence redundant. Arguments that presuppose faith, such as the teleological argument, would be acceptable to Climacus and, indeed, such an argument is put forward by Climacus himself. This is very wrong-headed. Climacus is not putting forward his remark about Socrates—'At least Socrates, who did indeed advance what is called the physico-teleological demonstration for the existence of God, did not conduct himself in this way. He constantly presupposes that the God exists, and on this presupposition he seeks to infuse nature with the idea of fitness and purposiveness.' (PF 44)—as an *argument* at all, for not only is this, as Climacus and Evans themselves point out, *qua argument*, entirely circular, it also directly follows Climacus' critique and rejection of attempting any kind of proof of the existence of God on the previous page. Consequently, what Climacus is saying here is that Socrates was wise enough *not* to attempt a demonstration of God's existence. His starting with the presupposition that God exists is therefore merely an indication, according to Climacus, that Socrates is really ironically rejecting the very idea of attempting such proofs. For a more detailed discussion of the teleological argument and Climacus' rejection of it (both in PF and in CUP), see chapter 4, section III.

[84] *Cool Place*, 28.

not go over that familiar ground again here. Instead, I would like to reopen the discussion by quoting the view of a different pseudonym on this topic, namely that of Anti-Climacus. This is what the latter has to say about the 'impossibility of direct communication' in PC:

> Indirect communication can be an art of communication in redoubling the communication; the art consists in making oneself, the communicator, into a nobody, purely objective, and then continually placing the qualitative opposites in a unity . . . For example . . . to bring attack and defence into a unity in such a way that no one can directly say whether one is attacking or defending, so that the most zealous supporter of the cause and its most vicious foe can both seem to see in one an ally—and then to be nobody oneself, an absentee, an objective something, a nonperson . . . yet he [the communicator] perhaps is an ingenious secret agent who with the aid of this communication finds out which is which, who is the believer, who the atheist; because this is disclosed when they form a judgement about what is presented, *which is neither attack nor defence.* (PC 133–4; emphasis added)[85]

So, similarly to his 'brother', Climacus, in CUP, Anti-Climacus is also in this passage drawing a link between the method of indirect communication and the *ethical* point of his authorship. The writing itself is, as he says, 'neither attack nor defence', and its object is to disclose the reader's heart. This purpose of holding a looking-glass up to the reader the production is able to fulfil precisely in virtue of the author's not taking sides on the issue and remaining a 'nobody' or 'purely objective something'. For in this way the reader is left entirely alone with the work and instead of having the author's point of view thrust upon her, all that she will, in the end, be confronted with is herself and the state of her own soul.

In other words, the different pseudonymous voices present us with different possible views of life in idealized form (in actuality there could not be as consummate an aesthete as Johannes, the Seducer, or as perfect a religious person as the Knight of Faith). Kierkegaard's dialectic virtuosity consists in its Janus-like quality: as Anti-Climacus says in the aforementioned passage, by continually placing the qualitative opposites in a unity, attack and defence of the view of life depicted come within a

---

[85] Compare what Kierkegaard says in a journal entry: 'Just as Johannes Climacus dialectically formulated the issue so sharply that no one could directly see whether it was an attack on Christianity or a defence, but it depended on the state of the reader and what he got out of the book, so also Anti-Climacus has carried the issue to such an extreme that no one can see directly whether it is primarily radical or primarily conservative, whether it is an attack on the established order or in fact a defence.' (PV 252)

hair's breadth of being one. Thus, it is up to the reader, as Climacus says, 'to put it all together by himself, if he so pleases, but nothing is done for a reader's comfort' (CUP 298). The reader's ethical self-examination is consequently made possible by the fact that the pseudonymous works admit of more than one interpretation. How—if at all—the reader uses Kierkegaard's words to examine her life is thus revelatory of the kind of person she is or, ideally, might become. If we therefore read Kierkegaard *à la* Phillips as someone who is only using the indirect method in order, in the end, to arrive at direct communication—that is to say, at communication of the view that Christianity is the superior life-view—then this is to annihilate the ethical point of the production by this one word.

Consequently, given that neither the pseudonymous works nor the signed ones engage in advocacy of any sort,[86] we would seem to be left only with Kierkegaard's assertion in PV that his authorship has an obvious religious end (in the sense of attempting to push his reader towards Christianity). But the very fact that Kierkegaard was so singularly dissatisfied with that work, which derived, in the end, from his realization that in it he was straightforwardly trying to conflate his personal existence with his production, constitutes the best evidence that this point of view cannot be the definitive one. For, as Kierkegaard says in an illuminating journal passage where he criticizes the attempt to publish PV, he is 'a poetic reflector of Christianity with the capacity to set forth the Christian qualifications in all their ideality' (PV 213). But a 'poetic reflector' is not an advocate and to engage in a 'qualitative dialectic' about Christianity is not the same as to endorse—or to get the reader to endorse—Christianity. If it were otherwise, conceptual investigation would become an absurdity.

It is for these reasons, as we have already seen in the first section of this chapter, that Kierkegaard and Wittgenstein don't want to make the reader *believe* something she won't believe, but to make her *do* something she won't do. Results, as Climacus says, are 'nothing but junk with which we should not bother one another' (CUP 242). But if so, then Phillips's reading of Kierkegaard cannot be correct. For arriving at the view that the Christian form of life is superior is a kind of result, and even if Kierkegaard, personally, believed this to be true,[87] it does

---

[86] With the exception, perhaps, of *Attack upon Christendom*, but then this constitutes an attack on the Church rather than advocacy of religion.

[87] It is unclear even whether Kierkegaard himself really did believe this. At least, at the time of writing CUP it seemed still to be unclear, because Kierkegaard has Climacus say,

not follow that the authorship as a whole therefore aims at showing such a thing. To lose sight of this distinction is to lose sight of the ethical point of Kierkegaard's philosophical activity.

In other words, to regard Kierkegaard's work as consisting of a *scala paradisi* with three main rungs—the aesthetic, the ethical and the religious, the latter constituting its culmination—is to turn his production into a kind of inverted Hegelian system and Kierkegaard himself into his dreaded 'premise-author'. But this is to commit the error that Kierkegaard himself, as well as all his pseudonyms, incessantly warn us against:

> just as it has not been understood why *Concluding Postscript* has a comic design—just as the matter is thought to be improved by taking particular theses and translating them into the didactic—so it will probably end with treating me, unto new confusion, as a cause and translating everything into the objective, making it into something new, that here is a new doctrine, rather than that the new is that here is personality. (PV 216)

Let us now return to our primary concern, namely, the question of whether there is an asymmetry between Kierkegaard's and Wittgenstein's conception of philosophy. More specifically, does the argument I have been developing in this section imply that Kierkegaard has a 'contemplative conception' in Phillips's sense? In the previous section I already suggested that the labels 'contemplative' and 'underlabourer' conception do no useful work when applied to Kierkegaard's and Wittgenstein's ethical conception of philosophical authorship, so I have no intention of reviving them again here. That is to say, to reject Phillips's arguments for the apparent asymmetries in Kierkegaard's and Wittgenstein's work is not thereby to endorse his notion of a 'contemplative conception'. In other words, while I think it can be shown that Kierkegaard and Wittgenstein have no underlabourer conception of philosophy (and I hope, in the previous section, to have shown it), I am unsure, in the end, what exactly Phillips's 'contemplative conception' amounts to. For, as we have seen, Phillips's insistence on the complete independence of philosophical problems presupposes the

---

'It is possible both to enjoy life and to give it meaning and substance outside Christianity, just as the most renowned poets and artists, the most eminent thinkers, even pious men, have lived outside Christianity' (CUP 293). And in a journal entry Kierkegaard says, ' "Johannes Climacus" was actually a *contemplative* piece, for when I wrote it I was contemplating the possibility of not letting myself be taken over by Christianity' (PV 221, emphasis added).

tendentious assumption that unless this is guaranteed, we are assigning to philosophy an instrumental role. But to accept this assumption is, as we have seen, not only to endorse a false dichotomy, it is also to rule out, on *a priori* grounds, that someone can be both a (serious/genuine) philosopher and a religious thinker—something that, coming from a philosopher of a Wittgensteinian persuasion, is a very bizarre form of essentialism to buy into.

To be sure, as I have emphasized before, Kierkegaard doesn't, as it were, wonder at the 'possibility of discourse' in the *same way* as Wittgenstein, if what we mean by this is an awareness that our philosophical problems are lodged in the language we speak. But, if so, then, of course, no philosopher before Wittgenstein could have had a 'contemplative conception of philosophy' in Phillips's sense, for this idea constituted, as it were, Wittgenstein's 'Copernican Revolution'. Indeed, it emerges at the end of Phillips's book that *none* of the philosophers discussed in it, according to Phillips, apart from Wittgenstein, actually have a 'contemplative conception'. And this, more than anything else, would seem to make Phillips's claim about the asymmetry between Kierkegaard and Wittgenstein all but vacuous.

Finally, it also becomes apparent in the conclusion to Phillips's book that in formulating his 'contemplative conception'—especially the notion of 'trying to go nowhere'—Phillips ironically ends up borrowing rather heavily from Kierkegaard. Compare the following sentence from Phillips's last chapter with the penultimate one from Kierkegaard's 'A First and Last Explanation': 'So I am not reforming anything, not going anywhere, but contemplating an old, old story and seeing what gets in the way of telling it today.'[88] And here is the *soi disant* 'non-contemplative' Kierkegaard:

> What I in one way or another know about the pseudonymous authors of course does not entitle me to any opinion, but not to any doubt, either, of their assent, since their importance . . . unconditionally does not consist in making any new proposal, some unheard-of discovery, or in founding a new party and wanting to go further, but precisely in the opposite, in wanting to have no importance, in wanting, at a remove that is the distance of double-reflection, once again to read through solo, if possible in a more inward way, the original text of individual human existence-relationships, the old familiar text handed down from the fathers. (CUP 629–30).

---

[88] *Cool Place*, 165.

CONCLUSION

By way of concluding, I would like, first of all, to stress what I have *not* attempted to do in this chapter. I have not defended a 'symmetrical' reading of Kierkegaard's and Wittgenstein's philosophical activity in order to show that there are no relevant or important differences between the two authors. That would be absurd. Neither have I been concerned to show that Wittgenstein was directly influenced by Kierkegaard in his conception of philosophy (although he probably was). Rather, I hope to have made good on the claims advanced in the previous chapter that Wittgenstein and Kierkegaard are united in their common aim of paving the way, in their writings, for an *authentic existence*—an existence that is free of self-deception and illusion—and that hence their conception of philosophical authorship is fundamentally an *ethical* one. I also hope to have shown that the asymmetry that Phillips perceives between Kierkegaard's and Wittgenstein's philosophical endeavours is not, in the end, in the least damaging to the account I offer, for it either rests on very questionable premises or else is trivial (that is, it asserts what everyone would admit). This should have dispelled the widespread misconception, mentioned in chapter 1, that Kierkegaard and Wittgenstein are engaged in radically different projects in favour of the view that they ought rather to be regarded as kindred spirits. And this, it seems to me, is a modest, but, by no means, negligible conclusion.

3

Sense and Ineffabilia—Kierkegaard and the *Tractatus*

> My work has expanded from the foundations of logic to the essence of the world.
>
> Ludwig Wittgenstein, Notebooks[1]

INTRODUCTION

In the previous chapter I argued that Kierkegaard and Wittgenstein share an ethical conception of philosophy. Although the *Tractatus*, Wittgenstein's early work, is in many ways very different from his later writings, one thing remains constant throughout his authorship and this, in the words of Alice Ambrose, is the fact that 'doing philosophy was a moral matter for him [Wittgenstein]'.[2] That the point of his first book is ethical is announced by Wittgenstein himself in a now famous letter to Ludwig von Ficker who Wittgenstein was hoping would publish the *Tractatus*. He says:

Because you won't understand it; the content will be strange to you. In reality, it isn't strange to you, for the point of the book is ethical. I once wanted to give a few words in the foreword which now actually are not in it, which, however, I'll write to you now because they might be a key for you: I wanted to write that my work consists of two parts: of the one which is here, and of everything which I have *not* written. And precisely this second part is the important one. For the Ethical is delimited from within, as it were, by my book; and I'm convinced that, *strictly* speaking, it can ONLY be delimited in this way. In

---

[1] In Werkausgabe Band 1, 174, translation mine.

[2] Alice Ambrose, 'Ludwig Wittgenstein: A Portrait', in Alice Ambrose and Morris Lazerowitz (eds), *Ludwig Wittgenstein. Philosophy and Language* (Bristol: Thoemmes Press, 1996), 25.

brief, I think: All of that which *many* are *babbling* today, I have defined in my book by remaining silent about it.[3]

Unfortunately, it is not entirely clear from the letter itself which Tractarian gate Wittgenstein's key is supposed to unlock: the traditional or 'standard' one, which, according to James Conant, 'guards the sanctity of the ineffable'[4] or the 'new', *trompe l'oeil* door which, appearances notwithstanding, shuts out nothing. For according to 'resolute readers',[5] such as Cora Diamond and James Conant, what lies beyond the bounds of Tractarian sense is not the promised land of ineffable truth, but the arid desert of mere nonsense. That is to say, on the interpretation that Diamond and Conant[6] share, the real point behind the *Tractatus*[7] is not, as the traditional (or 'standard') view would have it, to delimit what can be said (what is the case) from what is ineffable (which can only be 'shown'); nor is it to draw a distinction between 'mere' and 'substantial' nonsense, the latter being somehow revelatory of what cannot be said. Instead, it is to reveal that any such ambitions are nonsensical, and that those in thrall to such ambitions are captivated, merely, by an 'illusion of sense'. On this reading, that is, the point of the TLP is to show that the project in which the TLP itself appears to be engaged is, indeed, and as the later Wittgenstein would certainly have agreed, fundamentally misconceived. The TLP is thus an ironic exercise in self-refutation.

From this perspective, it is not surprising that the notorious 'ladder' metaphor with which the TLP (all but) ends figures large. Wittgenstein claims that 'anyone who understands me eventually recognizes [the foregoing propositions] as nonsensical, when he has used them—as steps—to climb beyond them. (He must, so to speak, throw away the ladder after he has climbed up it.) He must transcend these propositions, and then he will see the world aright' (TLP §6.54).[8] Wittgenstein's 'ladder' is to be thrown away, Conant says, 'not because it has outlived its purpose of conducting the reader into the heights of a higher understanding'—the standard view—'but because the reader

---

[3] Quoted in Monk, *The Duty of Genius*, 178.

[4] James Conant, 'Kierkegaard, Wittgenstein and Nonsense', 216, hereafter KWN.

[5] The term 'resolute reading' was coined by Warren Goldfarb, in 'Metaphysics and Nonsense: On Cora Diamond's *The Realistic Spirit*', *Journal of Philosophical Research* 22 (1997): 57–73.

[6] See James Conant, 'Elucidation and Nonsense in Frege and Early Wittgenstein', in Alice Crary and Rupert Read (eds), *The New Wittgenstein* (London: Routledge, 2000), 174–217, and also 'The Method of the *Tractatus*', in Erich Reck (ed.), *From Frege to Wittgenstein* (Oxford: Oxford University Press, 2002a), 374–462.

[7] Henceforth TLP.   [8] Translation by D. F. Pears and B. F. McGuinness.

comes to recognize that its rungs are unable to bear the weight they appeared to support. He comes to recognize that he has been captivated by an illusion of ascent, that the services of philosophy have furnished him with only an appearance of ethical or religious progress.'[9] On Conant's reading, that is, the TLP ends by revoking (most of) itself. And it is in this that Conant finds the prompt to relate his reading of the TLP to Kierkegaard's *Concluding Unscientific Postscript*, for that work too includes a 'revocation': 'what I write', says Climacus, 'contains the notice that everything is to be understood in such a way that it is revoked, that the book has not only an end but has a revocation to boot' (CUP 619). It is Conant's proposal that we should read CUP as if it too, like the TLP, represented 'an elaborate *reductio ad absurdum* of the [very] philosophical project' (KWN 207) in which it itself appears to be engaged.

In the present chapter I will argue that Conant's way of construing the parallels between Kierkegaard and (the early) Wittgenstein does no justice to the intentions—ethical or otherwise—of either author and in fact comprises a severe distortion of their texts. I hope to show that there are indeed interesting parallels between Kierkegaard and the early Wittgenstein, but that the exposure of a doctrine of 'substantial nonsense' (or of ineffable truth) isn't one of them. Getting the exegesis straight here isn't just an important exercise in its own right, it also has wide-ranging implications for an interpretation of Kierkegaard's and Wittgenstein's conception of religious belief. For the attempt to dismiss all talk of the ineffable as unintelligible seems to align Conant with those who, like Carnap and the Positivists, seek to expose religious language as devoid of sense, while Conant's claim that most of the *Postscript* consists of patent nonsense plays into the hands of those who, like Mackie and Plantinga,[10] regard Kierkegaard as an irrational fideist. Much, therefore, hangs on how we construe what, precisely, it is that Wittgenstein has *not* written in the TLP and what, exactly, it is that Climacus is asking us to revoke.

In the first half of this chapter I will sketch and criticize Conant's interpretation of the TLP and will then, in the second part, move on to a consideration and critique of his reading of CUP. Finally, in the

---

[9] James Conant, 'Putting Two and Two Together: Kierkegaard, Wittgenstein and the Point of View for Their Work as Authors' [already quoted on p. 60] 293.
[10] See the Introduction.

concluding sections, I will offer an account, based on the alternative readings of both works developed during the course of these criticisms, of what I take to be the central parallels between Kierkegaard's writings and Wittgenstein's early work.

I CONANT'S READING OF THE *TRACTATUS*

The central conundrum confronting a potential exegete of Wittgenstein's early text is: how can we understand a work that declares itself to be nonsense? We seem to be faced with a rather dire dilemma: if §6.54 is a correct description of the work, then it is impossible to understand it (as it is nonsense). If, however, it *is* possible to understand it, then it can't be nonsense, so §6.54 must be false. In other words, it seems that §6.54 can't both be true and it be possible to understand the work—and yet this appears to be what is required if we are to make any sense of the doctrine that seems to be propounded in the text. Matters are compounded further by the question of whether §6.54 applies to itself—that is, whether it itself is nonsense. For if it is, this would seem to constitute a *reductio* of any attempt to read the book. It appears that we have to give up before we even start.

According to Conant, responses to the predicament posed by §6.54 have traditionally involved one of two strategies:[11] either the penultimate proposition of the TLP—what he calls 'the final gesture of revocation' (KWN 198)—is more or less ignored and the work explicated 'as if it were an ordinary philosophical treatise' (ibid.); or the claim that it is impossible to understand nonsense is considerably watered down. To this end, a distinction tends to be made between 'plain' nonsense (mere gibberish) and 'important' nonsense which, according to Anscombe,

---

[11] In KWN Conant speaks of four (strategic) groups. However, three is really just a variant of two and four can be dismissed on the grounds that it makes any kind of reading of the TLP impossible. The four groups, in Conant's own words, are: '1) Those who simply ignore the final gesture of revocation and who explicate the work as if it were an ordinary philosophical treatise. 2) Those who acknowledge the problem of the work's nonsensicality but in their own interpretative practice end up treating it as a mere technicality . . . 3) Those who take the gesture very seriously and insist that the important things are truly ineffable, but who then nonetheless go on to tell us what those things are. 4) Those who insist upon the ineffability of the work's teaching and who then quite consistently, but also quite unhelpfully, have nothing further to say on the matter; except perhaps to offer an exclamation of hushed awe, betokening that their further silence is pregnant with meaning.' (KWN 198)

for example, consists of nonsensical propositions that would be true, if what they were an attempt to say were, *per impossibile*, things that could be said. For this reason, Anscombe believes, 'Wittgenstein regards the sentences of the *Tractatus* as helpful, in spite of their being strictly nonsensical according to the very doctrine that they propound.'[12] Peter Hacker, too, distinguishes between 'what might (somewhat confusingly) be called illuminating nonsense, and misleading nonsense. Illuminating nonsense will guide the attentive reader to apprehend what is shown by other propositions which do not purport to be philosophical; moreover it will intimate, to those who grasp what is meant, its own illegitimacy.'[13] This, however, and as Hacker himself admits, has the rather unfortunate consequence that 'apparently what someone means or intends by a remark can be grasped even though the sentence uttered is strictly speaking nonsense'.[14]

Cora Diamond has famously called this interpretative strategy 'chickening out'.[15] She believes that the notion of gesturing at an *it*, such as, say, the logical form of reality, that is there but that cannot be expressed in words, is unintelligible. James Conant concurs: the 'standard reading' (such as Anscombe's and Hacker's above), he contends, mistakes 'the bait for the hook', that is to say, mistakes 'the target of the work for its doctrine'.[16] On the interpretation that Conant and Diamond propose instead, no metaphysical theories, effable or ineffable, are propounded in the TLP. Rather, the point of the work is to undermine the illusion that there is such a thing as 'substantial' (or 'illuminating') nonsense by means of which we can gesture, albeit ineffectually, at what is inexpressible.

Conant's account rests on four interrelated theses. First, the book can be divided up into 'framing material', which gives us directions on how to read it, and nonsensical elucidatory corpus. Second, the point of the latter is to show that what appears to be 'substantial' nonsense is 'plain' nonsense (mere gibberish) and hence that there is nothing that cannot be said. Third, mere or plain nonsense is the result of not having given a meaning to a sign in a proposition, not of a violation of the rules

[12] G. E. M. Anscombe, *An Introduction to Wittgenstein's* Tractatus (Indianapolis, IN: St Augustine's Press, 1971), 162.

[13] P. M. S. Hacker, *Insight and Illusion* (Bristol: Thoemmes Press, 1997), 18–19.

[14] Ibid., 26.

[15] Cora Diamond, *The Realistic Spirit* (Cambridge, MA: Massachusetts Institute of Technology Press, 2001), 181.

[16] Conant, 'Method', 381.

of logical syntax. Fourth, recognizing the sentences of the book to be nonsense does not require the application of a theory of meaning, but nothing more than ordinary recognitional capacities.[17] I will set these theses out in turn.

I.1 Thesis One

Following Cora Diamond, Conant takes his main interpretative cues from the preface and the conclusion of the TLP which serve, he says, 'as the frame in which we are provided directions for how to read th[e] book' (KWN 216). In the preface Wittgenstein tells us that the TLP *ist kein Lehrbuch* (which Conant translates as 'it is not a work of doctrine' (KWN 217))[18] and that what lies beyond the limits of what can be said will be *einfach Unsinn*—simply nonsense.[19] From these remarks, as well as from §4.112, Conant draws the conclusion that what Wittgenstein has given us in the TLP is the exemplification of an activity rather than a body of doctrine. Consequently, Conant asserts, no thoughts are expressed in the book.[20] What §6.54 therefore asks the reader to do is to understand the *author* of the text rather than the propositions contained in it, for these are nonsensical. This demand, Conant holds, must be taken completely literally and this implies that the TLP must be regarded as forming a continuous train of nonsense with 'the exception of those sentences[21] which comment on the overall

---

[17] In Conant's and Diamond's most recent paper, the two authors speak of 'two interrelated general features that suffice to make a reading "resolute".' Those are first, not taking those propositions of TLP 'about which Wittgenstein said, at §6.54, that they are to be recognized as "nonsensical" to convey ineffable insights', and second, rejecting the idea 'that what such recognition requires on the part of a reader of the TLP is the application of a theory of meaning that has been advanced in the body of the work—a theory that specifies the conditions under which a sentence makes sense and the conditions under which it does not.' (See James Conant and Cora Diamond, 'On Reading the *Tractatus* Resolutely: Reply to Meredith Williams and Peter Sullivan', in Max Kölbel and Bernhard Weiss (eds), *Wittgenstein's Lasting Significance* (London: Routledge, 2004), 47.) These two 'sufficient conditions' are a condensed version of the four theses I attribute to Conant. That is to say, theses one and two are contained in (or implied by) the first condition, and theses three and four are contained in (or implied by) the second condition. In the following critique of Conant's reading of the TLP I will only be referring to this joint paper when it introduces new material or significantly modifies or advances Conant's argument, otherwise not.

[18] Pears and McGuinness render *Lehrbuch* as textbook.

[19] KWN 217.   [20] Ibid.

[21] Conant cites §§3.32–3.326, 4–4.003, 4.111–4.112, 6.53–6.54 in addition to the preface. See 'Method', 457.

elucidatory strategy of the work'.[22] These, Conant says, 'belong to the frame . . . and are only able to impart their instructions concerning the nature of the elucidatory aim and method of the work if recognized as *sinnvoll* [meaningful].'[23]

I.2 Thesis Two

It follows from thesis one that the TLP only *appears* to propound a distinction between what Conant calls two kinds of nonsense: 'mere nonsense' and 'substantial nonsense'. Conant says:

Mere nonsense is simply unintelligible—it expresses no thought. Substantial nonsense is composed of intelligible ingredients combined in an illegitimate way—it expresses a logically incoherent thought. According to the substantial conception, these two kinds of nonsense are logically distinct: the former is mere gibberish, whereas the latter involves (what commentators on the *Tractatus* are fond of calling) a 'violation of logical syntax'.[24]

Since Conant believes that there is no such thing as violating the rules of logical syntax in the TLP[25] (see below), he proposes instead the 'austere conception of nonsense' which holds that 'mere nonsense is, from a logical point of view, the only kind of nonsense there is'.[26] The task of Tractarian elucidation, on this conception, therefore isn't—by producing a work composed of substantial nonsense—to 'show' something that can't be said, but rather 'to show that we are prone to an illusion of meaning something when we mean nothing'.[27] That is to say, the purpose of the TLP, on this interpretation, is 'to reveal (through the employment of mere nonsense) that what appears to be substantial nonsense is mere nonsense'.[28] Consequently, the TLP does not, on Conant's reading, provide insight into inexpressible features of reality, but rather, 'insight into the sources of metaphysics'.[29]

I.3 Thesis Three

On Conant's construction, logical syntax in the TLP is concerned 'neither with the proscription of combinations of signs nor with the

[22] KWN 223, footnote 85.   [23] 'Method', 457, footnote 135.
[24] Ibid., 380–1.
[25] With the exception of 'cross-category' equivocation which Conant defines as 'the result of allowing different occurrences of the same sign to symbolize items of different logical category' ('Method', 415).
[26] Ibid., 381.   [27] Ibid.   [28] Ibid., 421.   [29] Ibid.

proscription of combinations of symbols.[30] It is not concerned with the proscription of combinations of signs, because Tractarian logical syntax does not treat of (mere) signs; it treats of symbols—and a symbol only has life within the context of a significant proposition. It is not concerned with the proscription of combinations of symbols, because there is nothing to proscribe—"Every possible proposition is legitimately constructed" (§5.4733).'[31] Hence, Conant argues, there is no such thing as a conception of substantial nonsense in the TLP where substantial nonsense is conceived as 'a proposition composed of signs that symbolize, but which has a logically flawed syntax due to a clash in the logical category of its symbols'.[32] Rather, the only kind of nonsense that the TLP allows for is mere nonsense which is 'a string composed of signs in which no symbol can be perceived, and which hence has no discernible logical syntax'.[33] Consequently, Conant holds, on the Tractarian view, ' "Caesar is a prime number" suffers, from a logical point of view, from the same deficiency as "Caesar is blick": "if it has no sense this can only be because we have given no *meaning* to some of its constituent parts" (§5.4733), regardless of how strong our inclination may be "to believe that we have done so".'[34] On Conant's reading, therefore:

if a sentence is nonsense this is not because *it* is trying but failing to make sense (by breaking a rule of logic), but because *we* have failed to make sense with it: 'the sentence is nonsensical because we have failed to make an arbitrary determination of sense, not because *the symbol in itself* is impermissible'. (§5.473) [Conant's emphasis][35]

I.4 Thesis Four

It follows from thesis three that the TLP 'does not aim to show us that certain sequences of words possess an intrinsically flawed sense by persuading us of the truth of some theoretical account of where to locate the "limits of sense" '.[36] Rather, Conant claims, the TLP 'seeks to bring its reader to the point where he can recognize sentences within

---

[30] Conant defines a sign as 'an orthographic unit, that which the perceptible expressions for propositions have in common (a sign design, inscription, icon, grapheme, etc)', and a symbol as 'a logical unit, that which meaningful propositions have in common (i.e. an item belonging to a given logical category: proper name, first-level function, etc.)' (ibid., 400). See TLP §3.11–3.13 and §3.31–3.312.
[31] Ibid., 414.   [32] Ibid., 400.   [33] Ibid.   [34] Ibid., 412.
[35] Ibid., 421.   [36] Ibid., 423.

the body of the work as nonsensical . . . by harnessing the capacities for distinguishing sense from nonsense . . . implicit in the everyday practical mastery of language that the reader already possesses'.[37] Hence, on Conant's construction, the 'sentences' of the TLP are to be recognized as nonsensical, not because they violate the conditions of sense laid down by a previously developed theory of meaning—as the traditional or 'standard' view would have it—but rather because they are gibberish plain and simple like 'piggly wiggle tiggle'.[38] Consequently, there is 'no such thing as understanding the propositions in the book', but only 'the illusion of understanding them' and this involves entering 'into the point of view from which this piece of nonsense appears to say something'.[39] Conant suggests:

The criterion of our having successfully performed this act of imaginative identification with the utterer of nonsense is that we are able to successfully anticipate the (apparent) logical relations that he will imagine obtain between the nonsensical string in question and other (pseudo)propositions. Wittgenstein's aim in the *Tractatus* is to lead the philosopher from the original 'disguised' piece of nonsense (to which he is attracted) through this network of (apparent) logical relations to some more patently nonsensical (pseudo)consequence.[40]

Although it isn't therefore possible, on Conant's interpretation, to understand the nonsense contained in the TLP, the reader can momentarily be led to believe that it is in order to be 'deceived into the truth'[41] *à la* Kierkegaard: the reader is lured up a carefully crafted 'ladder' which, in the end, falls apart around him. Hence, on Conant's view, to throw away the ladder not only means to see through the nonsensical corpus of the TLP, but also to give up 'the idea of our enlightened perspective on the thought of would-be metaphysicians, realists, transcendental idealists, and solipsists', once we realize that 'many of the sentences that

---

[37] Conant defines a sign as 'an orthographic unit, that which the perceptible expressions for propositions have in common (a sign design, inscription, icon, grapheme, etc)', 423–4.

[38] This example is Diamond's.   [39] 'Method', 423–4.   [40] KWN 218.

[41] Hence the kinship that Conant perceives between Wittgenstein's method in TLP and the way Kierkegaard describes what he is up to in *The Point of View*: 'Generally speaking, there is nothing that requires as gentle a treatment as the removal of an illusion. If one in any way causes the one ensnared to be antagonized, then all is lost . . . [So] a corrosive must first be used, but this corrosive is the negative, but the negative in connection with communicating is precisely to deceive. What, then, does it mean "to deceive"? It means that one does not begin *directly* with what one wishes to communicate but begins by taking the other's delusion at face value.' (PV 43, 54; Conant's translation changed to the Hong version.) See KWN 217, 'Method', 420, 'Elucidation', 195.

we ourselves [are] initially inclined to come up with, in explaining how the book dispels philosophical illusions, will themselves . . . turn out to be nonsensical'.[42]

II A CRITIQUE OF CONANT'S READING OF THE *TRACTATUS*

In what follows I will attempt to show that none of Conant's theses stands up to scrutiny.

II.1 Thesis One: The 'Framing Material'

There are three main problems with the 'framing material'. First, as pieces of evidence designed to underwrite Conant's interpretation, the preface and conclusion of the TLP are at best ambiguous, at worst damaging. For at the end of the preface, for example, Wittgenstein flatly contradicts Conant's claim that the book expresses no thoughts. Wittgenstein says:

If this work has any value, it consists in two things: the first is that *thoughts are expressed* in it, and on this score the better the thoughts are expressed . . . the greater will be its value . . . On the other hand the *truth* of the thoughts that are here communicated seems to me unassailable and definitive. I therefore believe myself to have found, on all essential points, the final solution of the problems.[43]

Given that the preface is part of the frame, on Conant's reading, and hence ought to be neither nonsensical nor ironic, these remarks present Conant with a serious exegetical embarrassment[44] as a result of which he is confronted with a dilemma: he must either give up on the idea that the preface is part of the frame and treat it as if it, too, were part of the nonsense to be revoked, or he must insist that even within the preface, and not just in the main body of the TLP, some remarks are tongue-in-cheek.[45] Either horn is sufficient to invalidate Conant's account.

---

[42] Conant and Diamond, 'On Reading the *Tractatus* resolutely', 79.
[43] Translation by Pears/McGuinness; first emphasis mine.
[44] For a similar argument against Diamond, see P. M. S. Hacker, 'Was He Trying to Whistle It?', in Crary and Read (eds), *The New Wittgenstein*, 360.
[45] This dilemma incidentally exactly parallels the one Conant faces as regards the 'frames' in CUP. See section VI.1 of this chapter.

As regards §6.54 of the TLP, Conant is faced with a similar problem. Since, on his own admission, more sentences form part of the frame than preface and conclusion, it is curious that Wittgenstein says at §6.54, 'my propositions serve as elucidations in the following way: anyone who understands me eventually recognizes them as nonsensical . . .' instead of saying, which, on Conant's reading, would be more apt, '*some* or *most* of my propositions elucidate in the following way', or, indeed, 'my propositions—except for §§3.32–3.326, 4–4.003, 4.111–4.112, 6.53–6.54[46]—elucidate in the following way'. If the TLP were really meant to be the kind of 'two-tier system' (comprised of 'framing material' and elucidatory nonsense) Conant claims it is why did Wittgenstein give us no intimations of it? For preface and conclusion of the work certainly don't tell us that this is what Wittgenstein had in mind.

The second problem with the framing material is that Conant rather keeps us in the dark about which propositions he regards as constituting the frame. Since Conant openly admits that §§3.32–3.326, 4–4.003, 4.111–4.112 are to be considered framing material, given that his interpretation relies heavily on them, one wonders why he doesn't mention §§5.473–5.4733 in this list, for these remarks lie, after all, at the very heart of Conant's reading, as he himself avows.[47] What is more, apart from the passages already mentioned, Conant relies on the meaningfulness of a whole host of other propositions. During the course of 'The Method of the *Tractatus*', for example, Conant unselfconsciously tells us what the following remarks *say*: §3.142, 3.1432, 3.144, 3.203, 3.321, 3.22,[48] 3.3, 3.31, 3.314,[49] 3.334, 3.341, 3.344, 3.4,[50] 4.021, 4.022, 4.0621,[51] 4.4611, 4.462, 4.466,[52] 5.02, 5.451, 5.4611, 5.5563,[53] 6.1264, 6.52[54]—and this compilation is by no means exhaustive.

Now one might even, charitably, be inclined to forgive this, if the remarks thus exempted from the nonsense formed a homogeneous group. But this is far from the case. Not only are the passages collated

---

[46] For a similar argument against Diamond, see P. M. S. Hacker, 'Was He Trying to Whistle It?', 362.

[47] 'Method', 411.

[48] For citation of §3.142, 3.1432, 3.144, 3.203, 3.321, 3.22, 5.02, 5.451, see 'Method', 442–3.

[49] For citation of 3.3–3.314, see 'Method', 409.

[50] For citation of 3.334, 3.341, 3.344, 3.4, see ibid., 446.

[51] For citation of 4.021–4.022 and 4.461, see ibid., 429.

[52] For citation of 4.4611, 4.462, 4.466 and 6.1264, see ibid., 448.

[53] See ibid., 417.   [54] See ibid., 423.

willy-nilly from almost everywhere in the TLP (with the exception of the 1s and 2s), they also keep alternating with apparently ironical remarks. This, as Hacker points out, makes it puzzling that:

tucked in between the serious claim that philosophy must set limits to what can and cannot be thought and the claim that everything that can be put into words can be put clearly, Wittgenstein wrote: 'It will signify what cannot be said (*das Unsagbare*), by stating clearly what can be said' (TLP 4.115). It seems implausible to suppose that this is a sudden intrusion of irony into an otherwise serious sequence of remarks, and equally implausible to think that *das Unsagbare* intimates that there isn't anything that cannot be said.[55]

Similarly, given that Conant approvingly refers to §6.52, 6.521, 6.53 and 6.54, one wonders on what grounds he excludes §6.522: 'There is, indeed, the inexpressible (*das Unaussprechliche*). This *shows* itself, it is the mystical.'[56]

The same problem keeps recurring throughout the TLP, for whenever we have a piece of Conantian framing material, we immediately get, in the following propositions, remarks that Conant would have to consider ironic. Here is one more example, where the problem actually arises within a single remark. In order to show that in much of the scholarly literature on the TLP the mistake has been made of thinking that the say/show distinction is applicable to nonsensical propositions when it isn't, Conant cites §§4.021–4.022 of the book.[57] This, however, would seem to be self-defeating since we read at §4.021: 'A proposition is a picture of reality: for if I understand a proposition, I know the situation that it represents. And I understand the proposition without having had its sense explained to me.'[58] But the 'picture theory of meaning' is of course supposed to be part of the nonsensical metaphysics destined, on Conant's interpretation, to be seen through as illusory. Hence we are left with the curious result that §4.021, on Conant's reading, must

---

[55] 'Was He Trying to Whistle It?', 370.
[56] My translation here—apart from the punctuation—is almost identical to C. K. Ogden's, but differs quite markedly from the one by Pears/McGuinness. They render 6.522 as: 'There are indeed things that cannot be put into words. They make themselves manifest. They are what is mystical.' Although this captures the sense of 6.522, it is only a paraphrase of what Wittgenstein actually says. In order for the first sentence of the Pears/McGuinness translation to be truly accurate, Wittgenstein would have had to write 'Es gibt allerdings Dinge die sich nicht aussprechen lassen.' Also, I think that Wittgenstein used '*zeigen*' (to show) quite explicitly to hark back to the say/show distinction, so this should be kept in the translation as well. This is obscured by the otherwise elegant phrase 'they make themselves manifest'.
[57] 'Method', 429 (footnote 23).   [58] Translation by Pears/McGuinness.

simultaneously be serious and ironic, which must constitute a *reductio* of Conant's interpretation.

Consequently, and this is the third problem with the framing material, no salient criteria seem adducible at all which would allow a coherent way of separating 'the frame' of the TLP from the nonsensical corpus. For looking at the role that a given remark plays in the text—the only criterion Conant suggests—will, as we have just seen, provide us with no independent evidence for Conant's reading, as determination of that role in favour of Conant's interpretation already presupposes his interpretation. This is why Conant himself says that, in the end, it depends on the reader which propositions she will find meaningful and which nonsensical.[59] But, if so, the interpretation of the book would seem to become an entirely haphazard exercise devoid of textual constraints and we are left with no more than the appearance of serious interpretative practice.

II.2 Thesis Two: No Ineffabilia?

We have seen in the previous section that it is not possible to marshal any convincing internal evidence in favour of dividing the TLP into two tiers. Consequently, I will focus, in this section, on the available external evidence, in order to show that at the time of writing the TLP Wittgenstein did, indeed, *pace* Conant, believe that there are ineffabilia.

In both pre- and post-*Tractatus* writings we find countless reiterations of central Tractarian doctrines that Conant claims figure only as targets in that work. Furthermore, and as Hacker has already pointed out,[60] in none of these texts do we find so much as an allusion to the strategy that Conant suggests is at work in the TLP—quite the opposite, in fact. In the *Notebooks* from 1914–16, for instance, we find manifold discussions of the picture theory, solipsism, the say/show distinction as well as of the ineffable and the 'mystical'. Here are just two examples from among innumerable others. Wittgenstein writes in 1914: 'What *can* be shown, cannot be said'[61] and in 1915: 'Objects can only be *named*. Signs are their representatives. I can only speak *of* them [objects/*Gegenstände*], I cannot put them into words [*sie aussprechen kann ich nicht*].'[62] It won't do to claim, in order to explain these passages away, that these were the views not of Early Wittgenstein, but of *early* Early Wittgenstein—a strategy

---

[59] 'Method', 457.   [60] 'Was He Trying to Whistle It?', 371.
[61] 29.11.1914. See note 1.   [62] 26.5. 1915–27.5.1915.

that Conant and Diamond have recently adopted[63]—for Wittgenstein incorporated into his work[64] next to verbatim many remarks, both early and late, from the *Notebooks* and there is no reason to suppose that he did so in an ironic vein. The first sentences of the second passage just quoted, for instance, find exact reiteration at §3.221 and the quotation from 1914 is identical to §4.1212, apart from one added emphasis (the second 'can' is also italicized). What is more, we find many other passages in the *Notebooks* which, according to Conant, Wittgenstein *did* mean in the TLP.[65] The following two entries from 1914, for example, foreshadow two of Conant's favourite remarks from the TLP: 'Logic must take care of itself'[66] (compare TLP §5.473) and 'Frege says that any legitimately constructed proposition must have a sense. And I say that any possible proposition is legitimately constructed, and, if it has no sense, that can only be because we have failed to *give* a meaning to some of its constituents. Even if we think that we have done so'[67] (compare TLP §5.4733). Consequently, Conant owes us a (non-circular) explanation of why Wittgenstein is supposed to have retained *these* particular views from the *Notebooks* (when making the transition from *early* Early Wittgenstein to Early Wittgenstein), while apparently jettisoning those that would undermine Conant's reading.

   Given the somewhat flimsy nature of the evidence available in favour of a 'resolute reading', then, Conant and Diamond have recently emphasized that the main benefit conferred by their interpretation is the eschewal of the kind of toleration of contradiction that 'standard readings' must inevitably attribute to Wittgenstein. For such an ascription, they argue, means to cease 'to take seriously the thought that *early* Wittgenstein was, after all, early *Wittgenstein*'.[68] This is an interesting version of the *argumentum ad hominem*, but, unfortunately, it, too, simply isn't borne out by the evidence, as the 'toleration of

---

63 See Conant and Diamond, op.cit., 97: 'Some of the passages our critics adduce arguably involve doctrines held by the *very* early Wittgenstein, before he turns on his earlier (comparatively Russellian) self in the *Tractatus*.'

64 To cite just two examples, compare *Notebook* entry 23.5.1915 with TLP §5.6, 5.62, 5.631, 3.3442, 5.631, and entry 11.6.1916 with TLP §6.41, 5.621. (Ludwig Wittgenstein, *Notebooks*, ed. G. H. von Wright and G. E. M. Anscombe with an English translation by G. E. M. Anscombe, 2nd edn (Chicago, IL: The University of Chicago Press, 1984).

65 Another good example, apart from the passages quoted below, is the entry from 2.12.1916, i.e. the precursor of TLP §6.53, that according to Conant is part of the frame of the TLP.

66 22.8.1914.   67 2.9.1914.   68 Conant and Diamond, op.cit., 51.

contradiction' is admitted, in writing, by Wittgenstein himself and is also corroborated by the testimony of friends.[69] Let us look, for example, at the description that Paul Engelmann, a very close friend of Wittgenstein's with whom the latter discussed the TLP in great detail, offers us of the book:

A whole generation of disciples was able to take Wittgenstein for a positivist because he has something of enormous importance in common with the positivists: he draws the line between what we can speak about and what we must be silent about just as they do. The difference is only that they have nothing to be silent about. Positivism holds—and this is its essence—that what we can speak about is all that matters in life. *Whereas Wittgenstein passionately believes that all that really matters in human life is precisely what, in his view, we must be silent about.* When he nevertheless takes immense pains to delimit the unimportant, it is not the coastline of that island which he is bent on surveying with such meticulous accuracy, but the boundary of the ocean.[70]

In other words, according to Engelmann, the self-conscious attempt to utter the 'unutterable' undermines itself, not because there is nothing to be silent about, as the Positivists and Conant maintain, but precisely because there are things that cannot be put into words.[71]

Now we might not want to trust the word of a non-professional philosopher such as Engelmann. But first, Engelmann was no fool—for Wittgenstein neither suffered fools gladly, nor would he have bothered to explain his work to them—and second, much of what Engelmann says is said by Wittgenstein himself in various other places. Compare, for example, what Wittgenstein says in *A Lecture on Ethics* (given in 1929 shortly after he had returned to Cambridge and philosophy):

I see now that these nonsensical expressions [ethical or religious expressions] were not nonsensical because I had not yet found the correct expressions, but that their nonsensicality was their very essence. For all I wanted to do with them was just *to go beyond* the world and that is to say beyond significant language. My whole tendency and I believe the tendency of all men who ever tried to write

---

[69] See, for example, Russell's letter to Lady Ottoline Morrell, cited in the first chapter, as well as F. P. Ramsey, 'General Propositions and Causality', in R. B. Braithwaite (ed.), *F.P. Ramsey: The Foundations of Mathematics* (London: Routledge & Kegan Paul, 1931), where Ramsey famously said, 'But what you can't say, you can't say and you can't whistle it either.' Nevertheless, Ramsey was convinced that Wittgenstein *was* trying to whistle it. See Hacker, op.cit., 355.

[70] Paul Engelmann, *Letters from Ludwig Wittgenstein with a Memoir*, ed. Brian McGuinness, trans. L. Furtmüller (Oxford: Blackwell, 1967), 96–7.

[71] For a similar argument, see Hacker, op.cit., 372–3.

or talk Ethics or Religion was to run against the boundaries of language. This running against the walls of our cage is perfectly, absolutely hopeless . . . But it is a document of a tendency in the human mind which I personally cannot help respecting deeply and I would not for my life ridicule it. (PO 44)

What Wittgenstein, in other words, is claiming here is this:

1. Some expressions (such as ethical and religious statements) are *intrinsically* nonsensical.
2. Such statements attempt to go beyond the world and meaningful language.
3. Language has boundaries and limits.
4. All that is great and important lies beyond those limits.
5. Any attempt to articulate what this is is necessarily futile, as it is *eo ipso inexpressible.*
6. The vain attempt to try to utter the 'unutterable' is worthy of admiration and respect, not ridicule and contempt.

Not only does this contradict Conant's theses *in toto*, it also tallies fully with Engelmann's account. If this is still not corroboration enough, however, here is a piece of evidence that Conant himself relies on, without either realizing or wishing to realize that, rather than substantiating his position, it actually undermines it. While attempting to demonstrate that Wittgenstein would have been more sympathetic to Heidegger's notorious 'the Nothing nothings'[72] passage than Carnap is when he accuses Heidegger of having produced paradigmatic metaphysical nonsense, Conant cites the following conversation Wittgenstein had with members of the Vienna Circle[73] where he says, 'To be sure, I can imagine what Heidegger means by Being and Anxiety.' This, by itself, is of course insufficient to prove Conant's thesis. The passage—although Conant does not quote it—continues, however, and in a way entirely detrimental to the latter's account:

(Man has the urge to thrust against the limits of language.) Just think of wondering at the existence of something. This wonderment cannot be expressed in the form of a question and there is also no possible answer. Anything we might be tempted to say is *a priori* nonsense. Nevertheless we thrust against the limits of language. Kierkegaard, too, recognized this thrust and even described it in much the same way (as a thrust against paradox) . . . But the tendency, the

---

[72] 'Das Nichts selbst nichtet', in Martin Heidegger; 'Was ist Metaphysik?', in Wegmarken (Frankfurt: Vittorio Klostermann, 1976), 114.
[73] Conant, op.cit., 452, footnote 110.

thrusting, *indicates something* [*deutet auf etwas hin*]. St. Augustine already knew this, when he said: What, you swine, you don't want to talk nonsense? Just talk nonsense, it doesn't matter![74]

It would be very strange indeed had Wittgenstein meant the first sentence, but none of the subsequent ones. It would be stranger still to claim that in 1929 Wittgenstein all of a sudden endorsed views that according to Conant's conception he had already exposed as illusory in the TLP. What is more, even as late as 1931 we find a reference to the *Unaussprechbare*: 'The unutterable [*das Unaussprechbare*] (what I find mysterious and am not able to express) perhaps provides the background against which whatever I could express has its meaning' (CV 16e, translation emended).

Naturally, it is baffling that Wittgenstein espoused such peculiar views. But there can, I think, be no doubt at all that he did and the reasons for it aren't *completely* inexplicable either. For Wittgenstein's cleaving to these ideas is, I think, primarily to be explained by *ethico-religious* motivations rather than by narrowly 'philosophical' ones. This is how Engelmann, for example, describes Wittgenstein's attitude to life: 'an ethical totalitarianism in all questions, a single-minded and painful preservation of the purity of the uncompromising demands of ethics, in agonizing awareness of one's own permanent failure to measure up to them'.[75] In this respect, Wittgenstein was exactly like Kierkegaard and given this conception, it is not entirely mystifying why Wittgenstein should have found the notion of 'ineffabilia' intelligible. For, as Kant had already seen, if the 'absolute value' of value is not to be compromised, value can *ex hypothesi* have no place in a merely contingent empirical world, as value would otherwise only be one more part of this world and *ipso facto* on the same plane as 'the facts'. On the Tractarian scheme of things this therefore means that (ethical or aesthetic) value can have no place in the ordinary empirical world, but must, if it is to be anything, be a 'condition' of the world, like logic. Consequently, value must necessarily be inexpressible, since, according to the TLP, only that which can also be otherwise can meaningfully be expressed in propositions which, as §4.06 tells us, must be bipolar (capable of being true *and* capable of being false). Hence, there can be no propositions of ethics, for these would necessarily be true, if, *per impossibile*, they could be expressed.

[74] Conversation held on 30 December 1929; translation mine.
[75] Engelmann, op.cit., 109.

I therefore agree with Engelmann that in the case of Wittgenstein, 'logic and mysticism have . . . sprung from the same root, and it could be said with greater justice that Wittgenstein drew certain logical conclusions from his fundamental mystical attitude to life and the world'.[76] This attitude is also reflected in the epigrammatic and cryptic form the book takes which, in many ways, echoes the pronouncements and parables of the Bible.[77] Consequently, the ethico-religious demand for 'ineffabilia' is just as much a *requirement* (that the pristine purity of the Ethical not be sullied by contingency and empty babble but be forever assured of the protection of this most impregnable of fortresses: the bounds of sense) rather than the conclusion of an argument, as the demand for the determinacy of sense that Wittgenstein speaks of at §3.23.[78] Ascribing this commitment to early Wittgenstein therefore doesn't, *contra* Conant and Diamond, imply a rejection of the thought that early Wittgenstein was, after all, early *Wittgenstein.* It is rather the other way round: pretending that Wittgenstein was engaged in irony—or some sort of deception at the service of dispelling illusion—when putting forward these views is to turn him, not into early *Wittgenstein,* but into some kind of Derrida.

Furthermore, I believe that Wittgenstein—and this is my *ad hominem* argument—could not, given his temperament, have written the kind of work that Conant's reading turns the TLP into. For the strategy that Conant imputes to Wittgenstein runs counter to the latter's almost pathological craving for honesty, which would not, I think, have tolerated even a mild form of Kierkegaardian 'deception' for the sake of the truth. Here is my evidence for this claim. Of the few critical things that Wittgenstein said about Kierkegaard, two are directly relevant to the current issue. We have met one of them before (in the first chapter), but it bears repeating here. Wittgenstein says:

Kierkegaard's writings are teasing and this is of course their intention, although I am not sure whether the exact effect they produce in me is intentional.

---

[76] Ibid., 97.

[77] Ibid., 111. For a similar view, see Brian McGuinness, *Wittgenstein. A Life* (London: Penguin, 1988), 300–3. See also 'The Mysticism of the *Tractatus*', in McGuinness, *Approaches to Wittgenstein* (London: Routledge, 2002), 140–59.

[78] This is not to say that the notion of the inexpressible isn't also a consequence of certain philosophical views, such as the thought, for example, that language and world must share commonality of form (which can't be expressed in language) or that the meaning of signs can't feature in a *Begriffsschrift* (concept-script) since they must already be presupposed.

Undoubtedly, the person who is teasing me is forcing me to take notice of his cause and if this cause is important, then this is a good thing. Nevertheless, there is something in me that rejects this teasing... The idea that someone uses a trick in order to make me do something is unpleasant. I am sure that this (using the trick) requires great courage and that I wouldn't in the least have such courage, but it is questionable whether, if I had this courage, I would have the right to employ it. I *believe* that what would also be required, apart from the courage, is a lack of love for one's neighbour. One could say: What you call loving your neighbour is selfishness. Well, then I know no love without selfishness, for I cannot meddle with the eternal blessedness [*Seligkeit*] of someone else. I can only say: I will love him in such a way as I—who am concerned about my soul—would wish that he would love me.[79]

This passage shows, I think, that Wittgenstein considers a strategy that depends on 'deceiving the reader for the sake of the truth'—what Wittgenstein is doubtlessly referring to when he speaks of 'using a trick'—as in some sense 'unethical', but also as requiring a kind of courage that Wittgenstein believes he lacks. For such courage, Wittgenstein seems to be implying, must spring from an utter conviction in the importance and justness of one's cause and the dividing line between such faith and self-aggrandisement can be a thin one. This is, I think, what Wittgenstein is driving at when he says that 'the association with authors such as Hamann, Kierkegaard, makes their editors presumptuous. Such a temptation would never be felt by the editor of the *Cherubic Pilgrim* [a work by Angelus Silesius] or, indeed, of Augustine's *Confessions* or Luther's writings. It must be that an author's *irony* tends to make a reader arrogant.'[80]

Although this is not a direct criticism of Hamann and Kierkegaard themselves, but of their editors/readers, I think it comes out clearly here that Wittgenstein would nevertheless more want to emulate (what he perceives as) the honest simplicity of writers such as Augustine and Silesius rather than the wit and sophistication of a Kierkegaard or a Hamann, no matter how great Wittgenstein's admiration for both these writers otherwise was. And this, I think, is mirrored in the plain, oracular style of the TLP which would become a bizarre form of self-parody if read, *à la* Conant, as a work that sets out to ensnare the reader.[81]

---

[79] *Denkbewegungen*, 62.   [80] Ibid., 41, my translation.

[81] Conant has said to me in conversation that the Kierkegaard quote from the journals is compatible with his reading, if we read it as a critique of Wittgenstein's former self. However, there is nothing in the entry itself that would license such an assumption—Wittgenstein does not so much as *hint* that his earlier work is supposed

II.3 Thesis Three: Logical Syntax and Combinatorial Nonsense

Conant takes the context principle adumbrated at §3.3 ('only propositions have sense, only in the nexus of a proposition does a name have
meaning') in conjunction with §5.473, §5.4732 ('we cannot give a sign
the wrong sense') and §5.4733 of the TLP as underwriting his claim
that, from a Tractarian point of view, 'Socrates is identical' or 'Caesar
is a prime number' are linguistic strings with no discernible logical
syntax and hence that they are no different from 'Caesar (or Socrates) is
blick'. At the same time Conant admits that what Wittgenstein seems
to be saying at §5.473 and §5.4733 appears to run counter to his
interpretation.[82] Wittgenstein says:

Logic must take care of itself. If a sign is *possible*, then it is also capable of
signifying. Whatever is possible in logic is also permitted. (The reason why
'Socrates is identical' means nothing is that there is no property called 'identical'.
The proposition is nonsensical because we have failed to make an arbitrary
determination, and not because the symbol, in itself, would be illegitimate.) In
a certain sense, we cannot make mistakes in logic. (§5.473)[83]

And at §5.4733 Wittgenstein elaborates:

Frege says that any legitimately constructed proposition must have a sense. And
I say that any possible proposition is legitimately constructed, and, if it has
no sense, that can only be because we have failed to give a *meaning* to some
of its constituents. (Even if we think that we have done so.) Thus the reason
why 'Socrates is identical' says nothing is that we have not given *any adjectival*
meaning to the word 'identical'. For when it appears as a sign for identity, it
symbolizes in an entirely different way—the signifying relation is a different
one—therefore the symbols also are entirely different in the two cases: the two
symbols have only the sign in common, and that is an accident.

These passages make it sound as if Wittgenstein *is* saying, *pace*
Conant, that in 'Socrates is identical' we can recognize the symbol
in the sign, for we are able to diagnose its *misuse*: we can see that the
string means nothing *because* we have not given an *adjectival* meaning to
'identical' (or *because* there is no property called 'identical'), *not* because,

to be included, along with Kierkegaard's, in his criticism. Conant's suggestion therefore
strikes me as implausible.

[82] See Conant, 'Method', 451–2.
[83] Translation by Pears/McGuinness slightly emended.

as Conant maintains, the sign, in this construction, is as meaningless as 'blick'. But appearances are deceptive, Conant claims, since were we to take Wittgenstein at his word here, it would leave it a mystery why the example ['Socrates is identical'] is chosen by Wittgenstein to illustrate the point of the whole passage that 'we cannot give a sign the wrong sense' (§5.4732). Consequently, Conant suggests, we ought to read the term 'adjective' in §5.4733 as referring only to the *sign* 'identical' and not to the symbol. That is, we ought to read Wittgenstein as saying that in 'Socrates is identical' the sign 'identical' merely mimics the surface grammar of a sign symbolizing an adjective[84] (without actually doing so) which misleads us into thinking that we can recognize the symbol in the sign when, in fact, we are confronted by plain gibberish masquerading, as it were, as partial 'sense'.

We can, however, simply take Wittgenstein at his word here. For it is the Frege-Russell conception of logic as a kind of 'super-science' that Wittgenstein is attacking and not, as Conant supposes, a Carnap-type conception of 'substantial nonsense' (the attempt, as Conant says, 'to employ the identity sign . . . as if it were a concept-expression'),[85] [86] since this is the view, I will argue, that Wittgenstein is actually *endorsing*. That it is the traditional conception of logic that Wittgenstein is aiming at comes out very clearly at §5.4731 where Wittgenstein says, 'Self-evidence, which Russell talked about so much, can become dispensable in logic, only because language itself prevents every logical mistake.—What makes logic a priori is the *impossibility* of illogical thought.'[87]

Frege and Russell conceived of logic as a set of a priori general truths about logical entities—as laws, in other words, of a kind of super-physics. *This* is the notion that Wittgenstein is criticizing. On Wittgenstein's new conception, language prevents every logical mistake, not because, as Russell thought, when we think in accordance with the laws of logic, we think correctly, but rather because the logical syntax of language *determines* what is correct, once the relevant meanings have been assigned to words. Hence, *pace* Russell, logic can't be justified by appeal to self-evidence, for the 'laws of logic' are a *precondition* for

---

[84] 'Method', 451–2.   [85] Ibid., 411.

[86] Conant might of course say that Wittgenstein is attacking both conceptions (the Frege-Russell view as well as the Carnapian one) here, in which case other evidence needs to be adduced to show that he is also attacking the *Carnapian* conception and not just the Frege-Russell one.

[87] Translation henceforth always by Pears/McGuinness unless otherwise stated.

making sense in the first place. Logic therefore neither stands in need nor admits of further justification and the idea that we could so much as have a false or incorrect logic falls by the wayside: the logic of our language (logical syntax) is not a *theory* but a set of rules constitutive of what it is to *say* something. This disposes of Frege-Russell's mythological 'third realm' populated by logical entities whose antics make our logical propositions true or false—if a sign is possible, it is also capable of signifying. Consequently, we cannot make mistakes in logic. Naturally, this doesn't imply that we can't talk nonsense by producing meaningless strings like 'Socrates is identical'. But the reason why this is nonsensical is because an arbitrary determination has not been made—*we* have not given an adjectival meaning to the word 'identical' (although we could have done so). Once this determination has been made, however, the consequences that follow from it are *not* arbitrary, and hence there is such a thing as employing a sign *incorrectly*, that is, contrary to the rules for its use (and of course the sign does then not symbolize, for a symbol just *is* a sign used according to the rules for its correct use).[88] As Wittgenstein says, 'Although there is something arbitrary in our notations, *this* much is not arbitrary—that *when* we have determined one thing arbitrarily, something else is necessarily the case. (This derives from the *essence* of the notation)' (§3.342).

This answers Conant's question why 'Socrates is identical' is taken by Wittgenstein to illustrate the point of the passage that 'we cannot give a sign the wrong sense' (§5.4732). For the latter remark follows immediately upon the passage criticizing Russell's notion of self-evidence (§5.4731) and it therefore only seems sensible to assume that this is what it is referring to. To suppose, as Conant does, that the butt of the critique is (also) a Carnapian conception consequently stands in need of much more textual evidence—so much the more so given that Conant himself admits that the natural way to read §5.473 and §5.4733 is as propounding the view that Conant claims is singled out for reprobation in these remarks.

But all the other passages in which 'logical syntax' is mentioned in the TLP also make difficulties for Conant's reading. As against Conant's claim that logical syntax in the TLP is neither concerned with the proscription of the combinations of signs nor with the proscription of the combinations of symbols, we read at §3.325:

---

[88] See P. M. S. Hacker, 'Wittgenstein, Carnap and the New American Wittgensteinians', in *Philosophical Quarterly* 53 (2003): 13.

In order to avoid such errors [e.g. cross-category equivocations where the same sign is employed for different symbols as when we say, for example, 'Green is green'] we must make use of a sign-language that excludes them by not using the same sign for different symbols and by not using in a superficially similar way signs that have different modes of signification: that is to say, a sign-language that is governed by *logical* grammar—by logical syntax [*eine Zeichensprache also, die der* logischen *Grammatik—der logischen Syntax—gehorcht*]. (The conceptual notation [*Begriffsschrift*] of Frege and Russell is such a language, though, it is true, it fails to exclude all mistakes).

The German word *gehorchen* means 'to obey' which is rather stronger than the English 'to govern'. So what Wittgenstein is literally saying is that in order to avoid confusion in philosophy, such as might occur when 'to exist', for instance, figures as an intransitive verb like 'to go' or 'identical' as an adjective (§3.323), we need a sign-language that *obeys* logical syntax and thus excludes such *mistakes*. If Conant's reading were correct, it would be very hard to see why Wittgenstein talks of 'obeying' logical syntax and further, why, at §3.323, he again mentions employing 'identical' as an adjective in order to give an example of a fundamental confusion in philosophy (§3.324). For this contradicts two of Conant's central contentions: first, that the TLP only allows for cross-category equivocation, not for combinatorial nonsense (the illicit combination of two different logical categories) and second, that there is nothing for logical syntax to proscribe—since if there is nothing to proscribe, there is also nothing to obey: where there are no proscriptions, there are no rules either. Nevertheless Wittgenstein *does* speak of rules (at §3.334) and, moreover, he also talks of 'absolutely necessary signs':

The propositions of logic describe the scaffolding of the world, or rather they represent it. They have no 'subject-matter'. They presuppose that names have meaning and elementary propositions sense, and that is their connection with the world[89] . . . We have said that some things are arbitrary in the symbols that we use and that some things are not. In logic it is only the latter that express: but that means that logic is not a field in which *we* express what we wish with the help of signs, but rather one in which the nature of the absolutely necessary signs speaks for itself. If we know the logical syntax of any sign-language, then we have already been given all the propositions of logic. (§6.124)

This passage runs counter to Conant's claim that 'if a sentence is nonsense, this is not because *it* is trying but failing to make sense (by

---

[89] This passage of course also contradicts Conant's thesis that the TLP is not committed to a transcendental commonality of form between logic and the world.

breaking a rule of logic), but because *we* have failed to make sense with it', since what Wittgenstein is saying here is that in logic it is only the non-arbitrary that expresses—i.e. symbolizes—and the non-arbitrary consists of the rules of logical syntax which *determine* what makes sense. That is to say, our use of signs is *answerable* to logical syntax and if we (or our sentences) employ them in contravention of the latter, then we (or our sentences) have, indeed, *contra* Conant, broken a rule of logic. This is why Wittgenstein says that if we know the logical syntax of any sign-language, we have already been given all the propositions of logic. And this implies that we can tell *in advance*—that is, once we know the rules—that the 'sentence' 'Socrates is identical' is nonsense.[90] So we don't first need, as Conant supposes, to 'interrogate' the sentence, as it were, to see whether it makes sense.[91] Hence, as Wittgenstein says, 'there can *never* be surprises in logic' (§6.1251). Of course, as already emphasized, the rules of logical syntax are 'constitutive' rules and this means that breaking them will not, as Hacker says, result in doing something—such as describing something—the doing of which is illicit.[92] But not all rules prohibit something that can be done but that should not be done.[93] To claim otherwise, as Hacker so aptly points out, would be like saying that 'the pawn in chess can't be moved three squares at a time, since if one were to move a piece thus, it would not be a pawn—a transcendental argument to prove that one cannot cheat in chess'.[94] [95]

---

[90] Of course, if we assign a different meaning to the sign 'identical', such as say, 'a great philosopher', then naturally 'Socrates is identical' will no longer be nonsense. So, if we retained the standard meaning of 'identical' as well, we would get an instance of cross-category equivocation as in the case of 'Green is green'. But these examples are completely irrelevant to the issue at hand, for the point here is, precisely, that as long as 'identical' means what it currently means, 'Socrates is identical' is nonsense. Therefore imagining new contexts for the sentence where it will not be nonsense—something Conant and Diamond are fond of doing—is simply question-begging, for what we are talking about just *is* the 'normal' context. Otherwise the problem obviously wouldn't arise.

[91] See Conant and Diamond, op.cit., 64.   [92] 'Was He Trying to Whistle It?', 365.

[93] Ibid.   [94] Hacker, 'Wittgenstein, Carnap . . .', 16.

[95] In a recent article, Diamond has contested Hacker's analogy between the rules of logical syntax and the rules of a game claiming that it is question-begging. For the point of Conant's conception, according to Diamond, is precisely to deny that the rules of logical syntax are akin to the rules of a game. But, if so, then insisting on the contrary, as Diamond does, is surely just as question-begging. Furthermore, if the rules of logical syntax are not supposed to be constitutive rules, as Diamond here seems to imply, one wonders what *kinds* of rules they could possibly be, given that Wittgenstein does speak of rules (see TLP §3.334, §3.343, §3.344). See Diamond, 'Logical Syntax in Wittgenstein's *Tractatus*', *Philosophical Quarterly* 55/218 (2005a): 87.

The reason why Conant seems to be so keen to do away with the notion that the rules of logical syntax can be transgressed is that he appears to think that if you admit that this is possible, then you must automatically commit yourself to a conception of 'substantial nonsense'. This is false, however, if by 'substantial nonsense' Conant means 'a proposition with a sense that is nonsensical', the expression of an 'illogical thought' or the doing of something logically impossible. For, as has just been said, given that the rules of logical syntax are constitutive rules, contravening them does *a fortiori* not result in doing something 'positive' such as describing a metaphysically impossible state of affairs or an 'illogical' thought, since there are no such things.[96] As Wittgenstein says, 'thought can never be of anything illogical, since, if it were, we should have to think illogically' (§3.03) and, further, 'it is as impossible to represent in language anything that "contradicts logic" as it is to represent by its co-ordinates a figure that contradicts the laws of space, or to give the co-ordinates of a point that does not exist' (§3.032). Consequently, a metaphysical impossibility isn't a possibility that is impossible. Rather, logical impossibilities are expressed by logical contradictions (§4.462, §5.525) and these, as Wittgenstein points out, describe nothing for they are senseless (like tautologies): 'For all propositions of logic say the same thing. Namely nothing' (§5.43, my translation). Hence, commitment to the idea that the TLP allows for combinatorial nonsense in no way implies, *pace* Conant, commitment to an obviously nonsensical conception of nonsense.[97]

What is more, Conant's argument against the possibility of combinatorial nonsense not only rests on scant internal evidence, it also presupposes taking absolutely literally Wittgenstein's context principle and this, on Conant's construction of it, implies that words *only* have meaning in the context of a proposition, which just has to be false. For not only does this contradict the later Wittgenstein's dictum that

---

[96] Neither does it require a reification of 'meanings' or a meaning-body conception. See Hacker, 'Wittgenstein, Carnap . . .', 7–10, and Hans-Johann Glock, 'All Kinds of Nonsense', in *Wittgenstein at Work*, ed. Erich Ammereller and Eugen Fischer (London: Routledge, 2004), 221–45.

[97] That is to say, one can be committed to the idea that there is such a thing as combinatorial nonsense without believing that there is such a thing as Conant's 'substantial nonsense'—regardless of whether or not Wittgenstein himself, in the TLP, subscribed to a substantial conception or not. For to argue that Wittgenstein did espouse the 'substantial view', is neither to say that it makes sense nor that it is required in order for combinatorial nonsense to be possible.

the meaning of a word is its use in the language[98] (PI §43)—that is, that how it is used, not its occurrence in particular sentences alone, determines a word's meaning—but it also renders superfluous the employment of dictionaries, which, after all, tell one what individual words mean. Furthermore, such a principle leaves it altogether mysterious how a *sentence* gets to mean anything in the first place, since, although the whole (the sentence) can be said to be more than the sum of its parts (the individual words composing it), it would be absurd to conclude from this that the whole consists of individually meaningless parts or of parts that, by themselves, have no conceivable function *at all*. That is to say, it is one thing to claim, as the later Wittgenstein does, that the same word can take on different meanings in different contexts, it is quite another to insist that a word has *no meaning at all* outside a specific context. For if this were true, it would be impossible to explain how these parts (words/signs) suddenly acquired meaning simply in virtue of occurring within a particular proposition.

Perhaps Conant is misled into accepting Wittgenstein's restrictive principle from the TLP because in the PI Wittgenstein says things like: ' "I set the brake up by connecting up rod and lever."—Yes, given the whole rest of the mechanism. Only in conjunction with that is it a brake-lever, and separated from its support it is not even a lever; it may be anything, or nothing' (PI §6). This remark occurs within a discussion of ostensive definition and it is meant to show that teaching by ostension is only possible if at least a partial mastery of the language is already presupposed. What Wittgenstein is saying here is that attempting to set up a 'connection' between language and world *à la* TLP by, as it were, 'baptizing' objects by naming them, only makes sense 'given the whole rest of the mechanism', that is, the whole background of linguistic practice:

> For naming and describing do not stand on the same level: naming is a preparation for description. Naming is so far not a move in the language-game—any more than putting a piece in its place on the board is a move in chess. . . This was what Frege meant too, when he said that a word had meaning only as part of a sentence. (PI §49)

Hence, Wittgenstein is interpreting Frege's context-principle (which, Conant claims, Wittgenstein adopts unreservedly in both TLP and PI) *in the light of* his criticisms of ostensive definition and not, *pace* Conant, as a restrictive principle that is supposed to apply unreservedly across

---

[98] For a similar argument see Glock, op.cit., 228–9.

the board. Consequently, these passages from the PI lend no support at all to Wittgenstein's Tractarian dictum that 'only propositions have sense, only in the nexus of a proposition does a name have meaning'. Rather, Wittgenstein is claiming that only against the backdrop of a *whole network* of language-use, does a word acquire meaning, which is precisely why he says at PI §43: 'For a *large* class of cases—though not for all—in which we employ the word "meaning" it can be defined thus: the meaning of a word is its use in the language.' Thus, it is our entire linguistic practices that imbue our words with life, not their occurrence in particular sentences *alone*.

Of course, when they are listed in a dictionary, for example, individual words are, at that precise point, fulfilling no particular role in the language, except for being, as it were, ready for employment. But it would be odd to infer from this that therefore these words are utterly meaningless. In fact, it is only the mistaken Tractarian picture theory of meaning that lends plausibility to such a conception and it is precisely this position that is under indictment in the relevant remarks from the PI. Consequently, the context principle, as propounded at TLP §3.3, does not, *pace* Conant, mark a profound continuity between early and later Wittgenstein, but rather a profound *departure* by the later man from his earlier self.

In order to pre-empt a move frequently made by Conant at this point—that Wittgenstein in the PI is not criticizing his former self, but is only targeting a general philosophical illusion[99]—let me begin by first quoting what the PI say about the Tractarian conception:

What lies behind the idea that names really signify simples?—Socrates says in the *Theaetetus*: 'If I make no mistake, I have heard some people say this: there is no definition of the primary elements—so to speak—out of which we and everything else are composed; for everything that exists in its own right can only be *named*, no other determination is possible... But just as what consists of these primary elements is itself complex, so the names of the elements become descriptive language by being compounded together. For the essence of speech is the composition of names.' Both Russell's 'individuals' and my 'objects' (*Tractatus Logico-Philosophicus*) were such primary elements. But what are the simple constituent parts of which reality is composed?—What are the simple constituent parts of a chair?—The bits of wood of which it is made? Or the molecules, or the atoms?—'Simple' means: not composite. And here the point is: in what sense 'composite'? It makes no sense at all to speak absolutely of the 'simple parts of a chair'. (PI §46–§47)

---

[99] See, for example, Conant and Diamond, op.cit., 84–5.

These passages make it, I think, quite clear that Wittgenstein *did* hold in the TLP, *contra* Conant, that names refer to sempiternal objects constituting the substance of all possible worlds and hence that they have meaning only within the context of a significant proposition (see below). For compare what Wittgenstein says in the TLP with the account from the PI just cited:

A name means an object. The object is its meaning . . . In a proposition a name is the representative of an object. Objects can only be *named*. Signs are their representatives. I can only speak *about* them: I cannot *put them into words*. Propositions can only say *how* things are, not *what* they are. (TLP §3.202–§3.221)

If this doesn't qualify as *the same account* as the one that Wittgenstein is singling out for criticism in PI §46–7, then I don't know what *would*. And if, furthermore, Wittgenstein did not hold this view in the TLP, as Conant claims, then I don't see why Wittgenstein would have bothered to criticize it so extensively in PI—especially given that it is obvious from the context in which Wittgenstein refers to the TLP (at PI §46) that he means to say that he, as well as Russell, used to endorse this conception, *not* that he had already exposed it as incoherent in his early work.

Consequently, Wittgenstein is *not* being ironic when he says in the TLP that 'objects make up the substance of the world. That is why they cannot be composite. If the world had no substance, then whether a proposition had sense would depend on whether another proposition was true. In that case we could not sketch any picture of the world (true or false).'(TLP §2.021–§2.0211) That is to say, picture-theoretic considerations—being able to sketch a true or false picture of the world which Wittgenstein thought, at the time of writing the TLP, comprised the *essence* of language—*demand* that names have meaning by dint of referring to 'simple objects', as propositional analysis would otherwise be endless and sense indeterminate: 'the requirement that simple signs be possible is the requirement that sense be determinate' (§3.23). Given that, as Wittgenstein also believed, 'the substance of the world *can* only determine a form, and not any material properties, for it is only by means of propositions that material properties are represented'(§2.0231; punctuation changed), only propositions can portray facts (§2.19–§2.225). Names, on the other hand, are primitive signs which cannot be dissected any further (§3.26) and which therefore can only be understood if the meanings of these signs are already known (§3.263). This is effected by means of elucidations, which are propositions that contain the primitive signs (ibid.). Hence, and as the next proposition says, 'only in the nexus of a proposition does a name have meaning' (§3.3), for only within a proposition does a name stand for an object, just as only within a picture do coloured circles and squares represent people (§2.1–§2.14).[100] Outside such a context, they might mean anything or nothing.

If this account is correct, then it shows that the context principle plays a very different role in the TLP than it does later in the PI. Consequently, once the picture theory of meaning is abandoned and with it the misguided conception that language can be divided up into two kinds of 'component'—names and propositions—we no longer have any good reasons for adhering to such a restrictive dictum at all. For once individual words are no longer conceived as names that stand for objects, we will see that what confers meaning on them is not their reference to the indestructible furniture of the world in virtue of which they can figure as the representing proxies in the depiction of a possible state of affairs, but rather the myriad ways that words are actually employed in the language (both inside and outside of propositions). And this means that the context principle, as developed in the TLP, will become obsolete as well or will, at least, have to be substantially reinterpreted in the light of Wittgenstein's later conception of language.

Hence, as I hope to have shown, there are neither good exegetical[101] nor good philosophical grounds for accepting Conant's thesis that there is no such thing as violating the rules of logical syntax in the TLP. Wittgenstein does, *contra* Conant, allow for the possibility of combinatorial nonsense, but this doesn't (by itself) imply commitment to a nonsensical 'substantial' conception. Consequently, although both linguistic strings are, indeed, meaningless, the reason why 'Socrates is identical' is nonsense is different from the reason why 'Socrates is blick' is nonsense. For the latter is nonsense because it contains a meaningless word—a word that has *no* use in the language,[102] whereas the former contains meaningful words—words that do have a use in the language, but which are strung together in a meaningless way. Conant is therefore

[100] See also Hacker, ibid., 17.

[101] For external evidence for the view that Wittgenstein did hold, in the TLP, that there is such a thing as violating the rules of logical syntax, see Hacker, ibid.

[102] So, strictly speaking, 'blick' shouldn't even be called a 'word' or a 'sign' at all—it is just an arbitrary mark and hence not even, as it were, a *candidate* for sense. This distinguishes it from a word or sign such as 'identical', because even if it is used incorrectly in a sentence like 'Socrates is identical', it is nevertheless still a candidate for sense (albeit a failed one in these circumstances).

wrong to believe that there is only *one way* in which something can be nonsense, namely, by being mere gibberish.

II.4 Thesis Four: Is Wittgenstein's Ladder 'Real'?

Conant, as we have already seen, rejects the 'standard' or traditional account whereby the revocation of the TLP is thought to be the result of the book's not having room for the status of its own propositions. For, on Conant's reading, the only way a 'sentence' can be nonsense is by containing a meaningless word or words, not by violating the conditions of sense laid down by a previously established theory of meaning. And although this strategy would, if we disregard two-thirds of what Wittgenstein actually says, save the TLP from self-refutation, it generates two other, to my mind, insuperable problems. First, Conant needs to be able to explain why, if it is the case that there is only one kind of nonsense—plain gibberish—and most of the sentences of the TLP fall into this category, we nevertheless seem to be able to understand the work. Second, he needs to be able to show how said gibberish is supposed to form a 'ladder' that can be climbed and that will, as it were, be 'firm' enough to effect the dispelling of metaphysical illusion. *Prima facie*, both these things seem impossible to accomplish if the concomitant embarrassment of simply telling the reader what the nonsense *says*—the stick that Conant most enjoys beating the 'standard reading' with—is to be avoided as well.

Naturally, Conant's answer to the first question is that there is only the *illusion* of understanding the propositions in the TLP and that this involves entering into the point of view from which the various pieces of nonsense appear to say something. But if the pieces of nonsense literally say nothing, as Conant maintains, I don't see how this is possible, since there is no such thing as performing logical operations on plain gibberish (on strings such as 'piggle wiggle tiggle'). If the propositions of the TLP are therefore no different from 'frabble frabble', then they simply can't tell us anything.[103] Consequently, making a distinction between understanding the utterer of nonsense rather than the nonsense itself won't help us along, for even our 'imaginative acts of identification' with

---

[103] Given that Conant thinks that there is no such thing as combinatorial nonsense in the TLP, he cannot legitimately claim that the 'propositions' of the TLP are of the form: 'Socrates is identical'; 'Anything identical is a prime number'; therefore 'Socrates is a prime number'.

the utterer of nonsense have to be constrained by at least some minimal (propositional) content, as we could otherwise legitimately project any 'pseudo-sense' onto these nonsensical propositions we choose—in which case, how do we climb the ladder? Perhaps Conant thinks that given that the negation of a piece of nonsense is itself nonsense, there is some loose kind of logical implication to be got here, but this seems far from substantial enough to allow one to work through the network of the merely '(apparent) logical relations' he speaks of. For even '(apparent)' logical relations must be a function of some, however tenuous, content and given that Conant doesn't allow for this, it seems that all he can have is the *appearance* of '(apparent) logical relations'. These *appearances*, though, cannot begin to add up even to the flimsiest ladder.

Hence, Conant is again confronted with a dilemma: either he sticks to his guns and consistently holds that nonsense really cannot say anything, in which case the construction of even an imaginary ladder cannot get off the ground, or he does allow that it is, in some sense, possible to understand the propositions in the TLP, in which case he has to account for the propositions being nonsensical in some other way. Simply claiming that it is possible, via a method of projection, to understand the author rather than what he is saying, isn't going to do the trick. For if all the propositions in the work really lack a sense, not just a '(clear)' sense, then what materials have we got for understanding even the author? It seems that, ultimately, all we can do is guess what the author could have meant, in which case, we seem not to be left with even a *reductio* argument, but with the mere *appearance* of one.[104]

Conant is therefore in exactly the same position as the 'standard reading': if he wants to be able to project any kind of—however slender—sense onto the pseudo-propositions of the TLP, then he must allow them to have, at least, a vestige of content. But if so, then, just as the 'standard reading' has to, he must tell us what the nonsense says. And this is, indeed, what Conant goes on to do, but without acknowledging the fact that this is a case of wanting to have one's cake and eat it. In his joint paper with Cora Diamond, for example, Conant says, as regards the putative metaphysical commitments of the early Wittgenstein:

In our list below of metaphysical commitments embodied in the *Tractatus*, we shall be using sentences of the sort that occur in this passage, sentences that 'appear to be about' the essential nature of language. We are not claiming that

---

[104] And, in fact, Conant's conception of nonsense makes *reductio* arguments impossible anyway. See the following paragraphs.

these sentences are anything but plain nonsense, or that Wittgenstein in any way intended to communicate a metaphysics of language.[105]

So in this list, which incidentally is rather extensive, Conant and Diamond *tell* us what the plain nonsensical propositions in the TLP are committed to, that is, *say*, and then attempt to bring this into line with their interpretation by framing what these propositions say with scare quotes.[106] Hence, one may be forgiven for wondering how this is supposed, in any way, to be better than what the 'standard reading' does when it explains what the pseudo-propositions of the TLP say.

Furthermore, it seems difficult to fathom what the exact distinction is between sentences that *are* about the essential nature of language and sentences that only 'appear to be about' the essential nature of language. For Conant and Diamond both seem committed to the view that if certain sentences are shown, at a later stage, to be incoherent or absurd (such as the sentences about the essential nature of language), these sentences could never have meant *anything* in the first place. But this not only makes *reductio ad absurdum* arguments in philosophy, as well as impossibility proofs in mathematics, impossible, it also makes a mockery of what Wittgenstein is up to in the PI, since it implies that in this work, too, and not just in the TLP, Wittgenstein must be talking nonsense when he says, for instance, things like:

In what sense are my sensations *private?*—Well, only I can know whether I am really in pain; another person can only surmise it.—In one way this is wrong, and in another nonsense . . . It can't be said of me at all (except perhaps as a joke) that I *know* I am in pain. What is it supposed to mean—except perhaps that I *am* in pain . . . The truth is: it makes sense to say about other people that they doubt whether I am in pain; but not to say it about myself. (PI §246)

---

[105] Conant and Diamond, op.cit., 95.

[106] This is not the only problem this strategy faces, however. For, on the basis of what evidence is a distinction to be drawn between the 'unwitting metaphysical commitments' of early Wittgenstein that Conant and Diamond seek to ascribe to Wittgenstein and the 'traditional' metaphysical commitments that Conant and Diamond would want to eschew? Finding textual criteria for this endeavour would just reproduce the problems with the framing material discussed in section III.1. What is more, it is also highly implausible to suppose that the 'unwitting metaphysical commitments' can be easily separated from the 'obviously' metaphysical ones, as many of them clearly hang together philosophically. For example, it would require a lot of ingenuity to show that on early Wittgenstein's scheme of things, the 'unwitting' commitment, 'antecedent to logical analysis, there must be this logical order—one that is *already there* awaiting discovery—and it is the role of logical analysis to uncover it' (Conant and Diamond, op.cit., 83), can be prised away from Wittgenstein's notion that language and reality share a transcendental logical form.

In this passage Wittgenstein is clearly trying to show that the philosophical conception of the intrinsic privacy of sensation is nonsense, which means that, on Conant's and Diamond's interpretation, the original statement that Wittgenstein is trying to reduce to absurdity or incoherence—'sensations are private'—only appears to say something, but is actually no different, say, than 'sensations are frabble', 'frabbles are private' or, indeed, than 'frabble frabble frabble'. But, if so, then the whole passage must be nonsense, and given that Wittgenstein proceeds analogously in most of his other remarks in PI, the entire book must be nonsense as well. Small wonder that Conant's and Diamond's interpretation leaves us with nothing more than the injunction to give up 'the idea of our enlightened perspective on the thought of would-be metaphysicians, realists, transcendental idealists, and solipsists', for their conception seems tantamount to giving up philosophy full stop.

So, it must be false that there is no difference—apart from a psychological one—between philosophical nonsense and plain gibberish, as, for a start, you can immediately recognize gibberish when you see it, but you certainly can't, especially if untrained in philosophical argumentation, immediately recognize a philosophical claim such as, say, 'the world is all that is the case' to be nonsense. The fact that logical operations, that is, *arguments*, are required to make such a thing apparent already indicates that the sentence in question must have some content and therefore can't literally be saying nothing. Nevertheless, allowing for this does not imply commitment to a 'substantial conception' of nonsense, since thinking a thought which, unbeknownst to me, leads to absurd consequences is *not* to think a thought whose *sense* turns out to be nonsensical[107] rather, it is to make a mistake in one's reasoning. For just as a miscalculation is a *calculation*—not a nonsense!—gone awry, so an incoherent thought is a *thought* that has taken a wrong turn.[108]

---

[107] For this would presuppose that a sentence and its sense can be divorced from each other, such that, say, in meaningful sentences there is a 'match' between the sentence and its sense, whereas in nonsensical sentences we get a 'clash' or 'mismatch' between the former and the latter. But to think that there can be such a thing as philosophical nonsense which is not plain gibberish is not to buy into this confusion. For something can both have a sense *and* lead to (unforeseen) absurd (or impossible) consequences, just as the question 'is it possible to trisect an angle?' has a sense, although a proof exists to show that there can be no such thing. For an illuminating discussion of the apparent paradoxical nature of this fact, see Juliet Floyd, 'Wittgenstein, Mathematics and Philosophy', in *The New Wittgenstein*, 232–61.

[108] And intelligibility can of course come in degrees, i.e. there may come a point where a thought (or a calculation) indeed ceases to be a thought (or a calculation), as

To claim otherwise, is to offer a sophistical argument for the view that there can be no such thing as mistaken reasoning (or calculating) *at all*, since anything not clear and logically perspicuous does not, on this conception, qualify as a *thought* (or as a calculation). But not only is this confused, it also undermines Wittgenstein's whole procedure of transforming 'latent' into 'patent' nonsense (PI §464), since, on such a conception, Wittgenstein's remark that 'to say "He alone can know what he intends" is nonsense: to say "He alone can know what he will do", wrong' (PI, II, 223) would be as uninformative as saying 'To say "blick" is nonsense' and hence no distinction could be drawn here between what, according to Wittgenstein, is merely false and what nonsensical—a distinction that lies at the very heart of the later Wittgenstein's philosophical practice.

Hence, if a *reading* of the TLP (and, by parity of reasoning, of the PI) is supposed to be possible, Conant's 'austere conception of nonsense' must be abandoned. For it either falls into self-contradiction by covertly smuggling content into apparently *plain* nonsense, or it leaves the reader with no materials at all from which to construct a ladder.[109] We must therefore allow that there are many different reasons for why something can be nonsense[110] and, further, that Wittgenstein would have accepted this. Consequently, it is implausible to assume that the anti-essentialist (later) Wittgenstein would have subscribed to a 'nonsense essentialism' of the kind that Conant attributes to him. For, as Wittgenstein says, 'Even a nonsense-poem is not nonsense in the same way as the babbling of a child' (PI §282).[111]

---

in the case of someone who claims to be 'adding' and then says '2+2 = 35'. This is certainly no ordinary 'mistake'. But from such aberrant cases (where we might indeed end up concluding that someone is speaking *plain* nonsense), it does not follow that *all* 'mistakes' are of this form. For if they were, there would be no such thing as a mistake.

[109] Stephen Mulhall has recently attempted what he calls a 'resolute' reading of the PI. But although, on the one hand, he shares Conant's view that nonsense is plain gibberish, he also admits that 'on his [Wittgenstein's] taxonomy, not all nonsense is devoid of sense, or meaning, or point' (see Mulhall, *Wittgenstein's Private Language* (Oxford: Oxford University Press, 2007), 122). But, if so, Mulhall is either, after all, not completely accepting Conant's 'austere conception' of nonsense or he is, like Conant, smuggling content—albeit it 'openly'—into apparently mere gobbledygook.

[110] And this means, as Glock correctly points out, that we must 'abandon or modify [the] standard assumption . . . that everything that stands in logical relations with something meaningful is itself meaningful' (Glock, op.cit., 243).

[111] Given that Conant thinks that Wittgenstein's conception of nonsense remains the same throughout his authorship, it is legitimate to appeal to evidence from the PI when arguing against Conant's view.

III INTERIM CONCLUSIONS

I hope to have shown in the previous sections that Conant's way of reading the TLP faces insurmountable exegetical and philosophical difficulties. There is consequently no way, it seems to me, of avoiding the fact that the book ends in self-refutation. And if Wittgenstein, at the time at least, had no qualms about this, I don't see why we should go and clean up, as it were, what the author himself intended this way.[112] Hence, I agree with the traditional (or 'standard') conception—which is much more faithful to what Wittgenstein actually says—that the reason the author revokes his work is because its form and its content are at odds with each other. For the only propositions the TLP has room for are the bipolar, empirical (factual) ones that represent, truly or falsely, a state of affairs (§4.023, §4.06), or the 'formal' and 'empty' 'propositions' of logic which strictly speaking 'say nothing' (§5.43, §6.11, §6.13). Given that the sentences of the book itself fall into neither the first nor the second of these categories, as they employ formal concepts as if they were material ones (§4.124, §4.1272), they inevitably violate their own conditions of sense by attempting to *say* what can only be shown (§4.121–§4.1221) and thus produce metaphysical nonsense *par excellence*.

In other words, the book enacts a performative contradiction by attempting to say what, by its own lights, can't be said. Consequently, while I agree with Conant that there is no such thing as 'substantial' nonsense (conceived as a proposition with a 'nonsensical' sense or as a logically impossible thought), I would nonetheless insist, *pace* Conant, that this doesn't imply that if something is nonsense, then, necessarily, it involves saying nothing at all. For performative contradictions are, in

---

[112] Now one might think that this means that I am simply insufficiently bothered by the *Tractatus*' declaring itself nonsensical and in a certain sense this is true. That is to say, I am less worried by it than resolute readers (or those sympathizing with a resolute reading), because I believe, on good exegetical grounds, as I hope to have shown, that—whether we like it or not—this is what Wittgenstein himself intended. Furthermore, Wittgenstein himself, as he says in the preface to the PI, later came to see 'serious errors' (*schwere Irrtümer*) in his 'first book'. So, although, it would doubtless be more satisfying if the TLP did not enact a performative contradiction, if we are to remain faithful to what the text actually says and to what Wittgenstein himself said about it, there seems to be no escaping this fact—or if there is, no one has so far, to my mind, managed to show how this feat is successfully to be accomplished (without running into similar sorts of problems—such as simply telling the reader what the putative 'nonsense' says—as the standard view).

one sense at least, evidently nonsensical and yet they clearly do involve saying something and indeed have to say what they say in order to generate the kind of nonsense they do. As Johannes Climacus so aptly says in CUP: writing a work and revoking it is not the same as leaving it unwritten (CUP 612). That is to say, in order to be able see that the TLP is enacting a performative contradiction, I must first of all quite literally understand what the book is saying, for it is only once I have done that that I am in a position to realize that the TLP is propounding a self-defeating conception. And it is only once that has occurred to me that I can appreciate that the point of the revocation is, as it were, the author's sleight of hand for resolving that tension.

It is here, I think, that my main disagreement with Conant lies. Conant believes that the way to resolve the tension is by the reader's coming to realize that she was taken in by an illusion of sense and that the propositions in the TLP were never meant to say anything in the first place. I am saying that Wittgenstein literally meant to say everything he does say in the TLP, but that the work generates its own inconsistency.[113] So it is only in the latter sense that the book turns out to be nonsense—that is, it is only because of Wittgenstein's commitment to the extreme 'either/or' of the logical and the empirical that the work turns out to be nonsense. Without this commitment, it remains an open question whether the propositions of the TLP, by themselves, are ultimately nonsensical or not. And should it turn out that they are, an argument will be needed to show this.

In the next section I will turn to Conant's reading of CUP, whose revocation, Conant claims, functions analogously to that of the TLP. I will attempt to demonstrate that this, too, is false.

IV CONANT'S READING OF THE *POSTSCRIPT*

Conant's interpretative strategy in CUP revolves around two central questions: how to make sense of the work's pseudonymity and how to make sense of the revocation that is to be found in the Appendix. As regards the former, Conant says, 'if we wish to go into the business of interpreting one of these (pseudonymous) works, we would somehow be involved in a confusion if we were to ascribe (as, in fact, most commentators do) any assertions or arguments in the work to Kierkegaard' (KWN

---

[113] And that it does is related to its ethical point. See the conclusion to this chapter.

200). But it is not only attributing anything directly to Kierkegaard that is a problem in CUP. Given the revocation, Conant thinks, even ascribing anything to Climacus himself would be going astray. He says, 'To so much as quote the work appreciatively, to take it to be a partisan of some particular view, is a further sign that one has misunderstood it' (KWN 202). Uncovering what this misunderstanding consists in is, according to Conant, the key to understanding what CUP is ultimately up to.

The reading that Conant offers can again be understood as comprising four principal theses. The first one concerns what Conant calls the 'frame' of the work, the second concerns the nature of Climacus' targets, the third concerns the interpretation of Climacus' apparently substantive claims about Christianity, and the fourth concerns what it is that is 'difficult' about becoming a Christian. In the following I will set these theses out in turn.

IV.1 Thesis One

Directions on how to read the *Postscript*, Conant suggests, are to be found in the 'frames' of the book. These consist, on his view, of the Appendices to be found in the middle and at the end of the work which function '(as do the preface and the final sections of the *Tractatus*) as part of the frame of the work in which the author allows himself to comment on the work as a whole and provide directions for how to read it' (KWN 202). Conant takes three main interpretative cues from these pieces of 'framing' material. From the Appendix in the middle of the work, entitled 'A Glance at Danish Literature', he concludes, following Climacus' own remarks about *Either/Or*, that the *Postscript* 'is constructed as a mirror in which the reader can recognize his own confusions. The work will not have the transformative effect upon the reader to which it aspires unless the task of recognizing the relevant contradictions is left to him' (KWN 203). From the Appendix at the end of the work he takes note, of course, of the revocation, and also of the following passage: 'Consequently, the book is superfluous. Therefore, let no one bother to appeal to it, because one who appeals to it has *eo ipso* misunderstood it' (CUP 618). From this Conant draws the conclusion that 'it appears now that it is a sign that one has misunderstood the book not only if one invokes Kierkegaard's name, but even if one restricts oneself to an appeal to the persona of the pseudonym'(KWN 201). The reason for the misunderstanding, Conant believes, is failing to see that the point of the book is ethical: 'The problem is not one of teaching the reader something he does not know but rather of showing him that, with respect to the activity of becoming a Christian, there is nothing further he needs to *know*. His quest for knowledge is an evasion of the task of achieving . . . existential resolution' (KWN 202). Thus, Conant concludes, anything in the work that appears to make 'substantial' knowledge-claims of any kind is precisely what is to be understood as having been revoked.

IV.2 Thesis Two

It follows from the first thesis that the target of Climacus' rhetoric, according to Conant, must be the speculative philosopher *within the reader* who attempts to avoid the task of reflecting on his life by indulging in philosophical speculation about Christianity:

The purpose of Climacus' parody on speculative philosophy is to underscore what he takes to be the ludicrousness of the philosopher's attempt to advance our understanding of what it means to become a Christian. Climacus represents his literary task as one of 'taking away' insofar as his aim is to *deprive* the philosopher of the illusion that a well-conducted speculative inquiry will equip him with a deeper understanding of what it is to be a Christian. (KWN 206)

The point, then, of the *Postscript*, in Conant's eyes, is to dispel the illusion that a philosophical investigation of Christianity is possible. However, it appears to be the case that Climacus himself is engaged in the very project he seeks to undermine. In order to save Climacus, therefore, from refuting himself, Conant suggests we read all the passages where Climacus appears to propound a 'substantive conception' of Christianity as constituting an exercise in irony.

IV.3 Thesis Three

It follows from theses one and two, on Conant's reading, that while the first half of CUP can be read as Climacus offering us 'categorical distinctions' (which Conant likens to the later Wittgenstein's grammatical remarks) about what the difference between a secular and a 'religious' use of certain concepts (such as 'faith', 'revelation' etc.) consists in, by the second half, Climacus begins to speak nonsense, as he himself ends up running the relevant categories together:

Climacus, therefore, does not remain faithful to his own claim that all he is doing is marking categorical distinctions . . . It becomes clear that Climacus' remark about the 'essential incommensurability' of faith and objective reasoning will be invoked as a thesis, contesting the philosopher's counter-thesis that ordinary belief and religious faith represent commensurable kinds of cognitive states . . . Climacus himself is therefore driven in his polemic against the philosopher to *insist* upon something that by his own lights is a grammatical truth. He ends up representing what is a mere truism as his own intellectual discovery, *his* contribution to knowledge . . . Climacus' analysis therefore commits him to a distinction between mere absurdity and 'objective absurdity'—a category of deep nonsense which is supposed to be qualitatively more repellent to reason than ordinary nonsense. (KWN 211)

In an effort to rescue Climacus from espousing this unappetizing doctrine, Conant says, 'commentators have tried dutifully to water down and clean up Climacus' argument', but in so doing—and by 'ignoring Climacus' vehement warnings about the work's peculiar character'—they have inevitably gone astray. For, Conant claims, 'the dialectical ladder of the *Postscript* culminates in a demonstration and declaration of the nonsensicality of its doctrine. Its doctrine turns out to be a pseudo-doctrine. It is a ladder which once we have climbed up it, we are asked to throw away' (KWN 215–16).

Hence, Conant's suggestion is that Climacus, just like Wittgenstein, specifically wants to draw the reader into an illusion the better to reveal how powerful that illusion is. The 'difficulty' of understanding the work is consequently a matter of 'grasping the contradiction inherent in the relation between the work's form and its content' (KWN 207) which arises, according to Conant, because the form of the work consists of a parody on speculative philosophy, while its *content* seems to consist of something which is itself rather similar to that which it parodies—namely, the advancement of 'theses' (and indefensible ones at that) about the nature of Christianity. The way to 'grasp' this 'contradiction', then, and thus to understand the central aim of CUP, is to realize that 'the work as a whole represents an elaborate *reductio ad absurdum* of the philosophical project of clarifying and propounding what it is to be a Christian' (KWN 207). Hence, it is impossible to understand the theses[114] that Climacus appears to be propounding, as they reveal themselves, in the end, to the enlightened reader at least, as patently nonsensical. Consequently, on Conant's interpretation, CUP, just like the TLP, ends by revoking (most of) itself.

---

[114] Examples of such 'theses' are: 'truth is subjectivity', 'faith involves a crucifixion of the understanding', 'the absolute paradox is incomprehensible'.

IV.4 Thesis Four

Kierkegaard's aim in all of this, on Conant's reading, is 'to show him (the philosopher) that where he takes there to be a problem there isn't one. The solution to what he takes to be the problem of life is to be found in the vanishing of the problem . . . Climacus' aim is to reveal to the philosopher that for the simple task at hand no special application of the intellect is required' (KWN 206). Consequently, the 'difficulties' that Climacus creates for the reader are merely 'pseudo-difficulties'. Ultimately, there is no 'problem' with understanding Christianity at all, there is only the 'practical difficulty of living a certain sort of life'. That the philosopher is blind to this is what, on Conant's view, CUP and Kierkegaard hope to show.

V A CRITIQUE OF CONANT'S READING OF THE *POSTSCRIPT*

In what follows I argue that none of Conant's principal theses are sustainable and hence that Kierkegaard's text calls for an altogether different sort of reading.

V.1 Thesis One: The 'Framing' Issue

I agree with Conant—how could one not?—that CUP is an exercise in irony. However, as is not true of the TLP, there is not a single sentence in the book where Climacus says that anything in his work should be taken to be nonsense. Consequently, the only reason we have for supposing that Climacus wishes the reader to see that what he says about the 'absolute paradox' (the Christian Incarnation), for example, is tongue-in-cheek, is Conant's claim that this is indeed the case and his view that the apparent philosophical dubiousness of Climacus' 'thesis' must imply that this is, indeed, what he wants us to think. The distinction that Conant draws between the 'grammatical remarks' and the 'nonsense' in CUP therefore seems to come down, in the end, to a distinction between those remarks that Conant finds philosophically palatable and those that he doesn't. So unless we are already convinced by Conant's interpretation, there is no reason to suppose that Climacus' revoking the work means that he wants to dispel the illusion of there being such a thing as 'substantial nonsense'.

There is a further problem with the framing material. Given that Conant believes that in the Appendices Climacus is supplying us with directions on how to read the work, it seems sensible to assume that he can only do that if we can take what Climacus says in these passages at face value. What makes this problematic for Conant is that in the 'frames' themselves Climacus says a good deal about things that Conant classifies as nonsensical in the main text. If, therefore, Conant is right about which bits are nonsensical (and therefore part of what is revoked), then the 'frames' themselves cannot be immune from revocation. But, given that it is the 'frames' which, according to Conant, tell us what should be taken to have been revoked and what not, it now seems that Conant has sawn off the branch on which he was sitting. Here are two examples of this, both of which are to be found in the Appendix in the middle of CUP entitled 'A Glance at Danish Literature'. 'That subjectivity, inwardness, is truth,' Climacus says, 'was *my thesis*. I have tried to show how in my view the pseudonymous authors tend toward this thesis, which at its maximum is Christianity' (CUP 278–9, italics added). And further on in the Appendix Climacus adds (and this gives us a clue as to why he calls himself a 'humorist'): 'Humour does not take in the suffering aspect of the paradox or the ethical aspect of faith but only the amusing aspect. It is, namely, a suffering, faith's martyrdom even in times of peace, to have the eternal happiness of one's soul related to something over which the understanding despairs' (CUP 291–2). If these passages are supposed to be ironic too, then I think this constitutes a *reductio* of the view that the Appendices function as 'frames'. So Conant is presented with a dilemma. Either the 'frames' give us directions on how to read the work and therefore aren't ironic, in which case Climacus must be taken to mean the things that Conant says he later revokes; or the frames are ironic too, in which case it is unclear how they can function as 'frames', since they are then no longer capable of providing any salient criteria by which it is possible to distinguish what Climacus *means* from what is simply nonsense. Conant's interpretative strategy therefore fails on either horn.

V.2 Thesis Two: The Targets of the *Postscript*

It is true that what Climacus wants to achieve is to get the reader to engage with the question of Christianity on an *existential* level. In this respect I agree with Conant that the book has an ethical purpose. But Conant is wrong to believe that this is the *only* purpose of Climacus' book, for the targets that Climacus is shooting at are much more various than that. Firstly, Climacus does not only want to cure the philosopher's—*any* philosopher's—propensity for theorizing; rather, his polemic is aimed quite specifically at the *Hegelian* speculative philosopher who believes that he can use reason to 'mediate away' the Christian paradox and thus to employ his cognitive faculties to go *further* than faith. Secondly, Climacus attempts to show that the *Christians in Christendom* are deluding themselves into believing they are Christians, when they are, on his view, really nothing more than *pagans* or *idol-worshippers*:

> If God had taken the form, for example, of a rare, enormously large green bird with a red beak, that perched in a tree on the embankment and perhaps even whistled in an unprecedented manner—then our partygoing man would surely have had his eyes opened. . . All paganism consists in this, that God is related directly to a human being, as the remarkably striking to the amazed. (CUP 245)

About the latter issue Conant has nothing much to say, perhaps because this, too, would mean making some sort of 'substantive' claim.

Both of Climacus' aims outlined above can, however, only be achieved if we read him as actually *meaning* what he says rather than as setting an elaborate trap for us. Furthermore, it is simply not the case that Climacus then goes on to fall into his own trap, in order to take us with him, as Conant supposes, and that he himself consequently ends up being the target of his own polemic. For throughout CUP Climacus distinguishes sharply between knowing what Christianity is and knowing what it is to be a Christian. He says, 'That one can know what Christianity is without being a Christian must, then, be answered in the affirmative. Whether one can know what it is to be a Christian without being one is something else, and it must be answered in the negative' (CUP 372). And this claim is perfectly compatible with, and indeed is the reason for, Climacus' insistence throughout CUP that he is *not* a Christian. In the light of this, we can therefore read the book as an exercise in elucidating what Christianity is (in order, for example, to avoid the errors of the Hegelians and the Christians in Christendom) and not, *pace* Conant, as an 'elaborate *reductio ad absurdum* of the philosophical project of clarifying and propounding what it is to be a Christian'.[115] For again, the target here is the

---

[115] Especially, given that, as we have already seen, Conant's conception of nonsense seems to make *reductios* impossible anyway.

Hegelian philosopher who has made Christianity *easy* by doing away with its apparent paradoxicality and it is *this* idea that causes Climacus so much vexation. In order, therefore, to show that this thought is a misconception spawned by philosophical *hubris*, Climacus decided to make difficulties everywhere (CUP 187).

V.3 Thesis Three: Climacus' 'Substantive Claims'

That the foregoing is the central problem of CUP is revealed particularly aptly in a remark that Climacus makes in the book about *Either/Or*: 'That there is no conclusion and no final decision is an indirect expression for truth as inwardness and in this way perhaps a polemic against truth as knowledge' (CUP 252). For, as Climacus says:

> direct communication about what it means to exist and about inwardness will only have the result that the speculative thinker will benevolently take it in hand and let one slip in along with it. The system is hospitable! Just as a bourgeois-philistine, without regard to compatibility, takes along every Tom, Dick and Harry when he goes on an excursion to the woods, inasmuch as there is room enough in the four-seated Holstein carriage, so also is the system hospitable—there is indeed plenty of room. (CUP 250)

In other words, what Climacus seems to be worried about here is that the speculative philosopher will read Climacus' elucidations about the nature of Christianity as simply being one more addendum to the system, one more attempt at 'mediation', when the whole point of CUP is to challenge the very terms in which speculative philosophy poses the problem.

Effectively, what Climacus is trying to do in CUP is similar to Wittgenstein's description of his project in the preface to the TLP—that he wants to draw a limit to the expression of thought in language, not to thought as such, for in order to do *that* it would have to be possible to think what lies on both sides of the limit, that is, it would have to be possible to think the 'unthinkable'. In the same way, Climacus can only show what faith is indirectly, that is, negatively, by showing what it is *not*, as saying what it *is* would fly in the face of Climacus' own view, namely that Christianity is not a doctrine[116] and that the apostles were not a little professional society of scholars. He says:

---

[116] But see the discussion of the two senses of 'doctrine' operating in CUP in chapter 4, section III.

Just as for an existing person the highest principles of thinking can be demonstrated only negatively . . . so also for an existing person the existence-relation to the absolute good can be defined only by the negative—the relation to an eternal happiness by suffering, just as the certitude of faith that relates itself to an eternal happiness is defined by uncertainty. (CUP 455)

Consequently, it is not possible to *say* how one can become a Christian. Therefore, and strictly speaking, as Climacus himself says, 'the book is superfluous. Therefore, let no one bother to appeal to it, because one who appeals to it has *eo ipso* misunderstood it.' (CUP 618)

Conant naturally takes the misunderstanding that Climacus refers to in the latter quotation to consist in taking at face value what Climacus is apparently offering us in CUP: a dubious philosophical theory about the incommensurability between faith and reason—a piece of doctrinizing, when in fact the point of the book is ethical. That is, on Conant's reading, the reader must come to recognize that all appearance of doctrine is merely pseudo-doctrine. This is a misconceived interpretation of the foregoing passage. The misunderstanding that Climacus wants to avoid is the thought that he has anything to *teach* us, that he is an authority on matters of faith: precisely because faith cannot be reduced to a set of theses, however, there is no such thing as being an authority on it, just as no one can be an authority on 'existence'. 'Existential truths'—perhaps one way of understanding what early Wittgenstein meant by the 'ineffable'—cannot be directly communicated in the sense of giving someone a recipe for how to live. Therefore, it would be absurd, on Climacus' view, to suppose that someone could become a Christian as a result of reading CUP; and it is partly in order to guard against just this kind of absurdity, to which the theocentric nineteenth century seemed especially prone, that Climacus revokes the book. Therefore, *pace* Conant, Climacus does not revoke the book in order to signal to the reader that *he*, Climacus, has himself become mired in a conceptual confusion that has turned half the book into patent nonsense, but rather to prevent the reader from thinking that conceptual *clarification* about what Christianity is can somehow turn one into a Christian. Furthermore, Climacus wants specifically to prevent the Hegelian speculative philosopher from confusing Climacus' conceptual clarification with *speculative philosophy*—as if Climacus' remarks in CUP could simply be made into one more footnote to the all-encompassing 'system'.

In the light of this, it is also possible to make sense of the 'theses' that Conant takes to be obviously nonsensical. Climacus' polemic against 'objective truth', for example, should also be read against the backdrop of Hegelian speculative philosophy—the self-professed 'pinnacle' of objectivity. Climacus notoriously claims in CUP that in religious matters 'truth is subjectivity'. What he means by this is that because, according to him, the question of faith is not an objective, empirical issue which can be resolved by appeal to evidence, historical or otherwise, we have to concentrate instead on the 'existential' or personal significance that this question has for us. This is what Climacus means by 'subjectivity'—that is, pertaining to the subject—and this has nothing to do with relativism or irrationalism, as Conant seems to think. Climacus says:

> The way of objective reflection turns the subjective individual into something accidental and thereby turns existence into an indifferent, vanishing something. The way to objective truth goes away from the subject, and while the subject and subjectivity become indifferent, the truth becomes indifferent, and that is precisely its objective validity, because the interest, just like the decision is subjectivity. (CUP 193)

In other words, it is precisely because religious belief does not, on this view, consist of assenting to a set of propositions that Climacus holds that in order to resolve the question of faith I must be interested in it as an existing person, not as a lofty scholar. For religious belief, on this conception, is something much more fundamental than simply being of the *opinion* that God exists.[117] That is to say, Christianity, according to Climacus, does not call for an intellectual response (which would be entirely appropriate if the latter were a philosophical theory to be comprehended and assessed), but rather for an 'existential', that is, 'personal' or 'subjective', response along the lines of: do I, Johannes Climacus, believe that Christ is who he said he is? And this question cannot to be settled by, for example, deliberating on whether Christianity has presented the world with a true doctrine about the 'two natures' of Christ, since the Son of God has not come into the world in order to set Hegel a metaphysical riddle:

---

[117] See also a more detailed discussion of these points in chapter 4, section III.

Christianity is not a doctrine about the unity of the divine and the human, about subject-object, not to mention the rest of the logical paraphrases of Christianity. In other words, if Christianity were a doctrine, then the relation to it would not be one of faith, since there is only an intellectual relation to a doctrine. Christianity, therefore, is not a doctrine but the fact that the god has existed. (CUP 326)

So, even if, *per impossibile*, there could be such a thing as empirical evidence, say, for a religious claim, then, on Climacus' view, it would no longer be a *religious* belief, and belief in the Last Judgement, for example, would not be fundamentally different from the secular belief that one will be put into prison for certain crimes. Of course the very concept of 'belief' would then become obsolete too, as, on this conception, it makes no sense to say that I believe in something that is, as it were, before my very eyes. That is to say, in a world where 'God' could empirically manifest himself, our concept of a 'God' to be believed in would lose its point. Climacus puts it like this:

Without risk, no faith. Faith is the contradiction between the infinite passion of inwardness and the objective uncertainty. If I am able to apprehend God objectively, I do not have faith; but because I cannot do this, I must have faith. If I want to keep myself in faith, I must continually see to it that I hold fast to the objective uncertainty, see to it that in the objective uncertainty I am out on 70,000 fathoms of water and still have faith. (CUP 204)

What Climacus means here by 'objective uncertainty' isn't *empirical* uncertainty, but rather the kind of uncertainty that accrues to making certain 'existential' choices. The '70,000 fathoms of water' are not referring to the extreme degree of 'empirical uncertainty', then, but to the intellectual and existential risk you take when you stop pondering a question 'objectively' and rather want to resolve it by making a decision, that is, by changing the way you live in the relevant way. What Climacus is consequently referring to is the *risk of commitment*—and that is always a risk, be it in the religious domain or in other walks of life where you cannot remain dispassionate and disinterested (what Climacus means by 'objectivity'). Where something *can* be resolved objectively (that is, by appeal to empirical evidence), however, faith, on this view, becomes conceptually impossible and passion becomes madness. Hence, someone, says Climacus, who clings to something finite that could be settled objectively with the passion appropriate only to faith is on the brink of insanity (which is just what happens in the case of religious fanatics or religious fundamentalists).[118]

Now that we have made sense of Climacus' distinction between the 'objective' and the 'subjective', it is also possible to understand what Climacus means by the absurdity of the Christian paradox (the eternal—i.e. God—having entered time, having become a human being). When Climacus speaks of 'objective absurdity' he does *not* mean an absurdity that is somehow more 'absurd' than the absurd, as Conant seems to suppose. Rather, the use of the term 'objective' is supposed to alert us to the fact that the 'absolute paradox' cannot be comprehended, that is, made sense of, from the 'objective perspective'—from a disinterested, philosophical point of view. The reason why Climacus feels driven to use such high-pitched rhetoric in this passage is because the target of it is not, *pace* Conant, Climacus *himself*, that is, we are not supposed to be taken in by the illusion that he intends to advance a peculiar doctrine only to see in the end that we were led astray. Rather, the target is again the Hegelian philosopher who believes he can use reason to go 'further' than faith by sublating (*aufheben*) the paradox. But it is not possible to go further than faith, as faith, for Climacus, is not speculative (theoretical) and therefore, given that the Hegelian thinks that philosophy *is* speculative, it is not possible to use something speculative to 'outrun', as it were, something non-speculative. Climacus says:

Here the question is not whether Christianity is in the right but about what Christianity is. Speculation leaves out this preliminary agreement, and this accounts for its success with mediation. Before it mediates, it has already mediated, that is, changed Christianity into a philosophical theory. But as soon as the agreement establishes Christianity as the opposite of speculative thought, then *eo ipso* mediation is impossible, because all mediation is within speculation. If Christianity is the opposite of speculation, then it is also the opposite of mediation, since mediation is speculation's idea . . . But what is the opposite of mediation? It is the absolute paradox. (CUP 379)

In other words, what Climacus is saying here is that the Christian paradox is 'absolute', not because, as Conant supposes, it is 'maximally

---

[118] This shows, incidentally, that Conant is wrong to think that if we take Climacus' 'substantive claims' seriously, we must be licensing 'grisly forms of fanaticism' (KWN 214).

indigestible to reason'[119] or qualitatively the most 'absurd', whatever that may mean, but because, not being a *metaphysical* concept, there is no such thing as 'mediating' it. Hence, we are not confronted by an especially resilient species of philosophical concept; rather, because 'mediation' pertains only to speculative (that is, metaphysical) thought which, according to Climacus, is the very opposite of Christianity, we would be making a category mistake in Climacus' view, if we thought that the central question of Christianity—whether or not to believe in Christ—could admit of a theoretical (speculative) answer.[120] That the Hegelians thought it could is the central misunderstanding that CUP sets out to resolve.[121]

Consequently, what Climacus wants to get the reader to see is that because Christianity is not a philosophical theory, the issue of whether or not to believe in Christ can only arise for someone who wants *to be a Christian*, that is, it has to arise *subjectively*, for from the speculative point of view, the question doesn't even come up.[122] This does not imply, however, that the paradox thereby ceases to be a problem even for the person who has faith. In fact, what Climacus is suggesting, I think, is that it has to remain a problem, in order to prevent a person from relating to the Christian truth in the wrong way—namely objectively

---

[119] It is important to note here that Climacus doesn't use the word 'reason' (*Fornunft*) at all, but rather employs 'understanding' (*Forstand*). I agree with Walter Lowrie that Kierkegaard does this in order to prevent readers from thinking that 'believing against the understanding' has anything to do with believing logical contradictions, i.e. with believing something irrational. This is not to say, however, that Kierkegaard is drawing any kind of 'formal' distinction between the two terms or that he is using them in a Kantian or a Hegelian sense. In other words, it doesn't imply that 'reason' is consequently a higher principle for which the paradox is sublated. For a good discussion of the distinction, see Andrew Burgess, '*Forstand* in the Swenson-Lowrie Correspondence and in the "Metaphysical Caprice"', in Robert Perkins (ed.), Philosophical Fragments *and* Johannes Climacus, *International Kierkegaard Commentary* (Macon, GA: Mercer University Press, 1994), 109–28.

[120] For a more detailed discussion of these points, see chapter 4, section III.

[121] Kierkegaard in other material (e.g. in his preparatory notes and PF) sometimes seems to flirt with a stronger version of the notion of 'absolute paradox', but I think that the one I have developed here is (a) the one most likely to make sense and (b) what Climacus seems to have in mind in CUP.

[122] In 'Putting Two and Two Together' Conant holds that Climacus' distinction between 'subjective' and 'objective' problems comes down, in the end, to presupposing 'the existence of a category of problem that reason cannot penetrate; it seems as if we need to mark out that which reason can comprehend from that which it cannot' (292). This is a misunderstanding fuelled by pressing the analogy with a 'new' Wittgensteinian reading of the *Tractatus* too hard. A 'subjective' *point of view* or approach is *not* the 'logically alien' counterpart to 'objective thought'.

(as if to a theory), which would turn Christianity into paganism or idolatry. Climacus says:

> Suppose that Christianity does not at all want to be understood; suppose that, in order to express this and to prevent anyone, misguided, from taking the road of objectivity, it has proclaimed itself to be the paradox. Suppose that it wants to be only for existing persons and essentially for persons existing in inwardness, in the inwardness of faith, which cannot be expressed more definitely than this: it is the absurd,[123] adhered to firmly with the passion of the infinite. (CUP 214)

The emphasis on 'existence' is crucial here, because Climacus believes that it is impossible for any finite, existing being to apprehend truth *sub specie aeterni* (which is just what the Hegelians denied). And this provides us with another clue as to why Climacus calls the paradox 'absolute':

> But the absolute paradox, precisely because it is absolute, can be related only to the absolute difference by which a human being differs from God... But the absolute difference between God and a human being is simply this, that a human being is an individual existing being... whose essential task therefore cannot be to think *sub specie aeterni*, because as long as he exists, he himself, although eternal, is essentially an existing person and the essential for him must therefore be inwardness in existence; God, however, is the infinite one, who is eternal. (CUP 218)

The reason why Climacus is emphasizing the finitude of human beings here is, I think, because it is an awareness of finitude that tends to draw people out of and away from themselves, as it were, in the search of an objective point of view—of the God's eye view. Christians are just as finite as anybody else. Therefore Christians too exhibit this tendency, and this is why the absolute paradox represents a continuing challenge even from the perspective of the Christian way of living. The challenge, or the ongoing struggle, is continually to reaffirm oneself, as a Christian, as someone with the relevant unconditional commitments, sustained in the face of the temptations to objectivity (theorizing) with which one's finitude presents one. Thus, getting away from seeing the absolute paradox as an intellectual or philosophical problem is not something that one can do once and for all. Rather, it is something that one has to keep on doing, and it is in *that* process that the authentically Christian relation to the understanding (and indeed to the relation between faith and the understanding) can be recognized.

---

[123] By 'absurd' Climacus means something resistant to 'objectification' (and consequently 'mediation'). For a related point, see Annemarie Pieper, *Kierkegaard* (Munich: C. H. Beck, 2000), 48–60.

From the non-Christian perspective, then, the paradox cannot be understood.[124] From the Christian perspective, the paradox is Christ, the God-Man, the 'sign of contradiction',[125] who is a mere human being to non-believers but God to the faithful. But precisely because Christ is such a 'sign of contradiction', whether He is *in deed* God, is not something that can be settled by theoretical means and consequently faith does not consist of saying 'yes' or 'no' to the 'thesis' that 'Christ is the Son of God'.[126] When Climacus therefore speaks of the paradox as 'absolute', what he means is that only an existential ('subjective') response to the question is possible in the sense that I either become a follower of Christ or I reject Him: offence or faith. No theoretical ground is available here to determine whether the 'thesis' or its converse is philosophically defensible or not. Hence, to call the paradox 'gibberish', as Conant does, is to regard it as a philosophical thesis and this simply re-enacts the very error of the Hegelians. And if we will, for a moment, allow Kierkegaard himself to speak (for after all he is not only the 'editor' of CUP, but in actual fact its author), we will find further corroboration of my interpretation. Kierkegaard says to a reviewer who has objected to this notion:

But the absurd is a category, and a category that can have a restraining influence. When I believe, then assuredly neither faith nor the content of faith is absurd. Oh, no, no—but I understand very well that for the person who does not believe, faith and the content of faith are absurd, and I also understand that as soon as I myself am not in the faith, am weak, when doubt perhaps begins to stir, then faith and the content of faith gradually begin to become absurd for me.[127]

In other words, as long as I am in the faith, Kierkegaard seems to be saying, and have an existence-relation to Christ, the very idea that I should regard my religious commitment as commitment to a theoretical claim which may stand in the need of proof, will strike me as ludicrous and absurd. In moments of doubt, however, which are generally moments of detachment, I may indeed begin to see my faith in such terms, and from such a perspective it may indeed seem to me that

---

[124] But see chapter 4, section III—the remarks on 'external' and 'internal' understanding.
[125] See chapter 1, section II, for a discussion of this point.
[126] For further elaboration of this see chapter 4, section III.
[127] Quoted in the Supplement to FT, 262.

Christianity is a bizarre metaphysical doctrine about the 'two natures' of Christ.[128] But this is a temptation, a sign that I am beginning to lose my faith, not the 'correct', because 'objective', point of view.

Is this dangerously close to what Conant calls a 'substantive conception of nonsense'? I think not, *unless* one wants to maintain that *anything* which would count as a properly religious remark, on Climacus' view of religion, just *has* to be nonsense and that it is consequently not only impossible to say how one might become a Christian, it is impossible, too, to say anything (distinctive) about Christianity at all. And this is a position that Climacus evidently does not share. If this is what Conant would say, then just as the Hegelians settle the question in advance by assuming that everything meaningful can be made objective and speculative, so Conant settles the question in advance by assuming that anything non-objective and (non-Christianly) grammatical must be meaningless. And this would surely be simply a case of begging the question against Climacus, who, as I have emphasized before, nowhere says that the absolute paradox is gibberish.

Nor am I saddling Climacus with the view that CUP somehow provides us with insights into 'ineffable' religious truths—another corollary of the 'substantive conception'—for this is precisely the view that Climacus rules out when making the distinction between 'objective' and 'subjective' ways of approaching religious faith. For Climacus' account expressly denies that there are any truths to be 'glimpsed', as this would again reduce Christianity to aesthetics or paganism (to something that could, in principle, be 'directly perceivable' if one just had the relevant faculties).[129] He says:

If the paradoxical-religious address does not pay attention to this (the incomprehensibility), it abandons itself to the mercy of a legitimate ironic interpretation, whether the address peers behind the curtain with a revivalist's muzziness and spiritual intoxication, reads the obscure runes, catches a glimpse of the explanation, and now sermonizes it in a singing tone that is the echo of the seer's unnatural association with the marvellous . . . The basis of the misunderstanding is that, despite the use of Christ's name etc., Christianity has been shoved back into the aesthetic (something the superorthodox unwittingly are especially

---

[128] Of course I can also have moments of being, as it were, 'existentially' offended at Christ *à la* Nietzsche. Climacus' *alter ego*, Anti-Climacus, has quite a lot to say about this in PC, but Climacus is less concerned with it in CUP, as he is, in that work, taking on the 'speculative nineteenth century'.

[129] That is, what Climacus is saying entails a rejection of what I call the 'target view' of religion in chapter 4.

successful in doing) . . . which in time has its explanation in something higher behind itself, rather than in Christianity's being an existence-communication that makes existing paradoxical, which is why it remains the paradox as long as there is existing and only eternity has the explanation.[130] (CUP 562)

What I hope to have shown in this section is that it is perfectly possible to make sense of the remarks of Climacus' that Conant takes to be patently nonsensical and that Conant consequently has no reason to drive a firm wedge between the innocuous 'categorical distinctions' and the rest of CUP. On my reading, *all* of the remarks Climacus makes are on a par; they can all be read as conceptual elucidations of the nature of Christianity, whether we like them or not. The ever-present irony in the work is therefore not directed at Climacus' own theses, but at the misconceptions of the Hegelian (or neo-Hegelian) philosopher. In this sense, there is also nothing wrong with calling these remarks a 'contribution to knowledge'—what Conant is most averse to—as long as this is *not* taken to imply that Climacus is advancing a *theory* about Christianity or about how to become a Christian. That Conant seems to think that this is not even a remote possibility, stems, I believe, from his holding that philosophy can only do one of two things: peddle nonsensical metaphysical theories, or offer us a therapy for that tendency by advancing mere truisms and/or by dispelling those metaphysical illusions. I see no reason to believe, however, that the kind of conceptual clarification that Climacus (and also the later Wittgenstein) offers us need fall into either of these categories.

V.4 Thesis Four: The 'Difficulty' of Becoming a Christian

Climacus characterizes the difficulty of becoming a Christian in the following way:

My intention is to make it difficult to become a Christian, yet not more difficult than it is, and not difficult for the obtuse and easy for the brainy, but qualitatively and essentially difficult for every human being, because, viewed essentially, it

---

[130] What Climacus means by 'only eternity has the explanation' is unclear to me. But I think that Climacus' tendency sometimes to phrase things in an infelicitous way can be explained by the fact that, despite his quarrel with Hegelianism, the Hegelian framework has clearly left its mark on his thinking, so that certain inconsistencies in the text are due to vestiges of Hegelian categories creeping in now and again. These, though, do not pose a problem, I think, for a generally consistent interpretation of Climacus' work.

is equally difficult for every human being to relinquish his understanding and his thinking and to concentrate his soul on the absurd; and it is comparatively most difficult for the person who has much understanding, if one recalls that not everyone who has not lost his understanding over Christianity thereby demonstrates that he has it. (CUP 557)

The understanding, Climacus is suggesting here, is repelled by the very idea of having to let go of objectivity—of, as Climacus says in PF, 'surrendering itself' (PF 54). But given that, as I have argued, the paradox cannot be understood from the speculative perspective, if the understanding continues to cleave to pondering this question objectively, then the only possible response to it is offence.[131] If, however, the understanding realizes that the only correct response to the paradox is subjective appropriation, then the result will be the 'happy passion' (PF 54) of faith. But it is exactly this that, Climacus thinks, the understanding is loathe to do. In this much, then, becoming a Christian involves a 'crucifixion of the understanding': if we take the paradigm of 'understanding' to be the 'objective stance'[132]—a paradigm that Climacus shared with the Hegelians—then any non-objective response will naturally be something 'over which the understanding despairs' (CUP 292). Thus, the difficulty of becoming a Christian consists, among other things, of the ever-present struggle against the temptation to view the claims of Christianity objectively—a struggle so intense that Climacus calls it a 'martyrdom'.[133]

---

[131] Or the attempt to change Christianity into paganism, into something for which there could be evidence.

[132] Effectively, Climacus in CUP, is identifying understanding in the 'objective' sense with what I call 'external' understanding in the next chapter. Hence, 'subjective appropriation' would be something like what I have called 'internal' understanding in chapter 4. See chapter 4, section IV.

[133] It might be objected here that I seem to present the options Christianity confronts us with exclusively as being either 'subjective appropriation' or a confused attempt to 'view the claims of Christianity objectively'. This is a misunderstanding. I do not (as already mentioned in note 128) rule out the possibility of a properly existential offence at Christianity *à la* Nietzsche. The reason I am emphasizing the objective stance in this section, rather than speaking of existential offence, is because I am arguing against Conant's view that the only kind of offence there is is *existential* offence. Everything else, according to Conant, is plain gibberish. I, on the other hand, am trying to defend the view that when Climacus speaks of a 'crucifixion of the understanding' he is not, *pace* Conant, drawing attention to the fact that the absolute paradox is plain nonsense. That is to say, I am trying to give a coherent account of what Climacus might mean when he speaks of a crucifixion of the *understanding*—an account that will not commit him to an espousal of Conant's dreaded 'substantial nonsense'. So while it is the case that the 'problem of the objective vantage-point' exists for any existentially serious view in the sense that in

The problem with Christianity is therefore not simply a *practical* one, as Conant seems to urge. It is not simply a matter of deciding to lead a certain kind of life, for this life only becomes a possibility once we have realized that the objective point of view stands in the way of a genuine relationship to the Christian teaching. Furthermore, even the committed Christian has to keep battling against the seductiveness of the objective stance, according to Climacus, as there is no such thing as having faith once and for all: '(Faith is) the mortal danger of lying out on 70, 000 fathoms of water, and only there finding God' (CUP 232).

V.5 The Point of the Revocation

At this point I should make explicit what I take Climacus' reasons for revoking CUP to have been, since the revocation is, after all, the chief textual cue for Conant's interpretation. On my reading, the revocation serves three purposes. First, clearly to distinguish CUP from speculative philosophy. Second, to show that conceptual clarification about what Christianity is cannot turn one into a Christian, for in order to become one, one has to enter into an *existence-relationship* with Christ. In this respect, what Climacus is worried about is that the reader will be content to occupy the metaphilosophical stance CUP seemingly lets her occupy, that is, that she will be content simply to note the grammatical differences between genuine Christian faith and the travesty Hegelianism makes of it, without letting these differences impinge on her life in the relevant way. The third purpose of the revocation is this: Climacus is ironically[134] hedging his bets against attacks by the Danish Church, given that he is writing 'without authority' and given that what he says clearly flies in the face of orthodoxy. That this is one of the main reasons for the revocation—one that Conant, for obvious reasons, overlooks—is revealed by Climacus' juxtaposing his revocation with the way in which Catholic writers traditionally sought to avoid censorship or accusations of heresy:

such cases the emphasis is always on existential appropriation rather than intellectual contemplation, in the case of Christ, for example, intellectual (speculative) contemplation can only lead to offence—offence at an 'inherently incoherent' notion such as the God-Man—something that is not true in the Socratic case, for instance, where, even if entirely point-missing, some sort of 'intellectual' understanding of Socrates' ethics is still possible.

[134] Conant assumes throughout that Climacus' revocation is to be read 'straight', i.e. that he is not being ironic when apparently 'revoking' his work. However, if we take seriously Climacus' conception of himself as a humorist, then surely the possibility that the revocation itself is, as it were, part of the humour, cannot simply be dismissed offhand.

Just as in Catholic books, especially from former times, one finds a note at the back of the book that notifies the reader that everything is to be understood in accordance with the teaching of the holy universal mother Church, so also what I write contains the notice that everything is to be understood in such a way that it is revoked, that the book has not only an end but has a revocation to boot. (CUP 619)

On my reading, that is, the revocation has nothing whatever to do with Climacus' coming to realize that the majority of CUP is patently nonsensical; and that, it seems to me, is a strength of my reading. Nowhere, after all, does Climacus so much as *hint* that the distinction between sense and nonsense, or the non-distinction between mere and substantial nonsense, is any part of his concern. And that the revocation can be read—and read perfectly naturally—without imputing that concern to him confirms me in the view that that concern was, indeed, not his. The revocation does not depend for its sense upon the importation of any extra machinery at all, let alone upon the importation of the kind of machinery that Conant brings to it.

VI INTERIM CONCLUSIONS

Conant's interpretation of CUP fails. Climacus' assertion that 'what can be indirectly communicated, cannot be directly communicated' has nothing to do with the problem of 'ineffability' or of 'substantial nonsense'. That Conant thinks it has is, surely, due to his wanting to read the same strategy into CUP that he believes works for the TLP, as well as his implicitly wishing to do away with aspects of the book that he finds philosophically problematic. I have argued, however, that Climacus' concept of the absolute paradox, far from being a species of 'substantial' or 'mere' nonsense, rather undercuts the very standpoint from which such a distinction could be drawn. For, as Climacus has tried to show, attempting to 'understand' the paradox 'objectively'—by, for example, mediating it away or calling it nonsensical—is, from the Christian perspective, equally wrong-headed.

If this is correct, then we simply don't have to choose between ascribing to Climacus a form of irrationalism (*à la* Mackie and Plantinga, say) or read him, *à la* Conant, as the peddler of mere nonsense. Both alternatives involve the mistaken assumption that Climacus can't possibly mean (most of) what he says and that it is consequently a matter of realizing either that he never meant to say anything in the first place (Conant) or that he is just an incoherent thinker (proponents of 'irrationalist' readings). But if I am right, there is a third way and we need not collude with those who think that there is no such thing as Kierkegaard's religious *thought*.

VII KIERKEGAARD AND THE MYSTICISM OF THE *TRACTATUS*

So far we have seen that Conant's argument for the parallels he perceives in Wittgenstein's TLP and Kierkegaard's CUP depends on ascribing to both authors the desire to free the reader from the illusion that there is such a thing as 'logically alien thought' —conceived as ineffable truth in the case of Wittgenstein and a kind of 'super-nonsense' (such as the absolute paradox) in the case of Kierkegaard. I hope to have shown, however, that no such parallel is, in fact, discernible. For, whilst Wittgenstein is clearly committed to the notion of ineffabilia in the TLP, Climacus'/Kierkegaard's project in CUP has nothing whatever to do with such a conception. A profound disanalogy therefore exists, in this respect, between the early Wittgenstein and Kierkegaard. Wittgenstein himself is therefore guilty of imputing his own concerns to Kierkegaard when he said to Waismann, 'we thrust against the limits of language. Kierkegaard, too, recognized this thrust and even described it in much the same way (as a thrust against paradox)'.[135] Naturally, as we already saw in the first chapter, once Wittgenstein came to realize that language is not a cage against whose bars we can thrust, he also revised this particular interpretation of his favourite author. Consequently, the temptation to read Kierkegaard in Tractarian vein as either repudiating an ineffability conception (in the manner of Conant), or as espousing this (in the manner of Wittgenstein himself), needs very much to be resisted.

The points of contact that can therefore be perceived between the early Wittgenstein and the Danish philosopher cannot be located in the actual endorsement (or rejection) of similar views about the nature of language and what lies beyond its limits, but are rather to be found in a certain commonality of vision as regards ethics and religion. As I already mentioned in the third section of this chapter, Engelmann's

---

[135] See note 75.

characterization of Wittgenstein as an 'ethical totalitarian' can with equal justice be applied to Kierkegaard. Furthermore, there is much in their respective conception that appears, simultaneously, to be inspired by Kant as well as by a rigorous Augustinian conception of Christianity. For example, both Wittgenstein's[136] and Kierkegaard's view of ethics is radically anti-consequentialist: the ethical must be willed purely for its own sake and whatever effects my actions might have in the external world are completely irrelevant, since everything that happens in that world is utterly contingent and therefore, no matter how good my intentions are, they can always bring about a bad result. Consequently, what actually comes to pass is out of an individual's control and no blame or praise can legitimately attach to it. This is how Climacus puts it:

True ethical enthusiasm consists in willing to the utmost of one's capability, but also, uplifted in divine jest, in never thinking whether or not one thereby achieves something. As soon as the will begins to cast a covetous eye on the out-come, the individual begins to become immoral . . . —the individual demands something other than the ethical itself. A truly great ethical individuality would consummate his life as follows: he would develop himself to the utmost of his capability; in the process he perhaps would produce a great effect in the external world, but this would not occupy him at all, because he would know that the external is not in his power and therefore means nothing either *pro* or *contra*. (CUP 135–6)

That the external means nothing either *pro* or *contra* is also a consequence of Wittgenstein's Tractarian view of ethics that we have already touched upon. Given that Wittgenstein believes, in the TLP, that value is located outside the world and is, in this respect, transcendental like logic (§6.421), it follows that ethical actions cannot be events in the world, for if they were to be so construed, this would *eo ipso* strip them of all *ethical* content. In the *Lecture on Ethics* Wittgenstein explains:

Suppose one of you were an omniscient person and therefore knew all the movements of all the bodies in the world dead or alive and that he also knew all the states of mind of all human beings that ever lived, and suppose this man wrote all he knew in a big book, then this book would contain the whole description of the world; and what I want to say is, that this book would contain nothing that we would call an *ethical* judgement or anything that would logically imply such a judgement . . . all the facts described would, as it were, stand on the same level and in the same way all propositions stand on the

---

[136] When I say Wittgenstein in this section, I mean early Wittgenstein.

same level. There are no propositions which, in any absolute sense, are sublime, important or trivial . . . Ethics if it is anything, is supernatural and our words will only express facts; as a teacup will only hold a teacup full of water even if I were to pour out a gallon over it. (PO 39–40; compare TLP §6.41)

In other words, given Wittgenstein's dogmatic distinctions between what can and cannot be said and between fact and value, it cannot but follow that the ethical must either be a chimera or an inexpressible, mystical something. For Wittgenstein is trying to square the circle here by attempting to wed a positivistic view of language—sentences can only picture facts—to a romanticized absolutist conception of ethics. But, as Wittgenstein himself says, given that 'no state of affairs has, in itself, what I would like to call the coercive power of an absolute judge' (PO 40), such an attempt is *ex hypothesi* doomed to failure. And this is why Wittgenstein ends up drawing the same conclusion as Climacus when he says that 'the question about the *consequences* of an action must be unimportant.—At least those consequences should not be events. For there must be something right about the question we posed. There must indeed be some kind of ethical reward and punishment, but they must reside in the action itself' (§6.422). Notice how much this chimes with CUP:

Victory in the outer demonstrates nothing at all ethically, because ethically the question is only about the inner. Punishment in the outer is negligible, and far from insisting with aesthetic busyness on visible punishment, the ethical proudly says: I shall punish, all right, namely, in the inner, and it is plainly immoral to class punishment in the outer as something comparable to the inner. (CUP 297)

Hence, although both philosophers have followed entirely different paths—Climacus is here criticizing the Hegelian notion of the identity of the inner and the outer while Wittgenstein is simply following through on his logical commitments—they nevertheless end up arriving at the same destination. That is to say, in order to defend the absolute demands of ethics against the encroachment of the claims of contingency, the ethical is relegated, in both authors, to the realm of inwardness. The 'coercive power of an absolute judge' that both Kierkegaard and Wittgenstein require of the ethical is therefore to be found, on their conception, not in some external sanction, but rather within the individual himself in the sense that his good or evil willing becomes constitutive of the kind of world that individual inhabits. This is why Wittgenstein says:

if the good or bad exercise of the will does alter the world, it can alter only the limits of the world, not the facts—not what can be expressed by means of language. In short the effect must be that it becomes an altogether different world. It must, so to speak, wax and wane as a whole. The world of the happy man is a different one from that of the unhappy man. (TLP §6.43)

Without of course endorsing the concomitant Tractarian metaphysics, Kierkegaard seems to have something similar in mind when he distinguishes, for example, between the different existence spheres. For these, too, are in a relevant sense entire 'worlds' that require the use of different concepts which only become available once an individual has undergone an inner transformation. As Climacus says:

In the world of spirit, the different stages [spheres] are not like cities on a journey, about which it is quite all right for the traveller to say directly, for example: We left Peking and came to Canton and were in Canton on the fourteenth. A traveller like that changes place, not himself; and thus it is all right for him to mention and to *recount* change in a direct, unchanged form. But in the world of spirit to change place is to be changed oneself, and therefore all direct assurance of having arrived here and there is an attempt *à la* Münchhausen. (CUP 281)

Again, although the target here is Hegel and his 'direct assurance', in the system, of having reflected himself out of immediacy, the underlying idea is clearly the same as Wittgenstein's: ethical (or religious) transformation takes place in the inner and can't be cashed out directly, as it were, in philosophical propositions.

In other words, Kierkegaard's and Wittgenstein's emphasis on the inner is the result of a common moral absolutism that is to guard, as it were, the sanctity of the ethical, as well as of a shared sense of powerlessness in the face of the contingency of the world which can, at any moment, reduce my ethical striving to nothing. Wittgenstein speaks, in this context, of being completely dependent on an 'alien will' and in this way the ethical very quickly acquires a religious countenance:

To believe in God is to understand the question of the meaning of life. To believe in God is to see that the facts of the world are not the end of the matter. To believe in God is to see that life has meaning. The world is *given* me, i.e. my will approaches the world completely from the outside as something finished . . . That is why we have the feeling that we depend on an alien will. *However this may be*, we *are*, in any case, in a certain sense dependent and what we are dependent on, we can call God. God would, in this sense, simply be fate or, what is the same: the world independent of our will. I can make myself independent of fate . . . In order to live happily, I have to be in agreement [*Übereinstimmung*] with the world . . . I am then, as it were, in agreement with that alien will on which I seem dependent. This means: 'I am doing the will of

God'. . . When my conscience throws me off balance, I am not in agreement with something. But what is this? Is it *the world*? It must be correct to say: conscience is the voice of God.[137]

Sections §6.43–§6.4321 of the TLP are clearly modelled on these remarks from the *Notebooks*, without, however, identifying being in agreement with the world with doing the will of God. In fact, the only reference to God (in a religious context) occurs at TLP §6.432 where Wittgenstein says: '*How* things are in the world is a matter of complete indifference for what is higher. God does not reveal himself *in* the world.' But given that Wittgenstein goes on to say, at §6.4321, that the facts all belong to the task not to the solution, this makes it clear, I think, that he must have had something similar to what is in the *Notebooks* in mind. Indeed, as §6.43 cited above tells us, Wittgenstein, in the TLP, seems explicitly to identify the good will with being in agreement with the world (the facts), with being happy and with doing the will of God. In other words, what he seems to be saying is that when my conscience does not, as it were, throw me off balance, that is, my will is good, I am in agreement with the world, I am consequently doing the will of God and the world, to use his Tractarian metaphor, waxes as a whole. Hence, the important thing for Wittgenstein is not *how* the world is or *what* I do, but rather the *spirit* in which I view it and in which I perform my duties.

Climacus has a similar conception in mind when he writes, echoing Kant:

But freedom, that is the wonderful lamp. When a person rubs it with ethical passion, God comes into existence for him. And look, the spirit of the lamp is a servant . . . , but the person who rubs the wonderful lamp of freedom becomes a servant—the spirit is the Lord . . . So the resolving person says: I will—but I also want to have world-historical importance—*aber* [but]. So there is an *aber*—and the spirit vanishes again, because the rubbing has not been done properly, and the beginning does not occur. But if it has occurred or has been done properly, every subsequent *aber* must again be renounced, even if existence in the most flattering and inveigling way did everything to force it upon one. (CUP 138–9)

Climacus here voices, albeit more poetically, many of the same ideas as Wittgenstein above: the notion that to serve the ethical is to do the will of God as well as the thought that this only becomes a possibility once I

---

[137] 8.7.1916, translation mine.

renounce my stake in worldly affairs—once, as Wittgenstein would put it, I make myself independent of the facts. For, as Wittgenstein says in another *Notebook* entry, 'Even if everything we desired happened, this would only be the luck of the draw, as there is no logical connection between will and world' (5.7.1916). And a little later he adds, in Stoic vein, 'only that life is a happy one which is able to renounce the comforts of the world. For such a life these comforts are just so many mercies of fate' (13.8.1916).[138]

For both Wittgenstein and Climacus, then, the ethical life is a life of renunciation and in this sense it is very close to the religious. One would consequently be very much misled if one were to think that because the two authors emphasize, like Kant, the 'inner', or, as Climacus would say, 'subjectivity' (in the sense developed in section VI), as of paramount importance in ethics, the force of the ethical 'ought' is in any way diminished thereby. Quite to the contrary: if one's conscience is, indeed, conceived to be the voice of God, then its wrath is more terrible than any external punishment could be, since, as Climacus notes so perceptively:

If in my relationship with God I regard what I am doing as good and do not keep watch over myself with the infinite's mistrust of me, then it is just as if God, too, were content with me, because God is not something external that quarrels with me when I do wrong but the infinite itself that does not need scolding words, but whose vengeance is terrible—the vengeance that God does not exist for me at all, even though I pray. (CUP 162–3)

Hence, on the conception that Wittgenstein and Kierkegaard share, there is an internal connection between the good will (moral virtue) and faith and a lack of the latter, as has already been pointed out in the first chapter, is therefore tantamount to a moral failing. This is why Wittgenstein says in a letter to Engelmann from 1918 that 'it is obvious that someone who wants to invent a machine in order to become a better person, that such a one has no faith'.[139] For someone who shirks the painful process of inner transformation and would rather create a *deus ex machina* in order to do the work for him, is clearly still enslaved, in Climacus' words, to the '*abers*' of this world and consequently the spirit of the Lord vanishes again. The result is the hopelessness and despair that Wittgenstein felt—as the coded diary entries confirm—during

---

[138] Both translations mine.   [139] See chapter 1, note 23.

much of this time and that Anti-Climacus depicted so ably in *The Sickness unto Death*: terrible vengeance, indeed.

In other words, Kierkegaard's and Wittgenstein's quasi-religious conception of ethics implies what Anti-Climacus calls the 'upbuilding thought' of being a self 'directly before God': a self, that is, that has God and not the merely human as a criterion. As Anti-Climacus puts it:

[the] self takes on a new quality and qualification by being a self directly before God. And what infinite reality the self gains by being conscious of existing before God, by becoming a human self whose criterion is God! . . . Just as only entities of the same kind can be added, so everything is qualitatively that by which it is measured, and that which is its qualitative criterion [*Maalestok*] is ethically its goal [*Maal*]. (SUD 79–80)

That is to say, on such a conception, human guilt cannot but be infinitely magnified into sin, which perhaps explains the intense feelings of moral worthlessness that plagued Wittgenstein throughout his life. For with God or God's will as the measure of moral conduct, every failing becomes a sin against God. As Anti-Climacus confirms:

because sin is against God it is infinitely magnified. The error [of older Christian dogmatics] consisted in considering God as some externality and in seeming to assume that only occasionally did one sin against God. But God is not some externality in the sense that a policeman is. The point that must be observed is that the self has a conception of God and yet does not will as he wills, and thus is disobedient. Nor does one only occasionally sin before God, for every sin is before God, or, more correctly, what really makes human guilt into sin is that the guilty one has the consciousness of existing before God. (SUD 80)

Here Anti-Climacus repeats and religiously accentuates the point made by Climacus above that, because God is not something external, or, as Wittgenstein says in the TLP, does not reveal himself in the world, it is impossible ever to escape his scorching gaze, for this is located within. So, to continue with Climacus' metaphor, the wonderful lamp of freedom must be handled with care, as the spirit of the Lord, once conjured up, is here to stay. That is to say, once a self recognizes that it is before God, Wittgenstein and Kierkegaard seem to agree, it can never divest itself of this knowledge on pain of losing itself or, what amounts to the same, plunging into despair. Hence, and as has already been pointed out in the first chapter, Wittgenstein would also agree with Anti-Climacus that the opposite of sin and despair is not virtue, but faith, and that, as Wittgenstein said in 1914, 'Christianity is the only *certain* way to happiness.'[140]

Anti-Climacus' definition of faith as 'that the self in being itself and in willing to be itself rests transparently in God' (SUD 82) can therefore be seen to parallel Wittgenstein's identification, in the *Notebooks* and in the TLP, of being in agreement with the world (the facts) with doing the will of God and with being happy. For the 'faithful' self that wills to be itself is, in Wittgenstein's parlance, in agreement with itself and the world—that is, it 'happily' accepts the limitations and constraints imposed upon it from outside without viewing this as cause for despair. So the self, in faith, despite constantly struggling to better itself, bears a positive relation towards itself and the world. In this respect, the self's particular constitution and the way the world happens to be (the facts) becomes irrelevant in the sense that both these things, as Wittgenstein says, only belong to the task, not the solution. The self must therefore continue to work on itself—must, as Climacus puts it, continue to strive—but without regarding the way it is made or the tasks that the world sets it as reasons, as it were, to pick a quarrel with God. The attainment of such a perspective is consequently marked by not feeling at odds with the world (or alienated from oneself) and by ceasing to perceive life as a problem. This is why Wittgenstein says, 'the solution of the problem of life is seen in the vanishing of the problem' (TLP §6.521).

In order for such a perspective of faith to be a genuine possibility, however, Anti-Climacus would argue, real trust in God is necessary and this involves the conviction on the side of the believer that for God everything is possible:

The *believer* sees and understands his downfall, humanly speaking . . . , but he believes. For this reason he does not collapse. He leaves it entirely to God how he is to be helped, but he believes that for God everything is possible . . . The believer has the ever infallible antidote for despair—possibility—because for God everything is possible at every moment. This is the good health of faith that resolves contradictions. (SUD 39–40)

Hence, with this armour, so to speak, the self, in faith, avoids both possibility's despair, what Anti-Climacus characterizes as the failure to obey, 'to submit to the necessity in one's life', and necessity's despair, a kind of fatalism that can see nothing but unalterable facts (determinism). Wittgenstein's account in the TLP—although containing all other aspects of Anti-Climacus' formulation—is devoid of this dimension of possibility, for what it proposes is merely what Johannes *de Silentio* calls infinite resignation (the renunciation of all relative ends). And although *de Silentio* would agree that the dying to immediacy that early Wittgenstein proposes—renouncing the comforts of the world—is a necessary condition for faith, it is only the last step before faith and not equivalent to faith itself, as the knight of faith, in the end, regains the world after having renounced it. Wittgenstein's identification of the will of God with the world seems to preclude this, however, as, on his conception, happiness can only be achieved by making one-self completely independent of the facts. But if God and the world (the facts) are equated as in Wittgenstein's *Notebooks*, then this would seem to imply also having to make oneself independent of God. There consequently appears to be an unavoidable tension in Wittgenstein's position: on the one hand, in almost Spinozistic vein, he identifies God with the world and on the other he claims that God does not manifest himself *in* the world (in the TLP). Both views ultimately create imped-iments to Anti-Climacus' conception of faith, for they appear to leave God, as it were, with no room to manoeuvre at all.[141] Hence it seems that Wittgenstein, given his ethical-religious conception, has contracted Anti-Climacus' disease—the sickness unto death—but without, in the end, being able to reach for the 'radical cure' that Christianity would provide.

So far we have seen, then, that Kierkegaard and Wittgenstein share a Kant-inspired absolutist conception of ethics, which, however, ulti-mately goes beyond Kant's, for it is inextricably bound to the notion of God's inexorable presence and constant admonishment. Furthermore, Wittgenstein and Kierkegaard both reject the German philosopher's rationalistic view that even God is subject to the decrees of human reason[142] (see below). In a conversation with the Vienna Circle from 1930 Wittgenstein makes this clear:

---

[141] This parallels the problem that Wittgenstein's conception of ethics faces: if ethics is transcendental and can only alter, as it were, the limits of the world, this would seem to leave one with a very impoverished notion of agency indeed. In fact, the problem is in many ways analogous to Kant's problem of how there can be interaction between the noumenal realm of ethics and the empirical world. It is no part of my concern in this section, however, to argue for the consistency of Wittgenstein's views, but merely to point out interesting continuities with Kierkegaard's.

[142] See, for example, Immanuel Kant, *Die Religion innerhalb der Grenzen der bloßen Vernunft* (Stuttgart: Reclam, 1974), 201–6; 245–53.

Schlick says that there are two conceptions of the essence of the good in theological ethics: according to the more superficial view, the good is good because God wills it; according to the more profound view, God wills the good because it is good. I believe that the first conception is the more profound: good is what God commands. For it cuts off the way to any kind of explanation of why the good is good, whereas the second conception is precisely the superficial, rationalistic one which pretends that reasons can be given for this. The first conception clearly states that the essence of the good has nothing to do with the facts and can consequently not be explained by a proposition. If there is a sentence that expresses precisely what I mean, it is this: good is what God commands.[143]

That God is the *terminus ad quem* or final arbiter on what is good or absolute, and that no further grounds can be given for this, is also Johannes *de Silentio*'s view in FT, where the issue is presented in a particularly radical way using the biblical story of Abraham and Isaac as a paradigmatic example. In the section entitled 'Is There an Absolute Duty to God?' *de Silentio* says:

The ethical is the universal, and as such it is also the divine. Thus it is proper to say that every duty is essentially duty to God, but if no more can be said than this, then it is also said that I actually have no duty to God . . . God comes to be an invisible vanishing point, an impotent thought, his power is only in the ethical, which fills all of existence.[144] Insofar, then, as someone might wish to love God in any other sense than this, he is a visionary, is in love with a phantom, which, if it only had enough power to speak, would say to him: I do not ask for your love—just stay where you belong. (FT 68)

If Kant and Hegel are right, in other words, then, as *de Silentio* goes on to point out, Abraham cannot be the father of faith he is commonly hailed to be, but ought rather to be regarded as an especially abhorrent type of potential murderer. For Abraham conceived his duty to God as absolute, i.e. as something over and above all his other duties, even the duty to his son. And on such a conception, *pace* Kant and Hegel, it must at least in principle be possible that a collision can occur between one's duty to God and all one's other ethical commitments. If this is deemed impossible *ab initio*, then, as *de Silentio* says, it implies that there actually is no duty to God, but then of course there is also no

---

[143] *Wittgenstein und der Wiener Kreis*, 115, translation mine.

[144] Notice how this echoes the Kantian view: 'There are no special duties to God in a common [*allgemeinen*] religion; for God cannot receive anything from us; we cannot act upon or for him', *Die Religion innerhalb der Grenzen der bloßen Vernunft*, 202, translation mine.

such thing as faith, as the 'coercive power of the absolute judge' then becomes nothing more than the impotent power of an underlabourer of the ethical (and hence, on the Kantian view, of reason).

Consequently, what both Kierkegaard and Wittgenstein are rejecting here—and this is a feature that remains constant throughout the latter's authorship—is the craving for explanation and the idea that everything can be justified by appeal to the high court of reason. And this temptation, both philosophers believe, is all-pervasive: it is a deep-seated *malaise* that is not only to be found in ethics and religion, where, both would argue, it is especially pernicious, but in philosophy and science as well. It is surely not coincidental that in the sections directly preceding Wittgenstein's remarks on ethics and the mystical in the TLP, he says:

There is no compulsion making one thing happen because another has happened. The only necessity that exists is *logical* necessity. The whole modern conception of the world is founded on the illusion that the so-called laws of nature are the explanations of natural phenomena. Thus people today stop at the laws of nature, treating them as something inviolable, just as God and Fate were treated in past ages. And in fact both are right and both wrong: though the view of the ancients is clearer in so far as they have a clear and acknowledged terminus, while the modern system tries to make it look as if *everything* were explained. (TLP §6.37–§6.372)

Compare this with what Climacus says in CUP:

An objective religious person in the objective human mass does not fear God; he does not hear him in the thunder, because that is a law of nature, and perhaps he is right. He does not see him in events, because they are the immanental necessity of cause and effect, and perhaps he is right. But what about the inwardness of being alone before God? Well, that is too little for him; he is not familiar with it, he who is on the way to accomplish the objective. (CUP 544)

In other words, what both Kierkegaard and Wittgenstein are saying in these passages is that it is possible to see the world in two different ways: in terms of the 'so-called laws of nature' or as manifestations of the will of God or of Fate. Neither conception can be finally justified or absolutely grounded and this, at least, the religious perspective makes clear by acknowledging, as Wittgenstein says, 'a clear terminus'. In this respect, both authors believe, the religious conception is ethically superior to the scientific one, for it curbs philosophical (or scientific) *hubris* by recognizing a clear limit. What is more, both authors seem to urge, although there need not be a necessary conflict between the two points of view, that the scientific conception, just like metaphysical speculation, can stand in the way of seeing things from a religious perspective. For in order for a religious vantage point to be possible, one needs, as Wittgenstein says, to awaken to wonder, and in its desire to explain everything, 'science is a way of sending him [man] to sleep again' (CV 5e). And this is also the reason why, according to Climacus, the 'objective man' knows nothing about the inwardness of being alone before God, as the *spirit* in which science is carried on these days is not, in the end, compatible with such a conception.

Hence, it is precisely in order not to be the kind of philosopher who, as Climacus says, makes 'supernatural[145] things ordinary and banal' (PF 53) that early Wittgenstein banishes all that is great and important—ethics, aesthetics and religion—into the realm of the ineffable and eschews all theorizing about it. For in the sphere of value, Wittgenstein thinks, theories will necessarily bypass the problems which trouble us:

Whatever one were to tell me, I would reject it, and precisely not because the explanation is wrong, but because it is an *explanation*. . . One cannot teach the ethical. If I could only explain the nature of the ethical to someone else by means of a theory, then the ethical would have no value. . . *For me* a theory has no value. A theory does nothing for me.[146]

Or, as Climacus would say, the solution to the problem of life is not to be found in a *doctrine*—in a sum of propositions that gives me a recipe for how to live—but, rather, 'in the vanishing of the problem' (TLP §6.521), which, Kierkegaard and Wittgenstein agree, can only be brought about by the right way of life. And here we have re-established contact with the beginning of this chapter, for we are now in a position to understand the spirit in which the final 'proposition' of the TLP is intended. It is, as Wittgenstein writes in the letter to von Ficker, an *ethical* demand for silence which springs, like Wittgenstein's later work, from his identification of purity of thought with purity of heart: where only babble or transcendental twaddle is possible, it is a sin not to hold one's tongue.[147]

---

[145] This should not be taken to imply that Climacus thinks that religion is, in any ordinary sense of the word, 'supernatural'.

[146] *Wittgenstein und der Wiener Kreis*, 116–17, translation mine.

[147] Now one might think that I have, in this section, been 'chattering away', as Conant says, 'about the ethical insights that can only be "shown" but not said: thereby coming out and telling us what the (putatively) unsayable content of a given ethical utterance is' (see Conant, 'What "Ethics" in the *Tractatus* is *Not*', in D. Z. Phillips and Mario von der Ruhr (eds), *Religion and Wittgenstein's Legacy* (Aldershot: Ashgate, 2005), 58–9). And indeed I have. But, given that Wittgenstein himself is in exactly the same boat, I

CONCLUSION

We have, in this chapter, as Wittgenstein says in the preface to the PI, made some long and involved journeyings whose object has been to show that a 'resolute' way of conceiving of the parallels between Kierkegaard and the early Wittgenstein is mistaken. By way of concluding, I would now like briefly to say something about the continuities and discontinuities in Wittgenstein's work and their relation to Kierkegaard.

As we have seen, Wittgenstein not only subscribed to what I would like to call 'methodological dogmatism' in the TLP—Conant's view that certain metaphysical requirements are already lodged in Wittgenstein's conception of philosophical clarification[148]—but rather that he also held dogmatic metaphysical views about the nature of language and logic, which led to the rigid distinction between what can and cannot be said. Hence, it is not just that Wittgenstein's method and style changes from his early to his later work, there is also a profound philosophical disagreement about language between the early and the later author. For the early Wittgenstein believed, as we have seen, that the really deep things, such as logic, ethics and aesthetics, cannot be articulated in language at all, as they are in some sense a precondition of language and the world, and whatever is a precondition of language cannot be expressed in language, but can only be reflected by it, that is, can only be shown, but not said (TLP §4.121, §4.1212). For the later Wittgenstein, the 'preconditions of language' no longer have this mystical dimension. They rather become the rules that are constitutive of our various language-games. There is no agreement between language and the world which is made possible by a transcendental logical form: rather, there is only language and agreement in language (PI §241). If

am afraid that this problem cannot be avoided unless we are happy just to write off, in the manner of Conant, as literally nonsensical most of what it says in Wittgenstein's first book. This, however, seems to me to be a very high price to pay for getting round an interpretative problem: Wittgenstein's early views—mistaken and confused though they clearly are in many ways—are far too interesting and philosophically stimulating simply to be thrown away *tout court*. So, although, strictly speaking, one could say that in the light of his metaphysical commitments about language, Wittgenstein should not have written the TLP or, at any rate, should not have written more than proposition 7: 'what we cannot speak about we must pass over in silence', this would have hardly been very rewarding for the reader.

[148] See Conant and Diamond, op.cit., 82–5.

for the early Wittgenstein language is ultimately a mirror that reflects a transcendental logical form that language and world mysteriously share, then for the later Wittgenstein language is altogether more humble and no longer 'reflects' anything that might 'point' beyond it. Consequently, while the author of the PI is content simply to describe our actual practices and to make the reader see how and why we are bewitched by language, the author of the TLP tried to show how things *must* be. In other words, while the later Wittgenstein, by using models (language-games) merely as objects of comparison, is in fact content to hold up a mirror to the reader in which she can see all the deformities of her own thinking, the early Wittgenstein tried to construct a looking-glass that would ultimately reflect what *he* wanted to see.

Despite this profound disagreement about language, however, there is also some significant continuity in Wittgenstein's development and this is primarily to be located in his (ethical) conception of philosophical activity. It is precisely because the early and the later Wittgenstein agree that one must not advance theses in philosophy that Wittgenstein's earlier self gets into the predicament about ineffability in the first place. That is to say, despite claiming that the result of philosophy does not consist of philosophical propositions, but the elucidation of propositions (TLP §4.112), the early Wittgenstein did hold metaphysical views about the harmony between language and the world, which had, in some way, to be made explicit. Consequently, the only path open to Wittgenstein was to state these 'philosophical propositions' and then, as it were, to revoke them. In this respect the TLP exemplifies the last manifestation of 'man's eternal metaphysical urge',[149] for it not only attempts to bring metaphysics to an end, it also, at the same time, annihilates itself. Engelmann puts it well: '[Wittgenstein] nullifies his own world picture, together with the "houses of cards" of philosophy (which at that time at least he thought he had made collapse), so as to show "*how little is achieved when these problems are solved*".'[150] Just as in the case of Climacus' CUP, a personal appropriation of the book's (ethical) message is thus more important than its 'content': once it has been grasped that the TLP is trying to convey an impossible perspective, ethical progress is made by the reader when she gives up the futile attempt to 'utter the unutterable'. That is to say, the TLP's ethical point consists precisely in curbing metaphysical *hubris*

[149] Paul Engelmann, op.cit., 95.   [150] Ibid.

by constructing a self-refuting system: the ladder dissolves around us once we have scaled its rungs and have seen, as Wittgenstein puts it in the *Lecture on Ethics*, that 'this running against the walls of our cage is perfectly, absolutely hopeless' (PO 44).[151] In this respect, Wittgenstein, contrary to Climacus himself, is, as Kierkegaard says of Hegel, 'a kind of Johannes Climacus who wishes to storm heaven with his syllogisms'.[152]

Wittgenstein's later work no longer has a need for such ascensional devices, however, since it exposes the self-defeating Tractarian endeavour to capture 'the essence of the world' on paper as a transcendental illusion. As a result, there are no longer any hidden depths to plumb or any mystical heights to ascend to and the gap between the 'strictly correct method'(§6.53) and Wittgenstein's own philosophical practice is firmly closed. Hence Wittgenstein's rejection of the ladder metaphor in the draft for a foreword to *Philosophical Remarks* composed in 1930: 'If the place I want to get to could only be reached by way of a ladder, I would give up trying to get there. For the place I really have to get to is a place I must already be at now. Anything that I might reach by climbing a ladder does not interest me' (CV 7e). In this respect the shift from early to later Wittgenstein is a perfect example (as Wittgenstein notes one year later) of philosophy as (ethical) work on oneself (CV 16e), for it is primarily his own set of illusions and philosophical prejudices that Wittgenstein is dismantling in PI[153]—a paradigmatic case, in other words, of self-overcoming.

Once Wittgenstein has managed to rid himself of his peculiar attachment to ineffabilia and along with it of his dogmatic conception of the general form of the proposition and its concomitant fact/value distinction, it is possible for him to break the silence that the TLP had imposed on all discussion of questions of meaning and value. For the downfall of the aforementioned Tractarian commitments also spells doom for the idea that there is anything 'intrinsically nonsensical' (as the *Lecture on Ethics* insists) about ethical and religious statements and this paves the way for a more sophisticated and convincing account of how religious language, for example, might operate—an account which, as we shall see in the following chapter, is, in many ways, indebted

---

[151] Hence, what Conant and Diamond call early Wittgenstein's 'toleration of contradiction' is the upshot simultaneously of Wittgenstein's metaphysical entanglements as well as of his ethical commitments.

[152] See Introduction, note 1.   [153] See, for example, PI§89–119.

to Kierkegaard and which does not involve, *pace* Conant (and those inspired by him), either settling for a 'mere nonsense' conception or for a form of 'fideism'.[154]

In other words, although we have seen in the present chapter that if we are prepared to take at face value—rather than write off as nonsense[155]—Wittgenstein's remarks about ethics and the mystical in the TLP (and the *Notebooks*), interesting parallels can be discerned between early Wittgenstein's conception of ethics and religion and Kierkegaard's. But given that the Dane did not, contrary to Wittgenstein himself, espouse any form of ineffability conception, far more significant similarities can be perceived between the two thinkers once Wittgenstein has waved goodbye to this commitment and a whole cloud of philosophy has, as it were, been condensed into a drop of grammar (PI, II, 222). For the later Wittgenstein's fully-fledged anti-metaphysical bent is much more in keeping with Kierkegaard's own vision of things, both as regards philosophical authorship and in respect to the nature of religious belief.[156] Consequently, although both the early and the later Wittgenstein, as well as Kierkegaard himself, want to achieve the change

---

[154] Kai Nielsen, for example, who, as we shall see in the following chapter, is concerned to show that religious concepts are incoherent, would like the resolute reading of the TLP to apply across the board: 'This [the tendency to thrust against the walls of our cage that Wittgenstein mentions in LE] shows clearly enough Wittgenstein's respect for human beings and his sense for what deep needs such religious utterances and the experiences that go with them answer to, but it does nothing to show that there is any error in our claim that, on his *Tractarian* account, religious conceptions . . . must be just nonsense: straightforward nonsense. Seen clearly, that is, they are seen to be what they are, namely just nonsense though where seen through a glass darkly—seen confusedly—they remain *disguised* nonsense. But disguised nonsense is all the same nonsense' (*Wittgensteinian Fideism?*, 235). In other words, although Nielsen is aware that this account does not reflect Wittgenstein's mature views of religion, this is, in Nielsen's mind, what religious utterances really come down to: they are either plain nonsense or, at best, 'morality touched by emotion' (ibid., 314; see chapter 4, section III, for discussion of these points).

[155] Conant, of course, believes that there is no such thing as Ethics with a capital 'E' in the TLP and that all putatively ethical and mystical remarks are part of the book's nonsensical corpus. He does think, however, that the TLP has an 'ethical point', but that this is not to be found in anything that the 'ethical' propositions in it purport to say (see 'What Ethics in the *Tractatus* is Not', op.cit., 72). I believe, *pace* Conant, that there are ethical remarks in the TLP that deserve to be taken seriously, and also think, as has been shown, that the TLP has an ethical point. A book can both contain remarks about ethics *as well as* have an ethical point (and the two need not necessarily be connected in an obvious way). Indeed, this is true of most of Kierkegaard's works and especially, as we have seen, of CUP.

[156] Which is why I have devoted so much time to a discussion of both these issues in chapters 2 and 4.

in perspective that, in the end, makes all philosophical talk superfluous, Wittgenstein's Tractarian self never, ultimately, accomplishes the task of not giving in to metaphysical temptation. But it is precisely this failure that highlights the enormous pain and effort involved in bringing about the ethical self-transformation that Wittgenstein and Kierkegaard concertedly aspire to in their work. For, as it turns out, it is actually less difficult to throw away the ladder than it is not to construct one in the first place.

4

A Confusion of the Spheres—Kierkegaard's and Wittgenstein's Conception of Religious Belief

> Disobedience is the secret in the religious confusion of our age. This same disobedience also lies as the first falsehood, but more hidden and unconscious, at the base of what is the fundamental harm in modern speculation, that there has been a confusion of the spheres: profundity has been mistaken—for authority; the intellectual—for the ethical; being a genius for being an apostle.
>
> Petrus Minor, *The Book on Adler*[1]

INTRODUCTION

In one of his most controversial and misunderstood remarks Wittgenstein writes: 'If Christianity is the truth then all the philosophy that is written about it is false' (CV 83e). Not only could this statement serve as a second motto for the current chapter, it also comprises a fitting epitaph to Climacus' polemic against Hegel discussed in section V of the previous one. The remark, in other words, not only contains in a nutshell some of Wittgenstein's best insights on religion, it also testifies yet again to the Kierkegaardian pedigree of much of Wittgenstein's thought on this theme. In the present chapter I hope to cast further light on this connection by showing that Kierkegaard's and Wittgenstein's work on religion can be read as offering a trenchant critique of one of the most pervasive, but, to my mind, misconceived, ways of construing

[1] Petrus Minor, BA 5.

religious belief in both philosophy and theology. I shall call this the 'target view' of religion.

In the first two sections of this chapter I will focus on the claims that the 'target view' is committed to and on the criticisms that Kierkegaard and Wittgenstein bring forward against it. Subsequently, in section III, I will consider some of the most important objections levelled at Kierkegaard's and Wittgenstein's alternative vision, notably the charge that their account removes the 'content' from religious belief and reduces it to the expression of 'emotional attitudes', as well as Kai Nielsen's related objection that it gives rise to a 'fideism'[2] which renders religious belief 'incommensurable' with other forms of discourse and thus immunizes it against rational criticism. I intend to show that these kinds of criticism misfire, as they all spring from a false dichotomy between 'practice' and 'belief' or between 'living a certain way' and 'believing certain things' that, if we understand Kierkegaard and Wittgenstein correctly, cannot be upheld.

I THE 'TARGET VIEW' OF RELIGION

For a brief characterization of the kind of position that Kierkegaard and Wittgenstein are targeting in their work, we can turn to Richard Swinburne whose conception of religious belief exhibits all the hallmarks of what I am calling the 'target view'.[3] In his essay, 'Philosophical Theism', for example, Swinburne describes the 'theory that there is a God' in the following way: 'God is supposed to be roughly a person without a body, essentially omnipotent, omniscient, perfectly free, perfectly good, creator and sustainer of any universe there may be, a source of moral obligation, eternal and necessary.'[4] Of course,

---

[2] Kai Nielsen, 'Wittgensteinian Fideism', *Philosophy* XLII/161 (1967).

[3] This view is by no means peculiar to Swinburne. Other firm advocates of it, although coming from the opposite direction, are, among others, Anthony Kenny, J. L. Mackie, and Antony Flew (although he has apparently recently switched sides without, however, abandoning a version of the 'target view' of God). More nuanced proponents of the target view on the theistic side are, for example, Paul Helm (see his *Faith With Reason* (Oxford: Oxford University Press, 2000)) and the Reformed Epistemologists, such as Plantinga and Woltersdorff. For a detailed analysis and criticism of the Reformed project, see D. Z. Phillips's excellent book, *Faith After Foundationalism* (London: Routledge, 1988), especially Part One.

[4] Richard Swinburne, 'Philosophical Theism', in D. Z. Phillips and Timothy Tessin (eds), *Philosophy of Religion in the 21ˢᵗ Century* (New York: Palgrave, 2001), 8–9.

Swinburne concedes, 'to talk of the source of all being involves using words in somewhat stretched senses', but then, he adds, so does—albeit it in a 'humbler way'—'talk about photons and protons'.[5]

Given that (ordinary) persons, according to Swinburne, are 'beings with power to bring about effects intentionally, beliefs (true or false) about how things are, and some degree of freedom to exercise their power',[6] God, on Swinburne's conception, 'is postulated as a being with zero limits to his power, to his true beliefs, and to his freedom'.[7] The making of such an assumption is, to Swinburne's mind, good scientific practice which always prefers 'on grounds of simplicity hypotheses which postulate one entity rather than many, and entities with zero or infinite degrees of their properties rather than some finite degree thereof'.[8] And although Swinburne admits that the 'existence of anything at all is perhaps enormously improbable a priori, the existence of a very simple being [such as God] has a far higher prior probability than does the existence of anything else'.[9]

On Swinburne's construction, therefore, the claim that God exists is a scientific theory or hypothesis, which differs only in scope and not in kind from the question, say, of whether elementary particles exist or not. Furthermore, it is the purpose of philosophical theism, on Swinburne's conception, to provide cogent arguments for the existence of such a being[10] by way of appealing to the only 'true set of criteria' we have, the 'modern scientific criteria'. Swinburne says:

We all have the modern scientific criteria of what is evidence for what, and to say that we have these criteria is just to say that we believe that the results which they yield about what is probable to be correct results. If we thought that there are no true criteria of what is evidence for what, we would think it just as likely that if we jump from a window we will fly, as that we will fall to the ground. Our conduct shows that we do not think so.[11]

Swinburne's account, in other words, commits him to the following three interrelated theses which I take to be constitutive of what I am calling the 'target view':

1. God is the name of a super-empirical entity or being.
2. There is one correct way of describing the world and this description either contains an object (entity, item) such as God or it doesn't.

[5] Swinburne, 'philosophical Theism'.   [6] Ibid., 9.   [7] Ibid.   [8] Ibid.
[9] Ibid.   [10] Ibid., 3.   [11] Ibid., 18.

3. The proposition 'God exists' is a hypothesis to be investigated empirically and/or by a priori argument.

Kierkegaard and Wittgenstein, it should come as no surprise, would reject all three of these claims. In the next section, by way of developing their own distinctive account of religious belief, I will explicate their reasons for doing so.

II A CRITIQUE OF THE 'TARGET VIEW': THE KIERKEGAARD-WITTGENSTEIN CONCEPTION

So far we have seen that Swinburne, like Wittgenstein's Father O'Hara, 'is one of those people who make it a question of science' (LC 57). Wittgenstein's response to this account is brusque:[12]

I would definitely call O'Hara unreasonable. I would say, if this is religious belief, then it's all superstition. But I would ridicule it, not by saying it is based on insufficient evidence. I would say: here is a man who is cheating himself. You can say: this man is ridiculous because he believes, and bases it on weak reasons. (LC 59)

What Wittgenstein is saying here, in other words, is that if the Swinburne-O'Hara view of religious belief is correct, then religion is reduced to nothing more than superstition, that is to say, to a form of false science. Kierkegaard would concur: as we already saw in the previous chapter, Climacus castigates the Christians in Christendom precisely for deluding themselves into believing they are Christians, when they are, in his eyes, really nothing more than pagans or idol-worshippers who believe that God is some externality in the sense that a policeman is (SUD 80). Recall Climacus' sarcastic remark that:

if God had taken the form, for example, of a rare, enormously large green bird with a red beak, that perched in a tree on the embankment and perhaps even whistled in an unprecedented manner—then our partygoing man would surely have had his eyes opened . . . All paganism consists in this, that God is related directly to a human being, as the remarkably striking to the amazed. (CUP 245)

The error that Kierkegaard and Wittgenstein first and foremost seek to expose, then, consists in taking the existence of God to be on a par with the existence of some super-empirical object or entity which one

---

[12] See also chapter 1, section II.

could, in principle, encounter if only one possessed the relevant faculties. That is to say, the conception that Kierkegaard and Wittgenstein have within their sights is of the kind exhibited by the Soviet astronaut Yuri Gagarin's remark that God is an object he would have observed, had it existed, during his first space flight.[13] For, on this sort of view, there is no *qualitative* difference between being God and being some other kind of entity—that is, something one could encounter—but merely a quantitative one: God, as Swinburne says, is merely an (invisible) entity with 'zero limits to His power', as opposed to an entity (such as a human being) with infinitely many limits to its power. But such a view leaves open the possibility that, for all we know, God could, for instance, be a Giant Pumpkin since, as Swinburne himself concedes, if we allow that God is the name of a super-empirical something, the question immediately arises *which* 'super-empirical' entity—there might conceivably be more than one—the word 'God' is supposed to be referring to and it consequently becomes a matter of trying to distinguish belief in God from belief in other, similarly powerful, entities.[14] [15] This is none too easy a thing to do, though, for, *prima facie*, Swinburne's definition of God as a super-powerful person without a body, if it makes any sense at all,[16] does not appear to make any more (or less) sense than the idea of a super-powerful pumpkin. That is to say, if it were in fact possible to assign probability values to the existence of such supernatural entities, as Swinburne clearly seems to believe, then an argument is needed to show why the existence of a bodiless super-human should have more 'prior probability' than the existence of an omnipotent super-pumpkin. Swinburne's claim that the postulated 'simplicity' of God's nature gives us a presumption in favour of His

[13] See John Hick, 'Religious Belief and Philosophical Enquiry', in D. Z. Phillips (ed.), *Faith and Philosophical Enquiry* (London: Routledge & Kegan Paul, 1970); see also D. Z. Phillips, 'Wittgenstein and Religion: Some Fashionable Criticisms', in D. Z. Phillips and Kai Nielsen, *Wittgensteinian Fideism?*, 48.

[14] Ibid., 9.

[15] On Kierkegaard's and Wittgenstein's view the question of whether God might not be a Great Pumpkin doesn't so much as arise, since, on their conception, it is not a *matter of fact*—that is, something that could be otherwise—that God is *not* a Great Pumpkin. Rather, that He is not is ruled out by the grammar of the concept of God.

[16] For a very clear exposition of why it does not make sense, see Peter Geach, 'Immortality', in his *God and the Soul* (Indiana: St Augustine's Press, 1969). (I do not have space to go into this issue here). In this article Geach argues that the concept of a human person without a body does not make sense, but, if he is right, then *a fortiori* the concept of a super-human and super-powerful 'person' without a body does not make sense either.

existence clearly isn't going to do this trick. For why should the Great Pumpkin, or, let us say, in order to make the analogy to Swinburne's God closer still, the Great Bodiless Pumpkin, not be just as 'simple' an entity as Swinburne's person-without-a-body—whatever 'simple' could really mean in such cases.[17]

What is more, Swinburne's argument that having 'zero limits to one's power' is a criterion for 'simplicity', since scientists also postulate that 'photons have zero mass' rather than some very small mass,[18] is just fallacious, as this is to construct a pseudo-analogy that relies on equivocation on the word 'zero': having 'zero limits', that is, being unlimited or limitless, is clearly not the same thing at all as having no weight. That is to say, the 'postulate' that God has no limits to his power is not even remotely comparable to the 'postulate' that protons have no weight or zero mass. Otherwise we might just as well say that having a temperature of 0K[19]—having *zero* temperature—is analogous to being unlimited which is absurd. Consequently, *contra* Swinburne, there simply is no analogy with science here. But even if there were, this would not of itself solve the reference problem of the word 'God', as nothing is easier than simply 'postulating' that the Great Bodiless Pumpkin (or what have you) has 'zero limits to its power' (provided the latter is even a coherent notion which, I suspect, it is not).

Wittgenstein tackles (what I have called) the target view's (henceforth TV) first thesis head-on when he says that 'the way you use the word "God" does not show *whom* you mean—but, rather, what you mean' (CV 50e). In other words, on Wittgenstein's conception, the word 'God' does not denote some *thing* that one could encounter independently of having the concept in the sense that one could, for example, encounter a unicorn or the Great Pumpkin, if there happened to be such things. For, although, as Wittgenstein says in LC, the word 'God' is amongst the earliest learnt, I didn't learn the word 'God' by being shown a picture of him (LC 59). That is to say, even though the word is used like a word representing a person (God sees, rewards, etc.), 'it plays an entirely different role to that of the existence of any person or object I ever heard of' (ibid.). In the later Wittgenstein's parlance: the surface grammar of the word 'God' functions in many ways analogously to

---

[17] And here it is important to bear in mind Wittgenstein's warning that the mere fact 'that one can "imagine" something does not mean that it makes sense to say it' (*Zettel* §250) 250).

[18] Swinburne, op.cit., 9.   [19] That is, −273.15°C.

that of an outlandish person while its depth grammar is actually quite different. This is shown, for example, by the fact that it is impossible, even in principle, to paint a picture of God[20] or to hear Him speak to someone else (*Zettel* §717). Neither of these features are *contingent* descriptions of God as they would be if, *per impossibile*, they happened to apply to a human person. Rather, they serve to constitute (aspects of) the meaning of the word 'God'. Perhaps this is why Wittgenstein cites theology as his first example when he says in one of the most famous passages from the PI: 'Grammar tells what kind of object anything is. (Theology as grammar.)' (§373). Consequently, if Wittgenstein is right, it is a *grammatical* (conceptual/logical) feature of the concept 'God' that you can't hear him talk to someone else. It is not due to the fact that God is a person with an impossibly low voice (or, indeed, a disembodied one).

Climacus seems to have something similar in mind when he says that 'God is not a name but a concept, and perhaps because of that his *essentia involvit existentiam* [essence involves existence]' (PF 41). Existence, according to Climacus, is a temporal phenomenon that presupposes change: every *Existenz* (existing thing) comes into and goes out of existence, but God is said to be eternal and immutable. *A fortiori* he cannot be said to 'exist' in the same sense as human beings do. 'Can the necessary come into existence?' Climacus asks himself at PF 74 and responds:

Coming into existence is a change, but since the necessary is always related to itself and is related to itself in the same way, it cannot be changed at all . . . Precisely by coming into existence, everything that comes into existence demonstrates that it is not necessary, for the only thing that cannot come into existence is the necessary, because the necessary *is*.

Stripped of some Hegelian jargon, what Climacus appears to be saying here is this. What is necessary is changeless—it always is and couldn't

---

[20] And Michelangelo's painting of God creating Adam is not a 'picture of God' in the relevant sense. As Peter Winch says in his illuminating essay 'Wittgenstein, Picture and Representation': 'In other words, what makes the picture a religious picture is not its pictorial relationship to some event. If it is said that it is a relationship to a *supernatural* event, that of course makes a difference: but the chances are that in this context the speaker will be conceiving the 'supernatural' event as a weird sort of *natural* event. So it is best to leave aside talk about 'a relationship to an event' altogether . . . let us not overlook the fact that what makes the picture a representation of God the Father (rather than of a man in a queer blanket) is not itself something pictorial.' (In Peter Winch, *Trying to Make Sense* (Oxford: Blackwell, 1987), 79–80.)

be otherwise without changing its nature or essence. Consequently, it makes no sense to speak of its 'coming into existence', for if it came into existence, it would precisely thereby become subject to change and cease to be necessary, as everything that is actual exists only contingently—it could always not exist (but the necessary, *per definitionem*, always is). Hence, God's 'existence' cannot be analogous to that of human beings, say, for it is part of the definition of the concept 'God' that His 'existence' is non-contingent and changeless. This is why Climacus says that 'God does not think, he creates; God does not exist, he is eternal' (CUP 332). In a nutshell: 'necessary existence' is not a *kind* of existence.[21]

This is also the conclusion that Wittgenstein draws when he says—perhaps alluding to the aforementioned passage from PF:

God's essence is supposed to guarantee his existence—what this really means is that what is at issue here is not the existence of some *thing*[22] [*daß es sich um eine Existenz nicht handelt*]. Couldn't one actually say equally well that the essence of colour guarantees its existence? As opposed, say, to white elephants. Because all that really means is: I cannot explain what 'colour' is, what the word 'colour' means, except with the help of a colour sample. So in this case there

---

[21] Norman Malcolm is essentially making the same point as Climacus when he says in his article 'Anselm's Ontological Arguments': 'If God, a being a greater than which cannot be conceived, does not exist then He cannot *come* into existence. For if He did He would either have been *caused* to come into existence or have *happened* to come into existence, and in either case He would be a limited being, which by our conception of Him He is not. Since He cannot come into existence, if He does not exist His existence is impossible.' (In *The Philosophical Review* 69/1 (1960): 49.) However, Climacus would quarrel with Malcolm's drawing the conclusion from this that if the concept of God is not logically absurd, then the ontological argument is valid, for according to it God's existence is either logically necessary or logically impossible. So, if the former is false, the latter must be true. Climacus, who accepts the view that existential propositions are contingent would regard this as a confused way of putting the valid point that God's 'existence' is not akin to that of ordinary empirical objects (whose existence is contingent). Hence Climacus would reject the claim Malcolm makes later in the paper that the proposition 'God necessarily exists' is a kind of 'existential proposition'. This Climacus would regard as misleading, for it invites us to construe—something Malcolm himself would want to reject—the sense of 'God exists' *à la* Swinburne as meaning something like 'protons exist'. See also note 26.

[22] Peter Winch translates '*daß es sich hier um eine Existenz nicht handelt*' as 'what is at issue here is not the existence of something' which is ambiguous between '*daß es sich hier um keine Existenz handelt*' (or '*daß es sich hier nicht um Existenz handelt*') and the original. But the phrase Wittgenstein actually uses implies that what he means is that what is at issue is not the existence of some entity (an existing thing—*eine Existenz*), and this gets lost in Winch's translation which could also be read as saying that what is at issue here is that something doesn't exist rather than that it is not about the existence of something (some *thing*).

is no such thing as explaining 'what it *would* be like if colours *were* to exist'. And now we might say: There can be a description of what it would be like if there were gods on Olympus—but not: 'what it would be like if there were such a thing as God'. And to say this is to determine the concept 'God' more precisely. (CV 82e)

What Kierkegaard and Wittgenstein are suggesting, then, when they say that 'God' is not the name of an entity and that what is at issue is not the existence of something, is *not*, as a superficial reading of these remarks might lead one to believe, that there is no God, but rather that it makes no sense to construe God's existence as meaning something like 'a white elephant exists'. In other words, the grammar of the concept 'God' does not function, *pace* Swinburne and TV, like the grammar of *eine Existenz* (of an entity). For if it did and we also accepted that as regards the concept *essentia involvit existentiam*, then Descartes and Hegel would appear to be right and the ontological argument would seem valid.[23] But this cannot be the case, since, as Climacus rightly insists, the ontological argument is either a 'fraudulent form of developing a predicate, a fraudulent paraphrase of a presupposition' (CUP 334) or else a mere tautology: 'the more perfect, the more being; the more being, the more perfect'—that is, 'the more perfect the thing is, the more it *is*; but its perfection is that it has more *esse* in itself, which means the more it is, the more it is' (PF 41). The problem with the argument,[24] as Climacus goes on to point out, is that no distinction is made in it between 'factual being' [*Vaeren/Sein/*being] and 'ideal being' [*Vaesen/Wesen/*essence]: 'With regard to factual being, to speak of more or less being is meaningless. A fly, when it is, has just as much being as the god . . . Factual being is indifferent to the differentiation of all essence-determinants' (PF 41–2). Existence, in other words, doesn't come in degrees and therefore nothing that exists can have more 'being' than something else that exists. Hence, when Leibniz, for example, says that if God is possible, he is *eo ipso* necessary,[25] what he is really talking about, according to Climacus, is God's 'ideal being'—His essence—not His 'factual being' (PF 42). Consequently, the argument can't be employed, Climacus says, in the manner of Spinoza and Descartes in order 'to bring God's ideality into factual being' (ibid.) If, however, the argument is construed only as a means of developing a concept—a way of explicating

---

[23] But see notes 21 and 26.
[24] In PF Climacus uses Spinoza's version from *Principia philosophiae Cartesianae*.
[25] See, for example, *Monadology*, para 44–5.

the concept's grammar—then, according to Climacus, 'the tautology is in order' (ibid.).[26,27]

This is also the reason why Wittgenstein says that it is possible to describe what it would be like if there were gods on Mount Olympus, but not 'what it would be like if there were such a thing as God'. For in pagan religions, just as on TV, the deities are conceived as on a par with other empirical objects, only vastly more powerful.[28] There is therefore no grammatical difference between talk of Poseidon, say, and talk of an ordinary human being, except that Poseidon happens to have super-human powers. But, as we have already seen, this is not qualitatively different from encountering a new species from a distant planet who have powers surpassing our own or, indeed, from encountering the Great Pumpkin. In Christianity, however, as we have just seen, talk of God is not like that. Consequently, it is possible to give an account of what would have to be the case, if there were a Poseidon or if there were a Great Pumpkin—since the opposite of these scenarios can also be imagined and described—but not how it would be if there were a God, or how it would be if God existed, for in these cases there simply is no such thing as imagining or describing 'the opposite'; the 'phenomena' in the world remain the same whether there is a God or not. To become aware of God's presence is therefore nothing like becoming aware of the existence of some esoteric object whose presence had hitherto escaped one's notice. This is the significance of Wittgenstein's remark that:

Life can educate one to a belief in God. And *experiences* too are what bring this about; but I don't mean visions and other forms of sense experience which show us 'the existence of this being', but, e.g., sufferings of various sorts. These neither show us God in the way a sense impression shows us an object, nor do

[26] The ontological argument also comes out as a tautology on Malcolm's construal of it: 'The a priori proposition "God necessarily exists" entails the proposition "God exists", if and only if the latter also is understood as an a priori proposition: in which case the two propositions are equivalent. In this sense Anselm's proof is a proof of God's existence' (op.cit., 50). But it is precisely for this reason that Climacus thinks it is misleading to call this a proof, for ordinarily people who want a proof of God's existence want God's 'ideal being' brought into 'factual being' and it's just this that the ontological argument, *qua* tautology or conceptual development, can't give you.

[27] This concludes Wittgenstein's and Kierkegaard's critique of TV's first thesis that God is the name of a super-empirical entity or being (but of course discussion of all three theses hangs together and there is consequently no entirely non-arbitrary way of marking off one stage of the overall argument against TV from the others).

[28] That this is, indeed, Swinburne's view is shown by the fact that he conceives of God as a 'super-human', i.e. as possessing all positive human attributes in superlative (infinite) form. See Swinburne, op.cit., 12.

they give rise to *conjectures* about him. Experiences, thoughts—life can force this concept on us. So perhaps it is similar to the concept of 'object'. (CV 86e)

What Wittgenstein is suggesting here by drawing an analogy between the concept 'God' and the concept 'object' is that the former functions more like the *formal* concept 'object' (*Gegenstand*) than like a word referring to a particular thing, such as a table, chair, white elephant or what have you. In other words, the two concepts are grammatically similar, according to Wittgenstein, in the sense that they would both make for nonsense when employed in the subject-place of ontological assertions: it would make as little sense, on Wittgenstein's view, to assert (or to deny) that objects exist as it does to assert (or to deny) that God exists. The reasons for this, initially perhaps rather baffling, claim are as follows.

Contrary to Moore, who insisted on the truth of this proposition against the sceptic, Wittgenstein thinks that the proposition 'there are physical objects' is a piece of philosophical nonsense, as, according to him, it is not an empirical proposition for which one could have evidence. Wittgenstein says, 'But can't it be imagined that there should be no physical objects? I don't know. And yet "there are physical objects" is nonsense. Is it supposed to be an empirical proposition?—And is *this* an empirical proposition: "There seem to be physical objects"?' (*On Certainty*, §35).

In order for the proposition 'there are physical objects' to make sense, it would have to be possible to know or to explain what would have to be the case if there were *no* physical objects. Should the proposition make sense, then it would have to be a kind of *hypothesis*, for which one could have evidence. But what would such evidence look like? Moore held the view that it is possible to infer 'there are physical objects' from the proposition 'here is a hand', but this was an illusion. For the latter means no more than that a hand *is* a physical object, and far from being an ontological hypothesis, this, according to Wittgenstein, is no more than a grammatical proposition that tells us what kind of thing a hand is. If this were an ontological hypothesis, then we would have to be able to indicate what would count as evidence for it, what as evidence against it, how the question could be settled beyond any reasonable doubt. But it is just this that is impossible, for we cannot explain what would be different if there were *no* physical objects, and, consequently, we also cannot explain what is the case when physical objects *do* exist. Furthermore, it is even less possible to give criteria for what would have to be the case if physical objects only *seemed* to exist, but do not actually do so (the classical sceptical scenario). All of this indicates that the proposition 'there are physical objects' is not an empirical one. No sense-perception or impression of an object (such as a hand) can lead us to the conclusion that there are physical objects, for the concept of 'physical object' is not a theoretical one, nor is it employed in the same way as the concept of a particular object. Therefore it makes sense to say 'there are frogs' or 'there are no unicorns', as the opposite of these sentences also makes sense, but not to say 'there are physical objects'.

In other words, it only makes sense to doubt whether there are physical objects, if it also makes sense to assert it. But it only makes sense to assert it, if, at least in principle, there exists a means of settling the question. In the case of physical objects in general, we have no such means. For we might, for example, have evidence for the existence of life on Mars, but we couldn't have evidence for the existence of physical objects in general, as neither 'sense-data' nor Quinean 'surface irradiations' constitute such evidence. *Pace* Moore, I don't infer the existence of an object from the sense-impression. Of course I know that someone or something is present inasmuch as I see them. But to see an object is not a 'surface irradiation' or 'sense-datum' and although it involves perceptual stimuli, I am ignorant of them and make no inferences from them. That is to say, perceiving an object is not evidence for its existence in the way that fingerprints, for example, are evidence for someone's having been at the scene of a crime. Consequently, there is no such thing as 'demonstrating' that my hand exists.

Climacus is essentially making the same point as Wittgenstein when he says that:

it is generally a difficult matter to want to demonstrate that something exists. Worse still, for the brave souls who venture to do it, the difficulty is of such a kind that fame by no means awaits those who are preoccupied with it . . . whether I am moving in the world of sensate palpability or in the world of thought, I never reason in conclusion to existence, but I reason in conclusion from existence. For example, I do not demonstrate that a stone exists but that something which exists is a stone. The court of law does not demonstrate that a criminal exists but that the accused, who does indeed exist, is a criminal. Whether one wants to call existence an *accessorium* or the eternal *prius*, it can never be demonstrated. (PF 40)

That is to say, there are cases where it makes sense to speak of having evidence for the existence of something—life on Mars, distant planets, Great Pumpkins, etc.—but where it is a matter of being directly confronted by something in ordinary circumstances, such as by a hand, say, it does not make sense, since in such cases doubt is logically excluded: talk of evidence is only meaningful if there is also logical space for being wrong and here there is none. As Wittgenstein says, 'If Moore were to pronounce the opposite of those propositions which he declares certain, we should not just not share his opinion: we should regard him as demented' (*On Certainty* §155).

The implications of Wittgenstein's conception are quite radical. For, if his account is correct, there is no such thing, nor could there be such a thing, as a wholesale validation of our practices: our language-games or forms of life are not metaphysical or ontological theories that can 'track' or fail to 'track' what is the case in the world—as Phillips emphasizes, we do not stand in an *epistemological* relation to our world-picture.[29] But, if so, then it obviously makes no sense to demand evidence for the 'correctness' of this world-picture, as this would be as absurd as demanding evidence for the rules of a game (and no practice or set of practices can justify themselves). In Wittgenstein's words: 'I did not get my picture of the world by satisfying myself of its correctness; nor do I have it because I am satisfied of its correctness. No: it is the inherited background against which I distinguish between [what is] true and [what is] false' (*On Certainty* §95–6).

Consequently, if Wittgenstein is right, Swinburne is making the same mistake as Moore when he insists that 'there is one true set of criteria'—'the modern scientific criteria'.[30] For as Wittgenstein points out: 'Well, if everything speaks for an hypothesis and nothing against it—is it then certainly true? One may designate it as such.—But does it certainly agree with reality, with the facts?—With this question you are already going round in a circle' (*On Certainty* §191). That is to say, TV not only misdescribes religion, it misdescribes religion precisely *because* it misdescribes what it means to have a world-picture (whether it be that of 'modern science' or any other). And it is primarily for this reason that Wittgenstein draws the analogy between the concept 'God' and the concept 'object': for just as we can't infer 'there are objects' from the proposition 'here is a hand', in the case of religious belief it is also not a matter of making inferences from sense-experience or, as adherents of the cosmological and design arguments would have it, from the

---

[29] Afterword to Rush Rhees, *Wittgenstein's* On Certainty—*There Like Our Life*, ed. D. Z. Phillips (Oxford: Blackwell, 2003), 171.

[30] Swinburne, op.cit., 18.

existence of the universe or of human beings.[31] We are not, therefore, confronted by factual (or fictional) claims about the world, but rather with misbegotten attempts[32] at articulating something which 'can't be expressed like that' (*On Certainty* §37).[33]

It is for these reasons that Kierkegaard and Wittgenstein agree that it is a mistake to want to demonstrate God's existence. As Climacus so aptly puts it:

If, namely, the god does not exist, then of course it is impossible to demonstrate it [that he exists]. But if he does exist, then it is foolishness to want to demonstrate it, since I, in the very moment the demonstration commences, would presuppose it not as doubtful—which a presupposition cannot be, inasmuch as it is a presupposition—but as decided, because otherwise I would not begin, easily perceiving that the whole thing would be impossible if he did not exist. (PF 39–40)

That is to say, just as in the case of the ontological argument, I am either assuming what is to be proved or I cannot begin at all, since, contrary to what Hegel thought, I cannot begin with nothing.

If, for example, I wanted to demonstrate Napoleon's existence from Napoleon's works, I can only do this if I already assume that Napoleon's works are 'his' works, that is, if I already assume that Napoleon exists (PF 40). For, if I do not do this, all I can demonstrate is that the works in question have been accomplished by a great general, but this in itself is not sufficient to demonstrate *Napoleon's* existence (as opposed to someone else's), as another person could have accomplished the same works (ibid.). This is why Climacus says in the aforementioned passage that I can never reason in conclusion to existence, but only in conclusion from existence. And the same, of course, applies to demonstrating God's existence from his 'works', that is, from the existence of the universe: I cannot infer the existence of God from the existence of the universe, since God's works do not exist immediately and directly in the way that

---

[31] Swinburne appeals both to cosmological and design arguments. He says, for example, 'But unless there is a God, it is most unlikely that there would be a universe at all . . . That it should exist, on its own, uncreated, is therefore—by normal scientific criteria—very much less likely than that God should exist' (op.cit., 10). For a good criticism of this view (which accepts Swinburne's overall programme), see J. L. Mackie, *The Miracle of Theism*, 95–101.

[32] And in some sense the ontological argument qualifies as such a 'misbegotten attempt'—as Climacus has tried to show.

[33] This concludes Wittgenstein's and Kierkegaard's argument against TV's second thesis that there is one correct way of describing the world and this description either contains an object (entity, item) such as God or it doesn't.

tables and chairs do. Hence, even if we assume that nature is the work of God, only nature is directly present, not God (CUP 243). Therefore, just as in Napoleon's case, I can only demonstrate God's existence from these works (nature/the universe), if I already regard them ideally as *God's*, that is, if I already assume what is to be proved, namely that the universe is ordered according to providential or divine principles. Climacus says:

God's works, therefore, only the god can do. Quite correct. But, then, what are the god's works? The works from which I want to demonstrate his existence do not immediately and directly exist, not at all. Or are the wisdom in nature and the goodness or wisdom in Governance right in front of our noses? Do we not encounter the most terrible spiritual trials here. . . ? . . . Therefore, from what works do I demonstrate it [God's existence]? From the works regarded ideally—that is, as they do not appear directly and immediately. But then I do not demonstrate it from the works, after all, but only develop the ideality I have presupposed. (PF 42)

That I cannot, just as in the case of the ontological argument, get beyond a *petitio principii* here—I can only see divine governance in nature or the universe if I already believe in divine governance (and vice versa)—again shows that what is at issue is not something which could, even in principle, be amenable to empirical or philosophical investigation. For just as I cannot demonstrate to the sceptic that physical objects exist, neither can I demonstrate to the atheist that God exists—and the important thing here is to realize that this is not a shortcoming, but rather that it could not be otherwise. This is the whole point of Wittgenstein's analogy between the concept 'object' and the concept 'God': both concepts function as principles of judgement within the relevant form of life and therefore can't be 'demonstrated', since they must already be presupposed (or denied) in the demonstration itself. As Climacus ironically puts it:

Therefore, anyone who wants to demonstrate the existence of God (in any other sense than elucidating the God-concept. . .) proves something else instead, at times something that perhaps did not even need demonstrating, and in any case never anything better. For the fool says in his heart that there is no God, but he who says in his heart or to others: Just wait a little and I shall demonstrate it—ah, what a rare wise man he is! (PF 43)[34]

---

[34] Now one might want to object that while losing one's religious faith would neither wholly undermine one's ability to act in and think about the world, nor leave that ability entirely unaltered, denying that there are physical objects would (either undermine one's

Hence, if I am not religious already nothing will count as 'evidence for the existence of God' for me. Given that there is no such thing as a self-validating experience or a self-interpreting rule, the way I perceive certain events will itself already be shaped by my world-picture. I can therefore go on examining nature *ad infinitum* in order to find traces of God in it, but such an investigation will never be able to tell me whether nature is the work of God or the product of chance, just as a historical investigation of the New Testament will never be able to tell me whether Christ was God. As Anti-Climacus so perceptively points out:

a footprint on a way is indeed the result of someone's having walked this way. It may happen that I make the mistake that it was, for example, a bird, but by closer scrutiny, following the prints further, ascertain that it must have been another animal. But can I by close scrutiny and by following prints of this sort, at some point reach the conclusion: ergo it is a spirit that has walked along this way, a spirit—which leaves no print? (PC 28)

If this could be done, then, Anti-Climacus goes on to argue in Wittgensteinian vein, the following questions could also be answered: 'What results must there be, how great the effects, how many centuries must pass in order to have it demonstrated from the results of a "human being's" life (this, after all, is the assumption) that he was God?' (PC 27). Clearly, this question admits of no answer, for, I cannot, 'without somewhere or other being guilty of a shifting from one genus to another, suddenly by way of a conclusion obtain the new quality, God, so that as a consequence the result or results of a human being's life at some point suddenly demonstrate that this human being was God' (PC 27). Hence, Anti-Climacus concludes, one cannot come to know anything at all about Christ *qua* Son of God, that is, nothing that pertains to *faith*, from history or from biblical scholarship, since believing in the Gospels *qua sacred texts* is qualitatively different from treating them as

---

ability or leave it completely unaltered). This is true and in this respect there is indeed a significant disanalogy between the concept 'God' and the concept 'object'. But this is compatible with the view that Wittgenstein's analogy nevertheless shows something important, namely, that just as one can't make an inference from the existence of tables and chairs to the existence of physical objects, so one can't make an inference from the existence of the universe (or of religious experience, etc.) to the existence of God. 'There is a God' is consequently just as little an ontological (hypo)thesis as 'there are physical objects'. So there are no a priori reasons why a community should possess the concept of 'God', any more than a society need have our abstract concept of 'physical object'. That is to say, a tribe could perfectly well have the concepts 'chair', 'turnip', 'pigeon' and so on, and treat these things in the way that we do without thinking that they all have one property in common, namely, that they are all *physical objects*.

ordinary historical documents. This is also what Wittgenstein means when he says that:

> Christianity is not based on a historical truth; rather, it offers us a (historical) narrative and says: now believe! But not, believe this narrative with the belief appropriate to a historical narrative, rather: believe through thick and thin, which you can only do as a result of a life. *Here you have a narrative, don't take the same attitude to it as you take to other historical narratives.* Make a *quite different* place in your life for it.—There is nothing *paradoxical* about that! (CV 32e)

Consequently, if Kierkegaard and Wittgenstein are right, then, *pace* Swinburne and TV, there is no such thing as 'quantifying' oneself into faith (CUP 11). Rather, it is, in Petrus Minor's words, a 'confusion of the spheres'—a kind of category mistake—to believe that a scientific or probabilistic investigation of religious claims is possible:

> What is it that the erroneous exegesis and speculative thought have done to confuse the essentially Christian? Quite briefly and with categorical accuracy it is the following: they have shifted the sphere of the paradoxical-religious back into the aesthetic and thereby have achieved the result that every Christian term, which by remaining in its sphere is a qualitative category, can now, in a reduced state, serve as a brilliant expression that means all sorts of things. (BA 173)

Shoving the religious back into the aesthetic (the in-principle-directly-perceivable) is the cardinal sin of TV and this, according to both authors, is not just a philosophical error, but also, and much more importantly, tantamount to abolishing Christianity altogether. One could therefore be forgiven for (anachronistically) supposing that the following passage is aimed at Swinburne:

> If one were to describe this entire orthodox apologetic endeavour in a single sentence, yet also categorically, one would have to say: Its aim is to make *Christianity probable*. Then one must add: If this succeeds, then this endeavour would have the ironical fate that on the very day of victory it would have forfeited everything and completely cashiered Christianity . . . To make Christianity probable is the same as to falsify it. Indeed, what is it that atheists want? Oh, they want to make Christianity probable. That is, they are well aware that if they can only get Christianity's qualitative extravagance tricked into the fussy officiousness of probability—then it is all over with Christianity. (BA 39)

The very idea, in other words, of attempting to 'calculate the odds' for something as absolutely extraordinary as that God became man, is incoherent, for it betrays the qualitative (grammatical) confusion that the claims of Christianity are on a par with *secular* claims to which it is possible to assign probability values. But this is not only as confused as 'assuming that the kingdom of *heaven* is a kingdom along with all other kingdoms on *earth* and that one would look for information about it in a geography book' (CUP 391), it is also, in Anti-Climacus' eyes, *blasphemous* (PC 29), for it presupposes that we are in a position to tell what it is probable for *God* to do—the height of philosophical *hubris*—and according to which criteria should we ever be in a position to tell whether it is probable, for example, that Christ was God or that he rose from the dead? As Anti-Climacus' *alter ego* puts it: 'Comedies and novels and lies must be probable, but how could [the paradox] be probable?' (PF 52).

Hence, if Kierkegaard's and Wittgenstein's conception of religious belief is correct, it is not even remotely analogous to a form of correct (or false) science and neither is faith the result of scientific or philosophical speculation. Rather, both philosophers agree, Christianity is an existence-communication that demands not an intellectual, but an existential response, as truth 'in the sense in which Christ is the truth is not a sum of statements, not a definition etc., but a life' (PC 205). The Christian is called to exist in the truth as lived out by Christ, the paradigm or pattern—he is not supposed speculatively to 'comprehend' a teaching (PC 141). For Christ, according to Climacus, did not come to bring new speculative knowledge about God into the world, but in order to offer the promise of redemption and this is an *ethical* (that is, in Climacus' parlance, a 'subjective') category, not a metaphysical ('objective') one. Hence, Christianity, by providing a 'radical cure' (CUP 294) for the problem of life, requires something much more fundamental than assent to a sum of tenets. As Wittgenstein points out in LC, 'there is this extraordinary use of the word "believe". One talks of believing and at the same time one doesn't use "believe" as one does ordinarily. You might say (in the normal use): "You only believe—oh well..."' (LC 59–60). But in the religious case it makes no sense to say 'oh well', for, as Anti-Climacus approvingly quotes from the Bible: 'Thou *shalt* believe' (SUD 115). The call to have faith is therefore an ethical imperative—it is an injunction to repent and transform the self; it is not a demand to change one's ontology.

If Wittgenstein and Kierkegaard are right, therefore, atheist and believer do not diverge in *opinion*, but in form of life. And in this respect they are, to adapt a phrase of Davidson's, not *words*, but *worlds* apart: the believer looks at life in a different way, uses different pictures, holds other things dear than the atheist, all of which is something that goes much deeper than a simple difference in opinion does—an opinion alone does not regulate for all in one's life. This is why Wittgenstein says in a passage that is clearly indebted to the Danish philosopher: 'It strikes me that a religious belief could only be something like a passionate commitment to a system of reference. Hence, although it's *belief*, it's really a way of living, or a way of assessing life. It's passionately seizing hold of *this* interpretation' (CV 64e).

What Wittgenstein and Kierkegaard are saying, then, is that one does not come to Christianity through argument and intellectual deliberation, but that it is the shape of one's life and experiences that will (or will not) teach one a use for the Christian concepts. The exigencies of life may thrust these concepts upon one. As Wittgenstein says:

A man can . . . be in infinite torment and require infinite help. The Christian religion is only for the one who needs infinite help, solely, that is, for the one who experiences infinite torment. The whole planet can suffer no greater torment than a *single* soul. The Christian faith—as I see it—is a man's refuge in this *ultimate* torment. Anyone in such torment who has the gift of opening his heart, rather than contracting it, accepts the means of salvation in his heart. (CV 46e)

That is to say, the genesis of religious concepts does not, according to Kierkegaard and Wittgenstein, spring from metaphysical or quasi-scientific considerations, but from *transformations of soul*:

Christianity is not a doctrine, not, I mean, a theory about what has happened and will happen to the human soul, but a description of something that actually takes place in human life. For 'consciousness of sin' is a real event and so are despair and salvation through faith. Those who speak of such things . . . are simply describing what has happened to them, whatever gloss anyone may want to put on it. (CV 28e)

That the consciousness of sin is a necessary prerequisite for finding one's way to Christianity is of course also Anti-Climacus' view:[35]

'But if the essentially Christian is something so terrifying and appalling, how in the world can anyone think of accepting Christianity?' Very simply and, if you wish that also, very Lutherly: only the consciousness of sin can force one, if I dare to put it that way (from the other side grace is the force) into this horror . . . Admittance is only through the consciousness of sin; to want to enter by any other road is high treason against Christianity. (PC 67–8)

---

[35] See also Malcolm, 'Anselm's Ontological Arguments'.

In this respect it is interesting to note that Wittgenstein, who, on all accounts of him, was obsessed by his 'sins', nevertheless could not become a genuinely religious person. So, it seems that Anti-Climacus' claim that only 'consciousness of sin' can force one into Christianity leaves something rather fundamental out. It is not only consciousness of sin that is necessary, but also the belief that one's sins will ultimately be forgiven by Jesus Christ, the Redeemer.[36] It appears to be the latter that Wittgenstein could not bring himself to accept. As Wittgenstein says:

I read: 'No man can say that Jesus is the Lord, but by the Holy Ghost.'—And it is true: I cannot call him *Lord*; because that says nothing to me. I could call him the 'paragon', 'God' even—or rather, I can understand it when he is called thus; but I cannot utter the word 'Lord' with meaning. *Because I do not believe* that he will come to judge me; because *that* says nothing to me. And it could say something to me, only if I lived *completely* differently. (CV 33e)[37]

III OBJECTIONS TO THE KIERKEGAARD-WITTGENSTEIN CONCEPTION

Before we go any further, let us pause in order to dispel a common misapprehension of Kierkegaard's and Wittgenstein's religious thought which might be threatening at this point in the discussion. This is an objection that Climacus himself anticipates in a footnote: 'now, if only a hasty pate does not promptly explain to a reading public how foolish my whole book is, which is more than adequately seen in my alleging anything such as: Christianity is not a doctrine' (CUP 379). That is to say, Climacus seems to be warning: do not be misled into thinking, *à la* Kai Nielsen, for example, that because the 'existential' dimension of faith is emphasized, Climacus is really propagating a kind of 'attitudinal' conception of religious belief whose aim is to reduce religious claims to the expression of emotional attitudes (non-cognitivism) in the manner of the Logical Positivists[38] or of Braithwaite,[39] say. In other words,

---

[36] This is an issue that Anti-Climacus discusses in *The Sickness unto Death*.

[37] This concludes Kierkegaard's and Wittgenstein's critique of TV's third thesis that the proposition 'God exists' is a hypothesis to be investigated empirically and/or by a priori argument.

[38] See A. J. Ayer, *Language, Truth and Logic* (London: Penguin, 1971), especially chapter 6.

[39] See R. B. Braithwaite, *An Empiricist's View of the Nature of Religious Belief* (Cambridge, Cambridge University Press, 1953).

Climacus is at pains to head off the charge that 'the most crucial error common to both Nietzsche and Wittgenstein is to argue that Christian practice is everything and Christian belief, belief that involves doctrines, is nothing'.[40] For, as Climacus goes on to point out in the same passage:

Surely a philosophical theory that is to be comprehended and speculatively understood is one thing, and a doctrine that is to be actualized in existence is something else. If there is to be any question of understanding with regard to this latter doctrine, then this understanding must be: to understand that it is to be existed in, to understand the difficulty of existing in it, what a prodigious existence-task this doctrine assigns to the learner.

And in the main text he adds:

I cannot help it that our age has reversed the relation and changed Christianity into a philosophical theory that is to be comprehended and being a Christian into something negligible. Furthermore, to say that Christianity is empty of content because it is not a doctrine is only chicanery. When a believer exists in faith, his existence has enormous content, but not in the sense of a yield in paragraphs. (CUP 380)

Two senses of the word 'doctrine' appear to be in operation here. On the one hand Climacus says 'what a prodigious existence-task this *doctrine* assigns to the learner' (italics mine); on the other he admonishes: 'to say that Christianity is empty of content because it is *not* a doctrine is only chicanery' (my emphasis). So Christianity, according to Climacus, seems both to be and not to be a doctrine. To understand how this apparent inconsistency is to be resolved is, I will argue, to understand why Kierkegaard's and Wittgenstein's account is *not* an attempt to reduce religious belief to emotional attitudes. And this will also equip us with the means of providing a response to Kai Nielsen's objection mentioned above. But before I press on with an explication of this, a more detailed account of what it is to understand religious language is required and to this end I will examine what Wittgenstein has to say about 'religious pictures' in LC.

A good way into the discussion in Wittgenstein's third lecture on religious belief is his remark: ' "God's eye sees everything" —I want to say of this that it uses a picture . . . We associate a particular use with a picture' (LC 71). One of the students in the lecture, Smythies, isn't satisfied with this way of putting things and objects: 'This isn't all he

⁴⁰ Kai Nielsen, 'Wittgensteinian Fideism Revisited' in Kai Nielsen and D. Z. Phillips, *Wittgensteinian Fideism?*, 116.

does—associate a use with a picture' (ibid.). Wittgenstein's response to this interjection is curt since he appears to think that it betrays a misunderstanding:

Rubbish. I meant: what conclusions are you going to draw? etc. Are eyebrows going to be talked of, in connection with the Eye of God? 'He could just as well have said so and so'—this [remark] is foreshadowed by the word 'attitude'. He couldn't just as well have said something else. If I say he used a picture, I don't want to say anything he himself wouldn't say. I want to say that he draws these conclusions. (ibid.)

Smythies, in other words, like Nielsen and Climacus' 'hasty pate', is worried that Wittgenstein's account threatens to take the 'content'—the 'doctrine'—out of religious belief. That is to say, as Cora Diamond points out in an excellent essay, Smythies seems to think that there are only two possible ways of conceiving of the meaning of religious language:

either we allow that people really do mean what they say in such cases (and Wittgenstein thinks that Smythies takes him to reject that alternative), or we think of them as simply expressing a resolve to live in a certain way (or something of the kind), the expression of resolve being accompanied by a picture (and Wittgenstein thinks Smythies sees him as insisting on the correctness of this alternative).[41]

Smythies' either/or is misconceived, however, for Wittgenstein isn't denying that people mean what they say when making religious utterances. Rather, he is insisting that we cannot understand what *meaning* the utterances comes down to unless we understand the *use* to which the religious 'pictures' are put. As Wittgenstein explains at CV 85e: 'Actually I should like to say that . . . the *words* you utter or what you think as you utter them are not what matters, so much as the difference they make at various points in your life. How do I know that two people mean the same when each says he believes in God?. . . *Practice* gives the words their sense.'

In passages such as these Wittgenstein is really not saying anything different than when he is, for example, tackling the philosophical (or logical) problem of what it is to mean something in the PI: 'For a *large* class of cases—though not for all—in which we employ the word

---

[41] 'Wittgenstein on Religious Belief: The Gulfs Between Us' in *Religion and Wittgenstein's Legacy* ed. D. Z. Phillips and Mario von der Ruhr (Aldershot: Ashgate, 2005), 118.

"meaning" it can be defined thus: the meaning of a word is its use in the language' (PI §43). So, if Wittgenstein is denying anything in the LC, it is only the correctness of the familiar philosophical prejudice that meaning (or understanding) something consists of a peculiar 'mental process': 'In our failure to understand the use of a word we take it as the expression of a queer *process*' (PI §196). This explains why, in lecture III of LC, we get the apparent non sequitur of Wittgenstein suddenly asking, after a brief discussion of what it would be like to imagine oneself as a disembodied spirit, 'If you think of your brother in America, how do you know that what you think is, that the thought inside you is, of your brother being in America? Is this an experiential business?' (LC 66).

Wittgenstein is compelled to ask these questions at this point in the discussion, as Smythies has fallen into the trap of believing that you can talk of understanding a word 'without any reference to the technique of its usage' (LC 68). And the significance of Wittgenstein's interpolation is precisely to show that just as you cannot, as it were, 'read off' from your thought that it is the thought of your brother in America, so you can't find out the meaning of words (or sentences) by inspecting what goes on inside you while you utter (or 'mean') them. For, as Wittgenstein asks, 'What is the connection between these words, or anything, substitutable for them, with my brother in America?' (LC 67).

Smythies seems to think that when it comes to thought, we can be absolutely sure, right from the start (and independently of any sense-giving context), that *this* is a thought of *that*—as if 'thought' were an international, self-interpreting sign-language which left no question of interpretation (or connection) open, or as if it were a kind of 'super-picture' (LC 67) of reality that required no 'method of projection' in order to be understood. But, as Wittgenstein points out in the *Lectures on Aesthetics*:

If a Frenchman says: 'It is raining' in French and an Englishman also says it in English, it is not that something happens in both minds which is the real sense of 'It is raining'. [Rather,] (1) Thinking (or imagery) is not an accompaniment of the words as they are spoken or heard; (2) The sense—the thought 'It's raining'—is not even the words *with* the accompaniment of some sort of imagery. It *is* the thought 'It's raining' only within the English language. (LC 30)

That is to say, by ruling out options (1) and (2), Wittgenstein is also rejecting both sides of Smythies' dichotomy: meaning a word or phrase is not a mental 'accompaniment' to the written or spoken words and neither does it consist of merely acting in a certain way '*with* the accompaniment of some sort of imagery'—the conception Smythies erroneously believes Wittgenstein has in mind when he says that the person who says 'God's eye sees everything' is associating a particular use with a picture. This is why, in the *Brown Book*, Wittgenstein calls it 'a kind of general disease of thinking' to believe that meaning something is 'a mental state from which all our acts spring as from a reservoir'.[42]

Consequently, Wittgenstein is not denying that the religious person means what he says (as Smythies believes), but is rather rejecting Smythies' conception of what meaning something consists in. In other words, far from holding that the religious person *only* uses a picture—as opposed to something better—Wittgenstein insists that 'the whole *weight* may be in the picture' (LC 72). But what does this mean? In the PI Wittgenstein gives us some helpful clues:

If we compare a proposition to a picture, we must think whether we are comparing it to a portrait (a historical representation) or to a genre-picture. And both comparisons have point. When I look at a genre-picture, it 'tells' me something, even though I don't believe (imagine) for a moment that the people I see in it really exist, or that there have really been people in that situation. But suppose I ask: '*What* does it tell me then?' I should like to say 'What the picture tells me is itself.' That is, its telling me something consists in its own structure, in *its* own lines and colours. (PI §522–3)

In other words, Wittgenstein is suggesting here that there are two ways that a picture, and consequently, if his analogy is correct, a sentence, can 'tell' me something. It can either tell me something in the way that a historical portrait depicts a historical event—something that can also be described without using the picture—or it can 'tell' me something in a way that is not specifiable independently of the picture itself. Wittgenstein explains:

We speak of understanding a sentence in the sense in which it can be replaced by another which says the same; but also in the sense in which it cannot be replaced by any other. (Any more than one musical theme can be replaced by another.) In the one case the thought in the sentence is something common to different sentences; in the other, something that is

---

[42] Ludwig Wittgenstein, *The Blue and Brown Books* (New York: Harper and Row, 1965), 143.

expressed only by these words in these positions. (Understanding a poem.) (PI §531)

Now, when Wittgenstein says to Smythies that the whole weight may be in the picture, I believe that what he means is that the sentence in question cannot straightforwardly be replaced by another 'which says the same' and hence that the picture is irreplaceable in the sense of being non-paraphrasable. This is why Wittgenstein says:

Isn't it as important as anything else, what picture he does use? Of certain pictures we say that they might just as well be replaced by another—e.g. we could, under certain circumstances, have one projection of an ellipse drawn instead of another. [He *may* say]: 'I would have been prepared to use another picture, it would have the same effect'. (LC 71)

In this example the picture employed is therefore *not* essential to what is being communicated—it is not irreplaceable—for it can easily be swapped for another which 'has the same effect'. In this respect, to borrow Aaron Ridley's terminology, the picture is 'instrumentally intersubstitutable'[43]—it can be replaced by another which says the same thing (or brings about the same end). I take it that it is Smythies' worry that this is how Wittgenstein conceives of *all* pictures, namely, as being merely the means to some independently specifiable end (such as, say, living in a certain way),[44] whereas the whole point of Wittgenstein's distinction between 'essential' (irreplaceable/non-pharaphrasable) and 'inessential' (replaceable/paraphrasable) pictures in LC is precisely to show that 'religious pictures' are *not* instrumentally intersubstitutable in the way that Smythies fears.

Naturally, when Wittgenstein says in the aforementioned passage from the PI that in the case of paraphrasable sentences 'the thought in the sentence is something common to different sentences', while in the non-paraphrasable case 'the thought' can be 'expressed only by these words in these positions', we must not take this to mean, *à la* Smythies, that 'the thought' is something over and above *all* the sentences in which it occurs. That is to say, there is no way of 'independently specifying the thought' short of offering another sentence that also conveys it. As Wittgenstein says in 1931 in CV—still using the vestiges of Tractarian

---

[43] See *The Philosophy of Music. Theme and Variations* (Edinburgh: Edinburgh University Press, 2004), 28.

[44] Compare also Diamond's list of examples of the non-essential use of pictures in her 'Wittgenstein on Religious Belief', 119.

terminology—'The limit of language is shown by its being impossible to describe the fact which corresponds to (is the translation of) a sentence, without simply repeating the sentence' (CV 10e). But there is of course nothing mysterious or 'limiting' about this fact about thought. For the idea that 'thoughts' (or 'facts') should be specifiable independently of language-use is only lent credence by the incoherent 'mental process' picture of thought. If, however, as Wittgenstein says, we come to recognize that the thought 'it is raining' only is *this thought* within the English language (LC 30), then it becomes perfectly obvious why there is no other way of saying 'it is raining' than by saying 'it is raining' or by employing some paraphrase thereof—such as, for instance, to adapt a French expression, 'it is pissing from the sky'.[45]

So the point of Wittgenstein's distinction between the essential and the inessential use of pictures (sentences) is not to draw a distinction between sentences which can and sentences which can't latch on to independently specifiable thoughts or facts. Neither, therefore, is it to make a distinction between language-use which 'refers' to reality and language-use which doesn't. In other words, and *contra* most—including Smythies'—misreadings of him, Wittgenstein is *not*, as Putnam emphasizes, saying the following: 'in ordinary language we have pictures (and, of course, words) and uses of pictures and words, *and* something beyond the words and pictures, while in religious language we have only pictures and words and uses of pictures and words'.[46] We only ever have pictures and words and uses of pictures and words. There is no such thing as 'latching on to reality' *simpliciter*, say by correlating words with 'transcendent' or 'mental' objects that are supposed to 'anchor' our language to a non-linguistic 'beyond' (*pace* the author of TLP).[47] In this respect religious language is no different from 'ordinary' language. Where it *is* different, according to Wittgenstein, is that in the religious case I cannot do without the picture, I cannot

---

[45] The expression is *il pleut à vache qui pisse* which of course wouldn't be a paraphrase, but a qualification.

[46] See Hilary Putnam, *Renewing Philosophy* (Cambridge, MA: Harvard University Press, 1992), 159.

[47] That is, what Wittgenstein is rejecting here is the view that in ordinary language the meaning of a word is the object it stands for, while in religious language there is nothing for which the words stand and they therefore refer, at best, to emotional attitudes. That is to say, Wittgenstein is both rejecting a naïve realism as well as a naïve anti-realism about language here; he is not saying something Derridaesque such as 'there is nothing outside the text'.

describe my use of the picture without using the picture,[48] whereas in
'ordinary' language, I often can do without the 'picture' (or without
this particular turn of phrase—but not, of course, as we have just seen,
without *any* form of words) and use something else, a different picture
or another form of words, instead. In this sense 'ordinary' language
is often 'instrumentally intersubstitutable', whereas religious language
(generally) isn't. And this is a feature that religious language shares with
artistic[49] language-use—hence Wittgenstein's aside at PI §531 about
'understanding a poem'.

Two different senses of the word 'understanding' can therefore
be distinguished which mirror the 'essential' and 'inessential' use of
pictures discussed above. Following Ridley, I will call these two different
senses 'internal' and 'external' understanding respectively. That is to
say, Wittgenstein's notion of understanding a sentence 'in the sense
in which it cannot be replaced by any other' (PI §531) will be called
'internal', to register the fact, as Ridley says, 'that what is grasped
in it is, because "expressed only by these words in these positions",
understood as internal to *this* particular arrangement of words',[50]
whereas understanding a sentence 'in the sense in which it can be
replaced by another which says the same' (PI §531) will be called
'external' 'to mark the fact that what is grasped in it is, because
"something common to different sentences", not understood as internal
to any one specific formulation'.[51] Taken together, these two senses
comprise the concept of understanding (PI §533) which can therefore
be said to consist of both a paraphrasable and a non-paraphrasable
aspect.[52]

We can now apply this distinction in order to understand what
Wittgenstein means when he speaks of understanding religious utterances such as 'God's eye sees everything' or 'we might see one another
after death' (LC 70). If what I have been arguing so far is correct, then, if
I am to understand sentences of this kind, I must primarily understand

---

[48] See Diamond, op.cit., 128.

[49] The natural word to use here would, of course, be 'aesthetic', but in order not
to get the ordinary sense of 'aesthetic' confused with what Kierkegaard means by 'the
aesthetic' (a notion that plays a complex role in Kierkegaard's *oeuvre*, but that Julia
Watkin has usefully summarized as 'to do with the life of the senses; it [the aesthetic]
thus encompasses not only ordinary human instincts and desires but also their expression
through the arts, and through artistic creativity that at its highest achievement finds
its expression in works of genius', in *Historical Dictionary of Kierkegaard's Philosophy*
(Oxford: Scarecrow Press, 2001), 14. See also chapter 2.), I have used 'artistic' instead.

[50] Ridley, op.cit., 32–3.   [51] Ibid.   [52] Ibid., 26.

them 'internally', as a purely 'external' understanding based on a grasp of what the individual words mean in everyday contexts will not be sufficient to effect a real understanding of what is going on here. It is for this reason that Wittgenstein says:

In one sense, I understand all he [the person who says he believes in a Judgement Day] says—the English words 'God', 'separate', etc. I understand. I could say: 'I don't believe in this', and this would be true, meaning I haven't got these thoughts or anything that hangs together with them. But not that I could contradict the thing. (LC 55)

What Wittgenstein seems to be saying here is that in order to be able to contradict a religious statement, you not only need to understand what the 'atoms'–that is, the individual words—it is comprised of mean in ordinary contexts, but what the sentence as a whole means, and, for this to be possible, you must understand how the words are functioning in *this* specific context—you must, that is, understand their technique of application *here*—something that cannot be accomplished by, for example, simply hazarding a guess about what the words composing the sentence might or might not be 'referring' to.[53] This is why Wittgenstein says that in one sense he understands all the religious person says, because he understands, for example, the ordinary words 'God' or 'separate',[54] but that, in another sense, he doesn't understand the sentence *at all* for, in this particular context, he has no grasp of how these familiar words are used: 'my normal technique of language leaves me' (LC 55).

Wittgenstein's case, to borrow an example of Diamond's, is similar to someone who understands the ordinary use of the word 'beautiful', say, but who is at a loss when someone applies it to a person like George Eliot, for example. For according to the habitual criteria George Eliot obviously isn't beautiful. If I am therefore to understand this new application of a familiar concept, my ordinary vision must, as it were, first be transformed. In Diamond's words:

She [George Eliot], that magnificently ugly woman, gives a totally transformed meaning to 'beauty'. Beauty itself becomes something entirely new for one, as one comes to see (to one's own amazement, perhaps) a powerful beauty residing in this woman . . . In such a case, she is not judged by a norm available through

---

[53] See also Putnam, op.cit., 165.

[54] It is unclear why Wittgenstein speaks of 'separate' in connection with a discussion of a Last Judgement, but I presume he is thinking of sentences such as 'the soul is separate from the body' or some such thing, but of course this is only a guess. What exactly Wittgenstein meant is irrelevant to our discussion, though.

the concept of beauty; she shows the concept up, she moves one to use the words 'beauty' and 'beautiful' almost as new words, or as renewed words. She gives one a new vocabulary, a new way of taking the world in in one's words, and of speaking about it to others.[55]

That is to say, a 'conceptual reorientation'[56] must take place if I am to understand the application of the word 'beautiful' to George Eliot—a reorientation which, as Diamond says, makes possible new ways of speaking about the world. And something similar, if Wittgenstein is right, happens in religious contexts, when I am, for instance, suddenly brought to understand, perhaps through certain kinds of experiences of dependence and dependability,[57] what it means to call God 'Father'. In this respect, just as George Eliot 'moves one to use the words "beauty" and "beautiful" almost as new words', so, it could be said, does God move the religious believer to use the words 'father' or 'fatherly love' almost as new words.

Consequently, one could now say that for someone for whom this 'conceptual reorientation' does not occur, no real understanding of the sentence (or words) in question is possible. That is to say, someone like Wittgenstein, who does not know what to make of the 'after death man's'[58] words, can be said only to 'understand' such sentences in the sense that he recognizes, for example, the ordinary English words 'scrutiny', 'soul' and so on that might comprise them, but without being able to understand, to speak with Diamond, the 'renewed use' of these words. This would be similar to someone who knows that the sun is a star located at the centre of our Solar System, but who fails to see the aptness of the phrase 'Juliet is the sun'.[59] And such a failure of understanding cannot be remedied by, say, pointing at Juliet and at the sun and saying, 'she is like that', but rather by drawing attention to aspects of the sun that make the comparison with Juliet meaningful. If this still does not help, then perhaps getting the person to read more poetry will gradually make understanding dawn.[60]

It is ironic that in most philosophical domains, it is fairly common-place nowadays to appeal to context and practice when it comes to the

---

[55] Diamond, op.cit., 125.   [56] Ibid.

[57] Compare Wittgenstein's talk of 'feeling absolutely safe' in the *Lecture on Ethics*.

[58] This phrase is Diamond's.   [59] This example is Ridley's.

[60] Of course it is possible that regardless of what one tries, understanding will never occur. In such cases one may want to speak, like Wittgenstein, of a kind of 'aspect blindness'.

question of effecting an understanding of something; indeed, as regards understanding ethical and artistic concepts, for example, one even speaks of cultivating certain virtues of character said to be necessary for making such understanding possible. But when it comes to understanding religious language, these lessons are generally forgotten and it is assumed that here the only pertinent question to ask is whether religious language 'refers'—as if there were only *one* thing referring could be, as if what constitutes 'referring' doesn't itself, in many ways, depend on *context.* Noticing a 'religious fact', if one wants to talk that way, requires an understanding of theological concepts—such as, for example, seeing the point of calling God 'Father'—just as understanding a 'mathematical fact' needs the established practice of mathematics.[61] As Wittgenstein so aptly puts it in *Remarks on the Foundations of Mathematics*:

'If calculation is to be practical, then it must uncover facts.' But what things are 'facts'? Do you believe that you can show what fact is meant by, e.g. pointing to it with your finger? Does that of itself clarify the part played by 'establishing' a fact?—Suppose it takes mathematics to define the *character* of what you are calling a 'fact'! 'It is interesting to know *how many* vibrations this note has!' But it took arithmetic to teach you this question. It taught you to see this kind of fact. Mathematics—I want to say—teaches you, not just the answer to a question, but a whole language-game with questions and answers.[62]

Similarly, I would like to say, religion teaches you not just the answer to a question—say to the meaning of life—but a whole language-game with questions and answers.

So when Wittgenstein is, for example, saying that Christianity is not a doctrine, he does not mean that it has no conceptual—or paraphrasable—content. Rather, what he is suggesting is that being able, say, to recite the Creeds or Catholic dogma is not sufficient for having any real (that is, internal) understanding of religious concepts, as this requires being able to see religious utterances non-instrumentally, that is to say, it requires being able to see their *point* and aptness rather than their ability, as it were, to convey 'information' about God. And being able to see this is not possible, if Wittgenstein is right, independently of having some familiarity and grasp of the Christian

[61] The circularity involved here is analogous to that of paraphrase presupposing itself and is therefore harmless. For a good exposition of this, see Ridley, op.cit., 26–30.

[62] Ludwig Wittgenstein, *Remarks on the Foundations of Mathematics*, ed. G. H. von Wright, R. Rhees, G. E. M. Anscombe, trans. G. E. M. Anscombe (Cambridge, MA: Massachusetts Institute of Technology Press, 2001), Part VII, section 18, 381.

form of life and the phenomenology of experience that gave rise to it. Hence, when Wittgenstein says that the important thing with regard to the Christian 'doctrine' is to understand 'that you have to change your *life*' or 'the *direction* of your life', he is not implying that it is somehow possible to do this *without* committing oneself to the Christian claims. For to say that much more than rote-reciting is required, is not to say that therefore the 'doctrine'—the Christian claims—are irrelevant, as this would be as absurd as thinking that because a song can be sung both with and without expression, you could have the expression without the song (LC 29). Similarly, when Climacus states that the important thing with regard to the Christian doctrine is 'to understand that it is to be existed in, to understand the difficulty of existing in it, what a prodigious existence-task this doctrine assigns to the learner', what he means is that a proper understanding of what these claims actually amount to—what these claims *are*—is only possible from within the context of a lived religious life.[63] Hence, there is no tension in Climacus' position when he says that Christianity both is and is not a doctrine, for of course it is a doctrine, if by 'doctrine' we mean 'having paraphrasable content', but it is not a 'doctrine' in the sense of being a philosophical theory whose purpose is to be comprehended speculatively. Rather, the point of the 'doctrine' is to exist in faith, to acquire an understanding of it 'from the inside' as it were.

Consequently, it is simply not the case, as Nielsen seems to be assuming, that on the one hand we have the 'beliefs', while on the other we have the 'practice' and, if we are very lucky, there are a handful of religious believers for whom the two come in a package. For it makes no sense to think that the 'beliefs' can be specified (in anything but a purely minimalist—'external'—sense) completely independently of the practices in which they are embedded (and vice versa), just as it makes no sense to believe that 'the meaning or thought is just an accompaniment of the word' (LC 29), and word and thought, like 'belief' and 'practice', can therefore be divorced from each other.

This also helps us to understand what Wittgenstein means when he says that:

in religion every level of devoutness must have its appropriate form of expression which has no sense at a lower level. This doctrine, which means something at a

---

[63] This is why it makes no sense to think that one can first come to believe in God and then use this 'belief' as a reason for adopting the religious form of life. See also note 70.

higher level, is null and void for someone who is still at the lower level; he *can* only understand it *wrongly* and so these words are *not* valid for such a person. (CV 32e)

Here Wittgenstein is suggesting that there are different levels of understanding as regards religious doctrines corresponding to the relative depth of devoutness and spiritual development of the person concerned. So, for example, someone who thinks that the expression 'the Lord has given, the Lord has taken away, blessed be the name of the Lord' is a cheap attempt at trying to justify the caprice of the deity, is at a lower level of religious understanding than someone who sees it as a trusting acceptance of God's sovereignty.

If the idea that spiritual development is necessary for a proper understanding of religious expressions to occur strikes us as implausible, it may again be useful to remind ourselves of what goes on in artistic contexts. Someone, for instance, who lacks a musical education and does not possess a 'musical ear' will not be able to contradict the judgement of a connoisseur, as such a person will not have sufficient (musical) sensibility even really to understand what the connoisseur is saying. In other words, such a person will neither possess the vocabulary nor have the appropriate concepts that would enable them to say anything genuinely meaningful about a musical work, short, perhaps, of finding it 'pleasurable' or 'relaxing'.

For exactly analogous reasons Wittgenstein feels that he cannot contradict what the religious person is saying, since he, as yet, lacks a real grasp of the concepts involved. That is to say, just as there is musical sensibility and tone deafness (and, to be sure, much in between), there is also religious sensibility and blindness for religion, and neither musical nor religious sensibility is acquired by learning a set of theses, doctrines, by heart—about who the great composers were, about the laws of counterpoint or about transubstantiation—since this would only bring about an 'external', that is, purely intellectual, understanding of the subject comparable to having learnt a code.[64] But what is required here is the kind of understanding that makes the musical work or the prayer (the religious words) *live* for me, not the kind that allows me to parrot a form of words. And such an understanding can only be brought about by immersing oneself in the culture or practice that has given rise to these phenomena. This is why Wittgenstein says in the *Lectures*

[64] See also Ridley, op.cit., 31.

on Aesthetics: 'In order to get clear about aesthetic words you have to describe ways of living' (LC 11). If we understand that this is so in the case of aesthetics, it is only prejudice which prevents us from seeing that this applies in exactly the same way to religion. Hence Wittgenstein's remark that he could only utter the word 'Lord' with meaning, if he lived *completely* differently (CV 33e).

Consequently, neither Kierkegaard nor Wittgenstein is concerned with taking the 'content' out of religious claims and reducing it 'to merely living in a certain way'. Rather, both philosophers are at pains to show that the either/or we seem to be confronted with is really a false dichotomy. For no such thing as a fully fledged understanding of any domain of discourse is possible without both aspects of understanding being present, without, that is, both the 'external' and the 'internal' aspect being available to the 'understander'. Hence, it is simply not the case that we have to choose between a purely 'external'—that is to say 'doctrinal'—account of religious belief and a kind of arbitrary, 'mystical' commitment to living a certain kind of life, as both alternatives involve serious distortions: if we don't want to have a purely 'external', code-like understanding of religious beliefs—which is really no understanding at all—then religious beliefs cannot be understood and specified independently of the mode of life that gives them sense.

Conversely, if we do not want to have mere religious passion—a kind of 'internal' understanding without any 'external' aspect, something, I take it, that is either unintelligible or some bizarre sort of rapture—then religious feeling must be expressible within the Christian conceptual framework.[65] To put it in a more Kantian way: external understanding without internal understanding is empty; internal understanding without external understanding is blind. Or in the words of Petrus Minor:

One does not become a Christian by being religiously moved by something higher; and not every outpouring of religious emotion is a Christian outpouring. In other words, emotion that is Christian is controlled by conceptual definitions, and when deep emotion is transformed into or expressed in words in order to be communicated, this transformation must continually take place within the conceptual definitions. (BA 113)

---

[65] But this of course does not imply that the one can be described independently of the other, any more than practice and belief can be specified completely independently of each other.

These words are a far cry from the usual stereotyping of Kierkegaard as the advocate of 'blind' religious passion.

Kierkegaard and Wittgenstein agree, therefore, that, as with all ordinary (non-religious) cases of understanding, both the 'external' and the 'internal' aspects of it are necessary. That is to say, although, as I have argued, the internal aspect is crucial in religious (and artistic) contexts, this does not imply that it is possible to have this on its own. Consequently, *pace* Nielsen, if Wittgenstein and Kierkegaard are right, there is no such thing as 'simply living in a certain way' as opposed to 'believing certain things' or, indeed, vice versa. *Genuine* beliefs can never be divorced from and understood completely independently of the difference they make in one's life, for there is no such thing as believing something *in vacuo*—without a context (or practice)—unless one thinks, like Smythies, that believing something is tantamount to holding a certain mental image before one's mind (and we've already seen that this is confused). Hence, it is not the case, as is often supposed, that Wittgenstein denies that religious people believe different things to non-religious people. What he *is* denying is that any sense can be made of *what* those things *are* independently of paying attention to the form of life (or practice) which gives them sense. For there is no such thing, nor could there be such a thing—in religion or elsewhere—as simply inspecting the words alone in order to find out whether they make sense or not.

And it is just this that—despite making claims to the contrary—Nielsen does when attempting to dismiss 'God-talk' as incoherent:

It is not...that I think that God is an object among objects, but I do think...that he must—in some very unclear sense—be taken to be a particular existent among existents though, of course, 'the king' among existents, and a very special and mysterious existent, but not an object, not a kind of object, not just a categorical or classificatory notion, but not a non-particular either. Though he is said to be infinite, he is also said to be a person, and these two elements when put together seem at least to yield a glaringly incoherent notion. He cannot be an object—a spatio-temporal entity but he is also a he—a funny kind of he to be sure—who is also said to be a person—again a funny kind of person—who is taken to be a person without a body: a purely *spiritual* being. This makes him out to be a 'peculiar reality' indeed. He gets to be even more peculiar when we are told he is an *infinite* person as well. But now language has really gone on a holiday.[66]

---

66 Nielsen and Phillips, op.cit., 123.

In spite of repeatedly expressing contempt for what I have called TV, it seems that Nielsen has momentarily endorsed this conception, for, like advocates of the latter, he is, in this passage, taking religious language crudely *au pied de la lettre*. That is to say, Nielsen is simply assuming that because I can understand what 'person' and 'infinite' mean in ordinary contexts, I am able to understand the religious expression 'God is infinite'—as if this were just a matter of combining the two linguistic 'atoms' of 'person' and 'infinite' into a 'peculiar' complex.

But if what I have been arguing is correct, such an idea just doesn't make any sense. For if it did, it would, among other things, spell doom for most other domains of discourse as well. For example, we should be just as much at a loss about how it is possible to apply emotive language to music, say. That is, if Nielsen's 'analysis' of 'God-talk' is anything to go by, we would be confronted by the following dilemma: either we understand sentences such as 'the string quartet is tearful' because it makes sense for sounds or bits of marks on a page to be sad—an analogue to Nielsen's strictly literal rendering of religious language—or such sentences are, as Nielsen is fond of emphasizing, purely 'symbolic', that is, the 'tearful' is merely a fancy way of saying something like 'arousing feelings of sadness in most perceivers'—a correlate of Nielsen's claim that if religious language can't be construed literally, then it reduces to 'morality touched by emotion'.[67] But, although philosophers have at one time or another held such views,[68] Nielsen's dilemma is surely just as much of a false dichotomy as the one between 'practice' and 'belief' discussed (and dismissed) earlier.

So, if we have, as Mulhall puts it, such a 'remarkably impoverished conception of the kinds of non-factual or non-descriptive uses of language . . . there might be',[69] then it should, of course, come as no surprise that, on such a conception, 'God-talk'—along with moral and artistic language—will turn out to be incoherent. Rather than celebrating this fact, however, Nielsen should offer an argument showing why his narrow conception of language which can see no alternative to a factual (metaphysical)/symbolic divide should be the only game in town.[70]

---

[67] Nielsen and Phillips, 314 (for an especially stark expression of this either/or).

[68] See, for example, Mackie, *The Miracle of Theism*, 219–22.

[69] See Stephen Mulhall's critique in Nielsen and Phillips, op.cit., 308.

[70] I take the foregoing also to constitute an argument against John Hyman's very similar view that 'Wittgenstein defends two principal doctrines: first a doctrine about the meaning of religious discourse, and second, a doctrine about the epistemology of religious beliefs. The first is that the expression of a religious belief in words is

The odd claim to have followed 'the very logic of God-talk'[71] isn't sufficient here, for, if I am right, this is precisely what Nielsen has *not* done.[72]

If what I have been arguing so far is correct, this disposes of Nielsen's charge that Wittgenstein's most crucial error consists in claiming that 'Christian practice is everything and... belief that involves doctrines, is nothing.' It is therefore now time to address the related criticisms of incommensurability and fideism mentioned in the introduction to this chapter. That is to say, I will now confront Nielsen's objection that Kierkegaard's and Wittgenstein's conception, by turning religion into a form of life 'incommensurable' with other forms of life, has effectively sealed religion off from all possible criticism.[73]

III.1 'Incommensurability'

In Nielsen's words:

not a prediction or a hypothesis, but instead expresses "something like a passionate commitment to a system of reference". And the second is that religious beliefs are therefore immune from falsification and verification.' (See 'The Gospel According to Wittgenstein', 7) These remarks clearly imply that Hyman can also see no alternative to a factual (metaphysical)/symbolic (metaphorical) dichotomy and therefore simply assumes it without argument. (For a critique of the 'second doctrine' Hyman ascribes to Wittgenstein, see the discussion of Nielsen's charge of 'fideism' and 'incommensurability' in the main text below.) See also Stephen Mulhall's excellent critique of Hyman's paper, in his 'Wittgenstein and the Philosophy of Religion' (in D. Z. Phillips and Timothy Tessin (eds), *Philosophy of Religion in the 21ˢᵗ Century*), especially the following passage: 'But if, according to this [Wittgenstein's] approach, no one can so much as understand what a belief in God's existence amounts to without grasping the location of that concept in the grammatical network of religious concepts that Wittgenstein here describes as a system of reference, it makes no sense to think that one can first establish the truth of that belief and then use it as a reason for adopting the system of reference. On the contrary, one could not acquire a belief in God's existence without both understanding and committing oneself to the broader grammatical system in which the concept of God has its life. Consequently, Hyman's objection to Wittgenstein's remark simply begs the question against Wittgenstein's whole approach—not only to the philosophy of religion but to philosophy in general.' (101) And the same can of course be said of Nielsen.

71 Nielsen and Phillips, op.cit., 123.

72 Compare also Diamond's remark that talk of God having scattered his people 'no more depends on a metaphysical conception of how an incorporeal being can intervene in human history than does talk of Ford Motor Company as having acted [as when it was charged with manslaughter]', Diamond, op.cit., 129.

73 See, for example, ibid., 320–1. Whether Nielsen believes this objection also applies to Kierkegaard is unclear, but given Kierkegaard's conception of 'existence spheres', which I have argued is in many ways analogous to Wittgenstein's notion of a form of life, it seems to me that it must.

The distinctive domains of discourse (e.g. science, religion, morality) *initially* give us our criteria of reasonability, justifiability distinctive to each domain of discourse, but domains are not unconnected and the form of life that is there with their practices can, and should, be appealed to where some practice or practices in one domain of discourse fits or fit badly with another... This is what Wittgensteinian Fideism does not allow with its conception of incommensurable domains determining what constitutes a rational authority unique to each domain of discourse. Rejecting along Davidsonian lines incommensurability... we can assess whole domains of discourse... We need not, that is, be stuck with just saying that these are our practices and these are the language-games we play, this is where we stand, this is what we do around here, these are the rules we have and we can do no other.[74]

I will take the 'incommensurability' objection first and will then consider the 'stonewalling' charge.

Given that Nielsen has brought Davidson into the picture, let us first of all ask whether the Kierkegaard-Wittgenstein conception of religion implies that religious believers have a 'conceptual scheme' which is in some sense 'incommensurable' with that of the atheist. Two responses to this question are possible, neither of which advances Nielsen's case. If we take 'incommensurable' to mean what Davidson means by it, namely, 'largely true but not translatable',[75] then the answer to this question is 'no', as any good Wittgensteinian would take Davidson's 'short line' on this issue: 'nothing, it may be said, could count as evidence that some form of activity could not be interpreted in our language that was not at the same time evidence that that form of activity was not speech behaviour'.[76] That is to say, given that I have argued that you cannot have internal understanding without the 'external aspect', and 'external understanding' depends on the paraphrasable use of words, there can, *ex hypothesi*, be no *complete* failure of 'translation'. So, for example, I cannot explain what 'God's eye sees everything' means to someone who does not understand the habitual senses of the words comprising the sentence. Neither, *pace* Nielsen, could I explain what 'eye' means in this context by pointing, say, to God's 'anatomy', since it is obvious that the word 'eye' in the sentence 'God's eye sees everything' does not function

---

[74] Nielsen and Phillips, 128–9.

[75] Donald Davidson, 'On the Very Idea of a Conceptual Scheme', in *Inquiries into Truth and Interpretation* (Oxford: Oxford University Press, 2001), 194. By 'not translatable' Davidson means 'not translatable *at all*'.

[76] Davidson, op.cit., 185.

in the same way as the word 'eye' does in the sentence 'a racoon's eye can see in the dark'. It is equally obvious that I could not apply the word 'eye' to God, if I could not employ the word 'eye' in everyday contexts—if, that is, I could not understand 'a racoon's eye can see in the dark' and similar sentences. Religious discourse cannot, therefore, be 'self-contained' or 'sealed off' from other linguistic 'domains', for it is precisely the quotidian senses of words that make possible the 'renewed' uses or applications of these words in religious contexts. In this respect, religious discourse, like artistic language-use, involves an *extension* or *transformation* of everyday discourse[77] and consequently can't be 'incommensurable' with it.[78]

If all we mean by 'incommensurable', however, is that there can be a partial 'translation failure'—in the sense that religious expressions are not instrumentally intersubstitutable—then the answer to our question is 'yes', but unsurprising and harmless. For such a 'translation failure' would be similar to a lyrical novel's (or poem's) resisting translation into another language. That is to say, although it can of course be done, what is distinctive about the poetic work will get 'lost in translation', something that will be apparent to anyone who ever tried to translate Proust's *A la Recherche du Temps Perdu* into English.

If this is correct, then Nielsen's bringing Davidson into the discussion at all is either irrelevant or merely a diversionary tactic, for Davidson seems to allow for partial translation failure.[79] Furthermore, given that Nielsen seems, in some sense, to regard himself as a faithful

---

[77] In this (religious) respect Diamond speaks, following Franz Rosenzweig, of the 'conversion' of our concepts. Diamond, op.cit., 125.

[78] So, for example, if 'sun' did not, in ordinary contexts, denote the heavenly body, it would make no sense to call Juliet the sun.

[79] Some philosophers, such as Hanjo Glock and including presumably Nielsen, read Davidson as not allowing for partial translation failure. I believe, although I cannot argue it in detail here, that such a reading is not borne out by the text. It would, for example, be hard to square with the following passage: 'A language may contain simple predicates whose extensions are matched by no simple predicates, or even by no predicates at all, in some other language. What enables us to make this point in particular cases is an ontology common to the two languages, with concepts that individuate the same objects. We can be clear about breakdowns in translation when they are local enough, for a background of generally successful translation provides what is needed to make these failures intelligible. But we were after larger game: we wanted to make sense of there being a language we could not translate at all.' (Op.cit., 192; see also my quotation in the main text below.) Be that as it may, if Davidson were nonetheless (and in spite of what he just seems to have said) committed to the view that partial translation failure is impossible, then his view is just false, for we clearly get such translation failure all the

disciple of Davidson's, it is ironic that he himself, in his criticisms of Wittgenstein's conception of religious belief, ends up espousing a version of the scheme/content distinction that Davidson deplores. For Nielsen's first charge against Wittgenstein presupposes that it is possible to separate religious 'content'—the 'beliefs', the 'doctrine'—from the 'scheme' (the religious practice and form of life), but, if Davidson is right, then this is something we can't do:

If we choose to translate some alien sentence rejected by its speakers by a sentence to which we are strongly attached on a community basis, we may be tempted to call this a difference in schemes; if we decide to accommodate the evidence in other ways, it may be more natural to speak of a difference of opinion. But when others think differently from us, no general principle, or appeal to evidence, can force us to decide that the difference lies in our beliefs rather than in our concepts.[80]

So when Nielsen says that 'individual practices and clusters of practices forming whole domains of discourse, such as science, religion or morality, can be criticized by reference to their fit with the forms of language/forms of life taken as a whole',[81] this sounds suspiciously like a linguistic version of what Davidson is rejecting—'a neutral ground, or common co-ordinate system'[82] that we can appeal to when criticizing other practices (or 'schemes'). But, if that is so, then Nielsen just hasn't learnt Davidson's lesson.

Consequently, I can, of course, criticize other practices, including religious practices, but not by reference to their 'fit' or failure to 'fit' with the forms of life 'taken as a whole'.[83] For there is no such thing, nor could there be such a thing, as a form of life-in-general consisting of all our diverse practices taken together and supplying us with a 'neutral set of criteria' against which individual practices can be measured and found wanting.[84] But if this is so, then Nielsen's notion would seem

time, which is, for example, why we employ German words like *Dasein* when translating Heidegger into English.

[80] Ibid., 197.   [81] Kai Nielsen, op.cit., 128.   [82] Davidson, op.cit., 198.

[83] For example, one might, as Mulhall points out, share Nietzsche's suspicions of Christianity as embodying sado-masochistic self-hatred or Freud's suspicions of institutionalized religion as pandering to psychologically immature dependence on a father-figure ('Wittgenstein and Philosophy of Religion', 106).

[84] Now if Nielsen's suggestion that religion can be judged against forms of language/forms of life taken as a whole meant nothing more objectionable than that someone's religious beliefs should cohere with his/her views about the world generally, this would be a perfectly reasonable demand. Unfortunately, this is not the case. Nielsen is not concerned with the question of whether someone's religious beliefs might (or

to amount to little more than advocacy of a form of (thinly disguised) rationalistic imperialism.

CONCLUSION

If what I have been arguing in this chapter is correct, then Kierkegaard and Wittgenstein have shown that the target view is untenable. Furthermore, if my arguments against Nielsen have been successful, then this shows that Kierkegaard's and Wittgenstein's single most important criticism of traditional philosophy of religion is summarized in Petrus Minor's topical diagnosis of the 'fundamental harm in modern speculation' as 'a confusion of the spheres' (BA 5): in its efforts always to want to say that 'things which look different are really the same',[85] or, indeed, that 'things which look different are really *incoherent*', adherents of TV—and those who, wittingly or unwittingly, share some of its premises—only succeed in obscuring the qualitative dialectic (grammar) characteristic of religious faith such that this either, in the end, as Kierkegaard's pseudonyms have shown, serves to abolish Christianity, or, as Wittgenstein insists, makes it impossible to see religious practices as anything but sheer stupidity.[86]

Hence, we are now in an even better position to understand the rationale behind Kierkegaard's elaborate pseudonymous strategy: it is precisely because Kierkegaard believes, like Wittgenstein who was inspired by him, that ethical and religious concepts can mean nothing to someone who lives entirely in aesthetic categories, that his pseudonyms try, first of all, to prise the reader away from this particular way of looking at things. Thus, for instance, Judge William in the second part of *Either/Or*, does not attempt to coax the young aesthete out of his state of blissful irresponsibility by trying to demonstrate the existence of God to him, say, but rather by attempting to develop him ethically, by as it were preparing the ground 'existentially' in order to make it possible for the relevant concepts to acquire some bite. Similarly, Climacus insists

---

should) cohere with their other beliefs about the world, but rather seeks to distil a neutral set of criteria from all our practices taken together (whatever that could be) and then to employ this as a stick to beat religion with. That is to say, Nielsen wants to show that by the lights of this 'neutral set of criteria' religious beliefs can be found to be 'inherently incoherent'.

[85] See chapter 1, note 10.   [86] See also chapter 1, end of section II.

throughout CUP that he is not a Christian: given that he wants to show to his readers that, far from being Christians, they actually regard the Christian concepts in completely aesthetic terms, he starts from where they are and hopes in this way to produce the inward deepening necessary for a reconceptualization to take place. In other words, if Kierkegaard and Wittgenstein are right, no internal understanding of the most important human practices—aesthetics, ethics, religion and, indeed (as I have tried to show in the second chapter) philosophy—is possible without cultivation of character or, as Wittgenstein says in CV,[87] self-mastery.

[87] CV 35e. See chapter 2, end of section I.

Conclusion

> In relation to their systems most systematizers are like a man who
> builds an enormous castle and lives in a shack close by.
>
> From *The Journals of Søren Kierkegaard*[1]

> I may find scientific questions interesting, but they never really
> grip me. Only conceptual and aesthetic questions do that. At
> bottom I am indifferent to the solution of scientific problems; but
> not to the other sort.
>
> Ludwig Wittgenstein, *Culture and Value*[2]

This book, apart from attempting to reveal the extent of Kierkegaard's
influence on Wittgenstein, has been animated by two dominant themes:
tracing the parallels in Kierkegaard's and Wittgenstein's conception of
philosophy and examining the affinities in their thought about religious
belief. In the first chapter I showed that Kierkegaard directly influenced
Wittgenstein to a much greater degree than is commonly supposed. In
the second I argued that the two thinkers share an ethical conception
of philosophy and defended this against D. Z. Phillips's criticism that
philosophical problems are not 'personal' problems.

In chapter 3, on the other hand, I showed that a 'resolute' way
of construing the parallels between early Wittgenstein's philosophical
endeavours and Kierkegaard's is misguided: to regard their work as an
attempt to draw the reader into a web of nonsense in order to dispel
the illusion that there is such a thing as logically alien thought. For, as
we have seen, such an interpretation not only distorts the views of both

[1] *The Journals of Søren Kierkegaard*, trans. Alexander Dru (London : G. Cumberlege
and Oxford University Press, 1951.), 156.

[2] *Culture and Value* 79e; translation emended.

thinkers, it also lends ammunition to those who, like Nielsen, want to insist that religious concepts are either nonsensical or else 'purely symbolic'.

Finally, in chapter 4, I showed how Kierkegaard's and Wittgenstein's common conception of religious belief mounts a successful attack on the 'target view' of religion and I dispelled Nielsen's 'stonewalling' and 'incommensurability' charges. I hope thereby to have undermined some of the more tenacious myths surrounding Kierkegaard's and Wittgenstein's religious thought and to have shown that the two authors—especially when read in the light of each other—still present the greatest challenge to the received orthodoxies in the philosophy of religion as well as to the subject's (philosophy's) own conception of itself.

By way of concluding, I will now try to weave together the two main strands of the book—Kierkegaard's and Wittgenstein's reflections on the nature of philosophy and religion—by emphasizing, one last time, how the parallels between the two themes ought *not* to be construed. To this end, I will show that Nielsen's criticism encountered in the previous chapter—the objection that, for Wittgenstein, 'Christian practice is everything and Christian belief nothing'[3]—can be seen to match Frege's misreading of the TLP briefly mentioned in the second one. So let us recall Wittgenstein's remark in the Preface to TLP, 'this book will perhaps only be understood by those who have themselves already thought the thoughts which are expressed in it—or similar thought . . . it is therefore not a *Lehrbuch* [textbook]',[4] which Frege glosses thus: 'the pleasure of reading [Wittgenstein's] book can . . . no longer be aroused by the content which is already known, but only by the peculiar form given to it by the author. The book thereby becomes an artistic rather than a scientific [*wissenschaftlich*] achievement; what is said in it takes second place to the way in which it is said.'[5]

Nielsen's and Frege's collective error is instructive: both kinds of criticism spring from being taken in by a false dichotomy. In Nielsen's case, as we have seen, it is the mistake of assuming that religious beliefs can be understood completely independently of the form of life that gives them sense; in Frege's, it is thinking that a book's 'content' can be specified completely independently of 'the peculiar form' given to it by the author. But, just as when Kierkegaard and Wittgenstein say

---

[3] See chapter 4, note 40. [4] See chapter 2, note 35.
[5] See chapter 2, note 36.

that Christianity is not a doctrine, this should not be taken to mean that Christianity has no conceptual (paraphrasable) content, so when Wittgenstein says in the TLP that the book is not a *Lehrbuch*—or, indeed, when he says later in the PI that philosophy must not advance any *theses*—this should not be taken to imply that the 'content' of his works is consequently redundant. Rather, just as in the case of religious claims, if an internal understanding of them is to be possible, more is required than being able to cite dogma, if we wish to understand what Kierkegaard and Wittgenstein are up to in their work, more is required than being able, say, to quote the (so-called) 'private language argument' or Climacus' 'theses' about 'subjectivity' and the 'absolute paradox'. And this is so, not because these 'theses' cannot be put into words, but rather because these authors aren't *premise-authors*. That is to say, given Kierkegaard's and Wittgenstein's ethical understanding of the subject (of philosophy), believing that their work can be reduced to a set of claims would be as point-missing as rote-reciting is in the case of religion. For, as we have repeatedly seen, the two authors do not seek to construct new philosophical theories, but to root out the false pictures that aid and abet our enslavement to philosophical illusions. Consequently, the hold that these pictures have on us must first be undermined and this requires an effort simultaneously philosophical and ethical.

An internal understanding of the point of Kierkegaard's and Wittgenstein's work therefore becomes possible precisely when I stop regarding their writings as an attempt to convey new 'philosophical' information—an attempt to replace one theory with another—but regard them instead as an invitation to work on myself and 'the deformities of my own thinking' (CV 18e). But, to reiterate, none of this can be done without their works having exactly the kind of content they do, just as it's not possible to convert to Christianity without committing oneself to the Christian claims.

Neither philosophical nor religious problems are solved, then, by gathering together new information or 'finding things out' empirically as in science, since what is difficult about these questions is not, as Wittgenstein says, having to master some abstruse subject (CV 17e), such as, say, astrophysics, but being able to master oneself and the obstacles that stand in the way of seeing things as they are. I take it that it is this that provides the rationale for Wittgenstein's aforementioned remark: 'I may find scientific questions interesting, but they never really grip me. Only conceptual and aesthetic questions do that. At bottom I am indifferent to the solution of scientific problems; but not to the other sort' (CV 79e). For, in the scientific case, there is no internal connection between the character of the writer and the character of the writing: scientific results can be given without paying (much) attention to the way in which one gives them. But, given that conceptual and aesthetic questions cannot be solved by constructing theoretical systems, the way the 'old facts', as it were, are presented, is of paramount importance and revelatory of the kind of person and philosopher one is. This also motivates Kierkegaard's attack on speculative philosophy: by putting all the emphasis on the communication of results, the speculative thinker has no time for self-development or self-understanding. That is to say, he constructs a large castle, but continues to live in a shack.

Furthermore, Kierkegaard and Wittgenstein would univocally agree, it is characteristic of the 'darkness of these times'[6] to have got the categories confused and to believe that things are really the other way round. That is to say, people regard the communication of results or, in Petrus Minor's parlance, the multiplication of premises, as what *genuine* teaching consists in and think that the arts exist solely to give them pleasure (CV 36e). But, if Kierkegaard and Wittgenstein are right, all that is great and important can precisely not be taught in this way—by teaching someone to reel off formulae—as this would be tantamount to making the following kind of error:

Suppose it was the life-view of a religiously existing subject that one may not have followers, that this would be treason to both God and men; suppose he were a bit obtuse... and announced this directly with unction and with pathos—what then? Well, then he would be understood and soon ten would apply who, just for a free shave each week, would offer their services in proclaiming this doctrine; that is, in further substantiation of the truth of his doctrine, he would have been so very fortunate as to gain followers who accepted and spread this doctrine about having no follower. (CUP 75)

We couldn't have a better example of someone who doesn't understand the meaning of a religious (or philosophical) doctrine at all.

'Making it a question of science' (LC 57), if Kierkegaard and Wittgenstein are right, is therefore just as pernicious in philosophy as it is in religion. For it is the scientific paradigm that (more often than not) lies at the root of what Kierkegaard calls a confusion of the spheres: by trying to assimilate everything to this paradigm, what is distinctive about

---

[6] Preface to PI.

other forms of discourse either gets lost or distorted beyond recognition. So, for example, it is the attempt to render Christianity probable—an attempt modelled on the 'arguments of scientists'[7]—that gives rise to the target view of religion that Kierkegaard and Wittgenstein have gone to such lengths to discredit.

And here Marguerite Porète once again foreshadows an important dimension in Kierkegaard's and Wittgenstein's thought about religion—which, given how the present book began, makes a fitting note on which to end:

Now Reason, says this Soul, you ask us where we turn for guidance; and I answer you, says this Soul, that it is to him who alone is so mighty that he can never die, whose teaching is not written down either in books of examples or in the teachings of men, for his is a gift which cannot be given by formulation. He knows from all eternity that I indeed believed this without any need for proof. Is there, says the Soul, anything baser than to ask for proofs in love? Truly not, it seems to me, since Love is its own proof, and that is enough for me. If I ask for more, then I do not believe this.[8]

---

[7] See Swinburne, 'Philosophical Theism', 6.   [8] *The Mirror of Simple Souls*, 90.

Select Bibliography

Adorno, T., *Kierkegaard. Konstruktion des Ästhetischen* (Frankfurt: Suhrkamp, 2003).

Allison, H., 'Christianity and Nonsense', *Review of Metaphysics* 20 (1967): 432–60.

Ambrose, A., 'Ludwig Wittgenstein: A Portrait', in Alice Ambrose and Morris Lazerowitz (eds), *Ludwig Wittgenstein. Philosophy and Language* (Bristol: Thoemmes Press, 1996).

Anscombe, G. E. M., *An Introduction to Wittgenstein's* Tractatus (Indianapolis, IN: St Augustine's Press, 1971).

Anz, W., *Kierkegaard und der deutsche Idealismus* (Tübingen: Mohr, 1956).

Arrington, R. L., and Addis, M. (eds), *Wittgenstein and Philosophy of Religion* (London: Routledge, 2001).

Ayer, A. J., *Language, Truth and Logic* (London: Penguin, 1971).

Barrett, Cyril, *Wittgenstein on Ethics and Religious Belief* (Oxford: Blackwell, 1991).

Bell, R., and Hustwit, R., (eds), *Essays on Wittgenstein and Kierkegaard* (Wooster, OH: The College of Wooster, 1978).

Bouwsma, O. K., 'Notes on Kierkegaard's "The Monstrous Illusion"', in *Without Proof or Evidence*, ed. J. L. Craft and R. E. Hustwit (Lincoln, NB: University of Nebraska Press, 1984).

—— *Wittgenstein. Conversations 1949–51*, ed. J. L. Craft and Ronald E. Hustwit (Indianapolis, IN: Hackett, 1986).

Braithwaite, R. B., *An Empiricist's View of the Nature of Religious Belief* (Cambridge: Cambridge University Press, 1953).

Burgess, A., '*Forstand* in the Swenson—Lowrie Correspondence and in the "Metaphysical Caprice"', in Robert Perkins (ed.), Philosophical Fragments *and* Johannes Climacus, *International Kierkegaard Commentary* (Macon, GA: Mercer University Press, 1994), 109–28.

Burns, S., 'If a Lion Could Talk', *Wittgenstein Studien* 1 (1994).

Cavell, S., 'Existentialism and Analytical Philosophy', *Daedalus* 93 (1964): 946–74.

—— 'Kierkegaard's *On Authority and Revelation*', in *Must We Mean What We Say?* (Cambridge: Cambridge University Press, 1969), 163–79.

—— *The Claim of Reason* (Oxford: Oxford University Press, 1979).

Conant, J., 'Must We Show What We Cannot Say?', in R. Fleming and M. Payne (eds), *The Senses of Stanley Cavell* (Lewisburg, PA: Bucknell University Press, 1989), 242–83.

—— 'Kierkegaard, Wittgenstein and Nonsense', in Ted Cohen, Paul Guyer and Hilary Putnam (eds), *Pursuits of Reason* (Lubbock, TX: Texas Technical University Press, 1993), 195–224.

—— 'Putting Two and Two Together: Kierkegaard, Wittgenstein and the Point of View for Their Work as Authors', in *Philosophy and the Grammar of Religious Belief*, ed. Timothy Tessin and Mario von der Ruhr (London: Macmillan, 1995), 248–331.

—— 'Elucidation and Nonsense in Frege and Early Wittgenstein', in Alice Crary and Rupert Read (eds), *The New Wittgenstein* (London: Routledge, 2000), 174–217.

—— 'The Method of the *Tractatus*', in Erich Reck (ed.), *From Frege to Wittgenstein* (Oxford: Oxford University Press, 2002a), 374–462.

—— 'On Going the Bloody *Hard* Way in Philosophy', in John Whittaker (ed.), *The Possibilities of Sense* (Basingstoke: Palgrave, 2002b).

—— 'What "Ethics" in the *Tractatus* is *Not*', in D. Z. Phillips and Mario von der Ruhr (eds), *Religion and Wittgenstein's Legacy* (Aldershot: Ashgate, 2005).

Conant, J., and Diamond, C., 'On Reading the *Tractatus* Resolutely: Reply to Meredith Williams and Peter Sullivan', in Max Kölbel and Bernhard Weiss (eds), *Wittgenstein's Lasting Significance* (London: Routledge, 2004).

Copi, I. M., and Beard, R. W. (eds), *Essays on Wittgenstein's Tractatus* (London: Routledge, 2005).

Creegan, C., *Wittgenstein and Kierkegaard—Religion, Individuality and Philosophical Method* (London: Routledge, 1989).

Daise, B., *Kierkegaard's Socratic Art* (Macon, GA: Mercer University Press, 1999).

Davidson, D., 'On the Very Idea of a Conceptual Scheme', in *Inquiries into Truth and Interpretation* (Oxford: Oxford University Press, 2001).

Deuser, H., and Soderquist, K. B. (eds), *Kierkegaard Studies Yearbook*: Concluding Unscientific Postscript (Berlin: de Gruyter, 2005).

—— Stewart, J., and Tolstrup, F. (eds), *Kierkegaard Studies Yearbook:* Philosophical Fragments (Berlin: de Gruyter, 2004).

Diamond, C., *The Realistic Spirit*, 4th edn (Cambridge, MA: Massachusetts Institute of Technology University Press, 2001).

—— 'Ethics, Imagination and the Method of Wittgenstein's *Tractatus*', *The New Wittgenstein*, 149–73.

—— 'Logical Syntax in Wittgenstein's *Tractatus*', *Philosophical Quarterly* 55/218 (2005a).

—— 'Wittgenstein on Religious Belief: The Gulfs Between Us', in *Religion and Wittgenstein's Legacy*, ed. D. Z. Phillips and Mario von der Ruhr (Aldershot: Ashgate, 2005b).

Drury, M. O'C., 'Notes on Conversations with Wittgenstein', in Rush Rhees (ed.), *Recollections of Wittgenstein* (Oxford: Oxford University Press, 1981).

Eichler, U., 'Kierkegaard und Wittgenstein: Über das Ethische', in *Wittgenstein Studies* 2/97.

Engelmann, P., *Letters from Ludwig Wittgenstein with a Memoir*, ed. Brian McGuinness, trans. L. Furtmüller (Oxford: Blackwell, 1967).

—— *Ludwig Wittgenstein. Briefe und Begegnungen* (Vienna and Munich: Oldenbourg, 1970).

Evans, C. S., *Faith Beyond Reason* (Michigan: William B. Eerdmans, 1998).

—— *Kierkegaard's* Fragments *and* Postscript (New York: Humanity Books (imprint of Prometheus Books), 1999).

Fahrenbach, H., *Kierkegaards existenzialdialektische Ethik* (Frankfurt: Klostermann, 1968).

—— 'Grenzen der Sprache und indirekte Mitteilung: Wittgenstein und Kierkegaard über den philosophischen Umgang mit existentiellen (ethischen und religiösen) Fragen', in *Wittgenstein Studies* 2/97.

Ferreira, J. M., 'The Point Outside the World: Kierkegaard and Wittgenstein On Nonsense, Paradox and Religion', in *Wittgenstein Studies* 2/97.

Floyd, J., 'Wittgenstein, Mathematics and Philosophy', in *The New Wittgenstein*, 232–61.

Gardiner, P., *Kierkegaard* (Oxford: Oxford University Press, 1988).

Garff, J. 'The Eyes of Argus—The Point of View and Points of View with Respect to Kierkegaard's "Activity as an Author"', in *Søren Kierkegaard—Critical Assessments of Leading Philosophers*, ed. Daniel Conway and K. E. Gover (London: Routledge, 2002), 71–96.

Geach, P., 'Immortality', in his *God and the Soul* (Indiana: St Augustine's Press, 1969).

Gill, Jerry (ed.), *Essays on Kierkegaard* (Minneapolis, MN: Burgess Publishing, 1969).

Glebe-Moeller, J., 'Notes on Wittgenstein's Reading of Kierkegaard', in *Wittgenstein Studies* 2/97.

Glock, H.-J., *A Wittgenstein Dictionary* (Oxford: Blackwell, 1995).

—— 'All Kinds of Nonsense', in *Wittgenstein at Work*, ed. Erich Ammereller and Eugen Fischer (London: Routledge, 2004).

Goldfarb, W., 'Metaphysics and Nonsense: On Cora Diamond's *The Realistic Spirit*', *Journal of Philosophical Research* 22 (1997): 57–73.

Gouwens, D. J., *Kierkegaard as Religious Thinker* (Cambridge: Cambridge University Press, 1996).

Green, R., *The Hidden Debt: Kierkegaard and Kant* (New York: State University of New York Press, 1992).

Hacker, P. M. S., *Insight and Illusion* (Bristol: Thoemmes Press, 1997).

—— 'Was He Trying to Whistle It?', in Crary and Read (eds), *The New Wittgenstein*.

—— 'Wittgenstein, Carnap and the New American Wittgensteinians', *Philosophical Quarterly* 53 (2003).

Haecker, T., *Der Begriff Wahrheit bei Kierkegaard* (Innsbruck: Brenner Verlag, 1932).

Hannay, A., *Kierkegaard, The Arguments of the Philosophers* (London: Routledge, 1982).

Hannay and Marino, G. (eds), *The Cambridge Companion to Kierkegaard* (Cambridge, Cambridge University Press, 1998).

Heidegger, M., 'Was ist Metaphysik?' in *Wegmarken* (Frankfurt: Vittorio Klostermann, 1976).

Helm, P., *Faith with Reason* (Oxford: Oxford University Press 2000).

Hick, J., 'Religious Belief and Philosophical Enquiry', in D. Z. Phillips (ed.), *Faith and Philosophical Enquiry* (London: Routledge & Kegan Paul, 1970).

Hustwit, R., 'Wittgenstein's Interest in Kierkegaard', in *Wittgenstein Studies* 2 (1997).

Hyman, J., 'The Gospel According to Wittgenstein', in Robert Arrington and Mark Addis (eds), *Wittgenstein and Philosophy of Religion* (London: Routledge, 2001).

Janik, A., and Toulmin, S., *Wittgenstein's Vienna* (Chicago, IL: Ivan Dee, 1996).

Johnson, H., and Thulstrup, N. (eds), *A Kierkegaard Critique* (New York: Harper, 1962).

Kant, I., *Die Religion innerhalb der Grenzen der bloßen Vernunft* (Stuttgart: Reclam, 1974).

Kaufmann, K., *Vom Zweifel zur Verzweiflung. Grundbegriffe der Existenzphilosophie Søren Kierkegaards* (Würzburg: Königshausen and Neumann, 2002).

Keightley, A. W., *Wittgenstein, Grammar and God* (London: Epworth Press, 1976).

Kerr, Fergus, *Theology after Wittgenstein* (Oxford: SPCK Press, 1986).

Kierkegaard, S., *The Journals of Søren Kierkegaard*, trans. Alexander Dru (London: G. Cumberlege and Oxford University Press, 1951).

—— *The Attack Upon Christendom*, trans., with an introduction, by Walter Lowrie (Princeton: Princeton University Press, 1968).

—— *The Sickness unto Death*, ed. and trans. Howard and Edna Hong (Princeton: Princeton University Press, 1980a).

—— *The Concept of Anxiety*, ed. and trans. Albert B. Anderson and Reidar Thomte (Princeton: Princeton University Press, 1980b).

—— *Fear and Trembling*, ed. and trans. Howard and Edna Hong (Princeton: Princeton University Press, 1983).

—— *Philosophical Fragments*, ed. and trans. Howard and Edna Hong (Princeton: Princeton University Press, 1985).

—— *Either/Or*, I and II, ed. and trans. Howard and Edna Hong (Princeton: Princeton University Press, 1988a).

—— *Stages on Life's Way*, ed. and trans. Howard and Edna Hong (Princeton: Princeton University Press, 1988b).

Kierkegaard, S., *Practice in Christianity*, ed. and trans. Howard and Edna Hong (Princeton: Princeton University Press, 1991).
—— *Concluding Unscientific Postscript to Philosophical Fragments*, ed. and trans. Howard and Edna Hong (Princeton: Princeton University Press, 1992a).
—— *Eighteen Upbuilding Discourses*, ed. and trans. Howard and Edna Hong (Princeton: Princeton University Press, 1992b).
—— *Three Discourses on Imagined Occasions*, ed. and trans. Howard and Edna Hong (Princeton: Princeton University Press, 1993a).
—— *Upbuilding Discourses in Various Spirits*, ed. and trans. Howard and Edna Hong (Princeton: Princeton University Press, 1993b).
—— *Works of Love*, ed. and trans. Howard and Edna Hong (Princeton: Princeton University Press, 1995).
—— *Papers and Journals: A Selection*, trans. Alistair Hannay (London: Penguin, 1996).
—— *Christian Discourses*, ed. and trans. Jeroen Tromp and Howard Hong (Princeton: Princeton University Press, 1997).
—— *The Book on Adler*, ed. and trans. Howard and Edna Hong (Princeton: Princeton University Press, 1998a).
—— *The Point of View*, ed. and trans. Howard and Edna Hong (Princeton: Princeton University Press, 1998b).
Kirmmse, B. H., *Encounters with Kierkegaard* (Princeton: Princeton University Press, 1996).
Klemke, E. D., *Studies in the Philosophy of Kierkegaard* (Netherlands: Springer, 1976).
Law, D. R., *Kierkegaard as Negative Theologian* (Oxford: Clarendon Press, 1993).
Lee, H. D. P., 'Wittgenstein 1929–31', *Philosophy* 54 (1979).
Liessmann, K. P., *Kierkegaard* (Hamburg: Junius Verlag, 1993).
Lipitt, J., *Humour and Irony in Kierkegaard's Thought* (London: Macmillan, 2000).
Lipitt, J., and Hutto, D., 'Making Sense of Nonsense: Kierkegaard and Wittgenstein', *Proceedings of the Aristotelian Society* 98 (1998): 263–86.
Lotti, M., 'Going Back to the Religious Beginning', in *Wittgenstein Studies* 2/97.
Lübcke, P., 'Kierkegaard and Indirect Communication,' *History of European Ideas* 12 (1990): 31–40.
McGinn, M., 'Between Metaphysics and Nonsense: Elucidation in Wittgenstein's *Tractatus*', *Philosophical Quarterly* 49 (1999): 491–513.
McGuinness, B., *Wittgenstein. A Life* (London: Penguin, 1988).
—— 'The Mysticism of the *Tractatus*', in *Approaches to Wittgenstein* (London: Routledge, 2002).
McManus, D., *The Enchantment of Words. Wittgenstein's* Tractatus Logico-Philosophicus (Oxford: Oxford University Press, 2006).

Mackey, L, *Kierkegaard: A Kind of Poet* (Philadelphia, PA: University of Pennsylvania Press, 1972).

Mackie, J. L., *The Miracle of Theism* (Oxford: Oxford University Press, 1982).

McKinnon, A., 'Kierkegaard and the "leap of faith"', in *Kierkegaardiana* 16 (1993): 107–25.

Malcolm, N., 'Anselm's Ontological Arguments', *The Philosophical Review* 69 (1960).

—— *Wittgenstein, A Religious Point of View?* (New York: Cornell University Press, 1993).

—— *Ludwig Wittgenstein, A Memoir* (Oxford: Oxford University Press, 2001).

Monk, R., *The Duty of Genius* (London: Vintage, 1991).

Mounce, H. O., *Wittgenstein's Tractatus* (Chicago, IL: University of Chicago Press, 1990).

Mulhall, S., *Faith and Reason* (London: Duckworth, 1994).

—— 'God's Plagiarist: The *Philosophical Fragments* of Johannes Climacus', *Philosophical Investigations* 22 (1999): 1–34.

—— 'Wittgenstein and the Philosophy of Religion', in D. Z. Phillips and Timothy Tessin (eds), *Philosophy of Religion in the 21st Century* (New York: Palgrave, 2001a).

—— *Inheritance and Originality* (Oxford: Clarendon Press, 2001b).

—— *Wittgenstein's Private Language* (Oxford: Oxford University Press, 2007).

Nielsen, K., 'Wittgensteinian Fideism', *Philosophy* XLII/161 (1967).

Nielsen, K., and Phillips, D. Z., *Wittgensteinian Fideism?* (London: SCM Press, 2005).

Nientied, M., *Kierkegaard und Wittgenstein—'Hineintäuschen in das Wahre'* (Berlin: de Gruyter, 2003).

Pattison, G., *Kierkegaard's Upbuilding Discourses: Philosophy, Literature and Theology* (London: Routledge, 2002).

—— *The Philosophy of Kierkegaard* (Montreal: McGill Queen's University Press, 2005).

Pears, D., *The False Prison*, vol. I (Oxford: Clarendon Press, 1987).

—— *The False Prison*, vol. II (Oxford: Clarendon Press, 1989).

Perkins, R. L. (ed.), *International Kierkegaard Commentary: Fear and Trembling and* Repetition (Macon, GA: Mercer University Press, 1993).

—— *International Kierkegaard Commentary*: Philosophical Fragments *and* Johannes Climacus (Macon, GA: Mercer University Press, 1994).

—— *International Kierkegaard Commentary*: Either/Or Part II (Macon: Mercer University Press, 1995).

—— *International Kierkegaard Commentary*: Concluding Unscientific Postscript (Macon, GA: Mercer University Press, 1997).

—— *International Kierkegaard Commentary*: Works of Love (Macon, GA: Mercer University Press, 1999).

Perkins, R. L. *International Kierkegaard Commentary*: Stages on Life's Way (Macon, GA: Mercer University Press, 2000).
—— *International Kierkegaard Commentary*: The Concept of Irony (Macon, GA: Mercer University Press, 2001).
—— *International Kierkegaard Commentary*: Eighteen Upbuilding Discourses (Macon, GA: Mercer University Press, 2003).
Phillips, D. Z., *Faith After Foundationalism* (London: Routledge, 1988).
—— *Wittgenstein and Religion* (London: Macmillan, 1993).
—— *Philosophy's Cool Place* (New York: Cornell University Press, 1999).
Pieper, A., *Kierkegaard* (Munich: C. H. Beck, 2000).
Plantinga, A., 'Religious Belief as Properly Basic', in Brian Davies (ed.), *Philosophy of Religion. A Guide and Anthology* (Oxford: Oxford University Press, 2000).
Poole, R., *Kierkegaard: The Indirect Communication* (Charlottesville, VA: University Press of Virginia, 1993).
Porète, M., *The Mirror of Simple Souls*, translated from the French with an Introductory Interpretative Essay by Edmund Colledge, J. C. Marler, and Judith Grant (Notre Dame: University of Notre Dame Press, 1999).
Proops, I., 'The New Wittgenstein: A Critique', *European Journal of Philosophy* 9 (2001): 375–404.
Putnam, H., *Renewing Philosophy* (Cambridge, MA: Harvard University Press, 1992).
Raatzsch, Richard, 'Klarheit, Tiefe, Ironie—Oder wie man von Frege zu Wittgenstein kommt, in dem man den Weg über Kierkegaard nimmt', in *Wittgenstein Studies* 2/97.
Ramsey, F. P., 'General Propositions and Causality', in R. B. Braithwaite (ed.), *The Foundations of Mathematics* (London: Routledge & Kegan Paul, 1931).
Rée, J., and Chamberlain, J. (eds), *Kierkegaard: A Critical Reader* (Oxford: Blackwell, 1998).
Rhees, R., *Ludwig Wittgenstein. Personal Recollections* (Oxford: Oxford University Press, 1984).
—— *Discussions of Wittgenstein* (Bristol: Thoemmes Press, 1996).
—— *Wittgenstein's* On Certainty—*There Like Our Life*, ed. D. Z. Phillips (Oxford: Blackwell, 2003).
Ridley, A., *The Philosophy of Music. Theme and Variations* (Edinburgh: Edinburgh University Press, 2004).
Roberts, R. C., *Reason, Faith and History* (Macon, GA: Mercer University Press, 1986).
Rorty, R., *Contingency, Irony and Solidarity* (Cambridge: Cambridge University Press, 1989).
Rudd, A., *Kierkegaard and the Limits of the Ethical* (Oxford: Clarendon Press, 1993).

Schönbaumsfeld, G., 'Wittgenstein über religiösen Glauben', in *Der Denker als Seiltänzer*, ed. Anja Weiberg and Ulrich Arnswald (Berlin: Parerga, 2001a), 179–92.

—— 'Through the Looking-Glass: The Problem of Wittgenstein's Point of View', in *Beiträge der Österreichischen Ludwig Wittgenstein Gesellschaft*, vol. IX/2 (2001b), 276–80.

—— 'No New Kierkegaard', *International Philosophical Quarterly* 44 (2004): 519–34.

—— 'Das böse Alter Ego des Glaubens: Kierkegaard über "männliche" Verzweiflung und das Dämonische', in Florian Uhl and Artur Boelderl (eds), *Das Geschlecht der Religion* (Berlin: Parerga, 2005), Übersetzung von A. Boelderl, 127–50.

Schulte, J., *Wittgenstein* (New York: State University of New York Press, 1992).

Schweppenhäuser, H., *Kierkegaards Angriff auf die Spekulation* (Frankfurt: Suhrkamp, 1967).

Shields, P., *Logic and Sin in the Writings of Ludwig Wittgenstein* (Chicago, IL: University of Chicago Press, 1993).

Stegmaier, W., 'Denkprojekte des Glaubens. Zeichen bei Kierkegaard und Wittgenstein', in *Wittgenstein Studies* 2/97.

Stosch (von), K., *Glaubensverantwortung in doppelter Kontingenz* (Regensburg: Pustet, 2001).

Strawson, P. F., 'Freedom and Resentment', in A. P. Martinich and David Sosa (eds), *Analytic Philosophy. An Anthology* (Oxford: Blackwell, 2001).

Sullivan, P., 'On Trying to be Resolute: A Response to Kremer on the *Tractatus*', *European Journal of Philosophy* 10 (2002): 43–78.

Swinburne, R., 'Philosophical Theism', in D. Z. Phillips and Timothy Tessin (eds), *Philosophy of Religion in the 21st Century* (New York: Palgrave, 2001).

Taylor, M. C., *Journeys to Selfhood. Hegel and Kierkegaard* (New York: Fordham University Press, 2000).

Theunissen, M., *Der Begriff Ernst bei Kierkegaard* (Munich: Alber Karl, 1998).

Thompson, J. (ed.), *Kierkegaard, A Collection of Critical Essays* (Garden City, NY: Doubleday, 1972).

Thomte, R., *Kierkegaard's Philosophy of Religion* (Princeton: Princeton University Press, 1948).

Watkin, J., *Historical Dictionary of Kierkegaard's Philosophy* (Maryland: The Scarecrow Press, 2001).

Weston, M., *Kierkegaard and Modern Continental Philosophy* (London: Routledge, 1994).

Westphal, M., *Becoming a Self: A Reading from Kierkegaard's* Concluding Unscientific Postscript (Lafayette: Purdue University Press, 1996).

Winch, Peter, *Trying to Make Sense*, (Oxford: Blackwell, 1987).

—— *The Idea of a Social Science and its Relation to Philosophy* (London: Routledge, 1995).

Wittgenstein, L., *Philosophical Investigations*, trans. G. E. M. Anscombe (Oxford: Blackwell, 1953).

—— *The Blue and Brown Books* (New York: Harper & Row, 1965).

—— *Lectures and Conversations on Aesthetics, Psychology and Religious Belief*, ed. Cyril Barrett (Oxford: Blackwell, 1966).

—— *On Certainty*, ed. G. E. M. Anscombe and G. H. von Wright (Oxford: Blackwell, 1969).

—— *Culture and Value*, ed. G. H. von Wright (Oxford: Blackwell, 1977).

—— *Philosophical Remarks*, ed. Rush Rhees (Chicago, IL: University of Chicago Press, 1980).

—— *Zertel*, ed. G. E. M. Anscombe and G. H. von Wright, with an English translation by G. E. M. Anscombe, 2nd edn. (Oxford: Blackwell, 1981).

—— *Ludwig Wittgenstein und der Wiener Kreis*, conversations recorded by Friedrich Waismann, ed. Brian McGuinness (Frankfurt: Suhrkamp, 1984a).

—— *Notebooks*, ed. G. H. von Wright and G. E. M. Anscombe, with an English translation by G. E. M. Anscombe, 2nd edn (Chicago, IL: The University of Chicago Press, 1984b).

—— *Geheime Tagebücher*, ed. Wilhelm Baum (Vienna: Turia and Kant, 1991).

—— *Philosophical Occasions*, ed. James Klagge and Alfred Nordmann (Indianapolis, IN: Hackett, 1993a).

—— *Tractatus Logico-Philosophicus*, Werkausgabe Band 1 (Frankfurt: Suhrkamp, 1993b).

—— *Tagebücher 1914–16*, in Werkausgabe Band 1 (Frankfurt: Suhrkamp, 1993c).

—— *Ludwig Hänsel—Ludwig Wittgenstein. Eine Freundschaft*, ed. Ilse Somavilla, Anton Unterkircher, and Christian Paul Berger (Innsbruck: Haymon, 1994).

—— *Ludwig Wittgenstein: Cambridge Letters*, ed. Brian McGuinness and G. H. von Wright (Oxford: Blackwell, 1995).

—— *Wittgenstein Familienbriefe*, ed. Brian McGuinness, Maria Ascher, and Otto Pfersmann (Vienna: Hölder-Pichler-Tempsky, 1996).

—— *Denkbewegungen*, ed. Ilse Somavilla (Frankfurt: Fischer, 1999).

—— *Remarks on the Foundations of Mathematics*, ed. G. H. von Wright, R. Rhees, G. E. M. Anscombe, trans. G. E. M. Anscombe (Cambridge, MA: Massachusetts Institute of Technology Press, 2001).

—— *Licht und Schatten*, ed. Ilse Somavilla (Innsbruck: Haymon, 2004).

Wuchterl, K., and Hübner, A., *Wittgenstein* (Hamburg: Rowohlt, 1979).

Index